D0065368

Mercyhurst College Learning Resource Center

Presented By:

Mercyhurst College Community

IN MEMORY OF

Mrs. Eileen Keller

N. COONEY

American Historical Fiction
and Biography
for Children and Young People

by
Jeanette Hotchkiss

The Scarecrow Press, Inc.
Metuchen, N.J.   1973

Library of Congress Cataloging in Publication Data

Hotchkiss, Jeanette.
    American historical fiction and biography for
children and young people.

    SUMMARY: A chronologically and topically arranged
bibliography of historical fiction and biography of
North and South America, with emphasis on the United
States.
    1. United States--History--Bibliography.
2. United States--Biography--Bibliography. 3. United
States--History--Fiction--Bibliography. 4. North
America--History--Fiction--Bibliography. [1. United
States--History--Fiction--Bibliography. 2. United
States--Biography--Bibliography. 3. America--History
--Fiction--Bibliography] I. Title.
Z1236.H73   016.9173'03   73-13715
ISBN 0-8108-0650-9

TABLE OF CONTENTS

iv

PART III: INDEXES

INTRODUCTION

"All that Mankind has done, thought, gained or been:
it is lying as in magic preservation in the pages of
books."
Thomas Carlyle: Heroes and Hero Worship

The primary purpose of this bibliography is to en-
courage a love of history in young readers, from the very
beginners up through those in high school. With this purpose in mind the book is arranged in two main sections.
Readers who have already discovered the "joy of history"
may prefer a certain chronological period for intensive reading, while others who still think of history as a dry, obliga-
tory subject may find doorways to the American past opened
by their own special and individual interests in some of the
subjects listed in the second section of the book.

American history covers a large geographical area
(most of the western hemisphere, in fact) but a relatively
very short span of time. Part I: Chronology, except for the
beginning on early explorations, is confined for practical pur-
poses to the area now encompassing the United States, but
in Part II you will find books about Canada, Central and
South America, the West Indies and even the two poles as
well as the two newest members of the United States, Alaska
and Hawaii.

Compared to the rest of the world, what a short history it is! Though the Vikings came over around A.D. 1000,
they didn't "stay put" and it is less than 500 years since
Columbus discovered the New World. As for the United
States, 1976 will mark the 200th anniversary of its Declaration of Independence from England. Since there is no contemporary written history of the native Americans--the Indian
tribes and nations--we have to depend there on archaeology,
myths and legends.

The subject of Indians constitutes a sad chapter in
United States history as does the subject of slavery, and

each of these has its own heading, but biographies are not "segregated" as to color or previous nationality or sex. Poets, scientists, educators, and others are all placed in their special spheres of endeavor and achievement, though there is a special category for the pioneers in women's struggle for equality.

Historical authenticity, literary merit, readability (by which I simply mean good story-telling) and good taste have been my criteria. And by "good taste" in respect to both fiction and biography, I am thinking of the use of realism in contemporary writing for children. A novel can be realistic without being sordid and a biography can be fair and true to the subject's faults and weaknesses without being a "muckraker."

My sources were chiefly the children's rooms of nearby libraries, particularly my home town one of Highland Park, Illinois, where Mrs. Jo Hemsworth and her staff were of inestimable help. I also visited many book stores and was happy to find that publishers are now putting out attractive paperback editions of children's books, several of which have been out of print for some time. The Horn Book and Publishers Weekly have kept me up to date on new books, and for the "old favorites," I have happy memories of my own childhood reading and the more recent books enjoyed by my children and grandchildren. I have probably left out the titles of some excellent books which I simply could not or did not find, and for that I apologize to their authors.

For her helpful ideas and suggestions about the arrangement of this bibliography I express my thanks to my eldest granddaughter, Carolyn Hotchkiss, now a freshman at Mt. Holyoke College and an American history buff ever since she learned to read. Mr. Joseph Pollock, the Highland Park head librarian, started me off with some sound technical advice for which I have been constantly grateful. And a special "thank-you" goes to my husband, Eugene Hotchkiss, for his patience with my concentration on the Past.

The old Cheyenne story-teller, so I have read, used to tie one story on to another until the camp fire died down when he would say, "this cuts it off." In historical fiction and biography one story is not only tied to another but to many others, and the strands are so interwoven that whereas you may start out with a sole interest in spy stories you may find yourself, before too long, an authority on the American Revolution.

And so I "cut off" with the hope that you will find as much pleasure in using this book as I have had in compiling it.

Jeanette Hotchkiss
Highland Park, Illinois
December 1972

A NOTE ON USING THIS BOOK

Symbols designating approximate reading and interest levels:

E	Elementary; through second grade
I	Intermediate; through fifth or sixth grade
YA	Young Adult: Junior High School
YA and Up	Senior High School
A	Adult, but in many cases suitable for all ages

The spelling of proper names is given as used by the authors and vary in some cases--e. g. , "Vinland, " "Vineland, " and "Wineland"; "Dolly" or "Dolley. "

PART I: CHRONOLOGY

EARLY EXPLORATIONS AND CONQUESTS

VIKING STORIES

1 Best, Herbert. The Sea Warriors. Macmillan, 1959.
    A novel about Viking exploits in Greenland and Leif
    Ericsson's "Vineland the Fruitful." (YA)
2 Bond, Susan McDonald. Eric, The Tale of a Red
    Tempered Viking. Ill. by Sally Trinkle. Grove,
    1968. A mighty comical story, with equally funny
    drawings, about the father of Leif Eriksson.
    (Picture Book E)
3 Bulla, Clyde Robert. Viking Adventures. Ill. by Doug-
    las Gorsline. Crowell, 1963. A story of high ad-
    venture and a courageous boy who sailed to "Wine-
    land." (E)
4 Coblentz, Catherine Cate. The Falcon of Eric the Red.
    Ill. by Henry C. Pitz. Longmans Green, 1942. A
    story of the true meaning of freedom, in which a
    beautiful white falcon is given to Jon, a castaway
    lad, by Eric the Red, and is taken by Jon from
    Greenland to Vinland (possibly present Nova Scotia).
    (I and YA)
5 D'Aulaire, Ingri and Edgar Parin. Leif the Lucky.
    Ill. by the authors. Doubleday, 1941. A brightly
    illustrated biography of the Viking discoverer of
    North America, ca. A.D. 1000. (E)
6 Johanson, Margaret Alison. Voyagers West. Ill. by
    William Ferguson. Washburn, 1959. A novel
    about the Vikings led by Eric the Red in 982, and
    the discovery of Vinland by his son, Leif Ericson.
    (YA)
7 Liljencrantz, Ottilie. The Thrall of Leif the Lucky.
    McClurg, 1902. A story about a boy, son of an
    English earl, serving Leif Ericsson on his voyage
    to the new world. (I)
8 Pohl, Frederick J. The Viking Explorers. Ill. with
    drawings, maps (including the new Yale map of

11

Vinland from 1440), illuminations from ancient manu-
scripts and diagrams of archaeological discoveries.
Crowell, 1966. (YA and Up)
9 Schaff, Louise E. Skald of the Vikings. Lothrop, Lee
   and Shepard, 1965. A story about a 13-year-old boy
   taken on a voyage from Greenland to Vinland and
   about the colony established there, later attacked by
   the Indians. (I)
10 Schiller, Barbara. The Vinlander's Saga. Ill. by
    William Block. Holt, Rinehart and Winston, 1966.
    Inspired by the Yale Vinland map, a story about the
    early Norsemen, beginning with Eric the Red. (I)
11 Shippen, Katherine B. Leif Eriksson, First Voyager to
    America. Harper and Row, 1951. (I)
12 Treece, Henry. Westward to Vinland. Ill. by William
    Stobbs. S. G. Philips, 1967. From the Icelandic
    sagas, the story of Eric the Red, Leif Erikson and
    the voyages to America 500 years before Columbus.
    (YA)
13 Weir, Ruth Cromer. Leif Eriksson. Ill. by Harve
    Stein. Abingdon Press, 1951. A biographical
    story. (I)

A WELSH EXPLORER

14 Pugh, Ellen. Brave His Soul: The Story of Prince
    Madog. Ill. with photographs and maps; jacket by
    Ragna Tischler. Dodd Mead, 1970. An exceptional
    story about the possible discovery of America by a
    Welsh prince in 1170. A masterly piece of historical
    detective work, beginning with an old Welsh song and
    legend, still being pursued in America with a search
    for the origins of the "Welsh Indians." (YA and Up)

THE ITALIANS

15 Bailey, Bernardine. Christopher Columbus, Sailor and
    Dreamer. Ill. by Cheslie D'Andrea. Houghton
    Mifflin, 1960. An easy-to-read story of Columbus'
    life (1446?-1506), his discoveries and disappoint-
    ments. (I)
16 Baker, Nina Brown. Amerigo Vespucci. Ill. by Paul
    Valentino. Knopf, 1956. A biography (1451-1512),
    with a map of his voyage, of the man from whom
    the American continent derives its name. (YA)
17 Hill, Kay. And Tomorrow the Stars: The Story of

John Cabot. Ill. by Laszlo Kubinyi. Dodd Mead, 1968. A biographical novel about Giovanni Caboto, better known as John Cabot, who is credited with the discovery of North America in 1497 and who, in 1498, sailed south along the continent, never to be seen again. A Genoese whose life and dreams were entwined with those of Columbus, Vasco da Gama and Vespucci, it was only near the end of his adventurous life that he obtained a charter from Henry VII of England to explore the northern sea routes "to India" and plant the English flag in what may have been Newfoundland (ca. 1450-1498?). (YA and Up)

18 Carrison, Daniel J. Christopher Columbus, Navigator to the New World. Franklin Watts, 1967. A well organized and entertaining biography with emphasis on Columbus as a navigator and including a useful chronology (1451-1506). (YA)

19 D'Aulaire, Ingri and Edgar Parin. Columbus. Ill. by the authors. Doubleday, 1955. Another of the D'Aulaires' large colorful books. (E and I)

20 Hays, Wilma Pitchford. Noko, Captive of Columbus. Ill. by Peter Burchard. Coward McCann, 1967. A story of an Indian boy and the conflict between Indians and Spaniards, based on the diaries of the son of Christopher Columbus. (I)

21 Judson, Clara Ingram. Christopher Columbus. Ill. by Polly Jackson. Follett, 1960. A Beginning-to-Read Book, intended for second graders. (E)

22 Lowitz, Sadyebeth and Anson. The Cruise of Mr. Christopher Columbus. Ill. by the authors. Scholastic Book Services, 1967. An amusing little story and picture book for beginning readers and those not yet able to read themselves.

23 Sperry, Armstrong. The Voyages of Christopher Columbus. Ill. by the author. Random House, Landmark, 1950. An excitingly written biography in narrative form of the man who, though born in Genoa in 1446?, spent most of his life, when not at sea, in Portugal, first, and then Spain, where he died, neglected by King Ferdinand, in 1506. (I and YA)

24 Syme, Ronald. Columbus, Finder of the New World. Ill. by William Stobbs. William Morrow, 1952. A short biography.

25 Amerigo Vespucci. Ill. by William Stobbs. William Morrow, 1969. Surprisingly, the importance of this man--who first announced to the world the existence of the continent named for him--was not fully acknowledged until the early 19th century. (1451-

1512).   (I)

THE SPANISH

26 Baker, Betty. The Blood of the Brave. Harper and
    Row, 1966. A novel about a boy who went from
    Cuba with Cortez, his father and his dog. Based on
    a true 16th-century adventure, with a bibliography.
    (YA)
27 _____. The Treasure of the Padres. Ill. by
    Leonard Shortall. Harper and Row, 1964. Contem-
    porary children, in search of some "ghost bells,"
    come upon the real treasure of the Padres. (I)
              . Walk the World's Rim. Harper and Row,
28 1965. Novel about an Indian boy and the four sur-
    vivors of the Narvaez expedition--de Vaca, Castillo,
    Dorantes, and the Negro slave, Estaban--with inter-
    esting material about the Buffalo People and the Pima
    Indians. (YA)
29 Baker, Nina Brown. Ponce de Leon. Ill. by Robert
    Doremus. Knopf, 1957. Biography of the Spanish
    explorer (1460-1521) who discovered Florida in 1513.
    (YA)
30 Blacker, Irwin R. Cortez and the Aztec Conquest.
    Ill. with many paintings, drawings and artifacts of
    the period. American Heritage, 1965. (YA)
31 _____. The Bold Conquistadores. Bobbs-Merrill,
    1961. Brief biographies of Cortez, Cabeza de Vaca,
    Pizarro, Coronado and DeSoto, showing the sequences
    of their lives and discoveries. (YA)
32 Blassingame, Wyatt. Ponce de Leon: A World Ex-
    plorer. Ill. by Russ Hoover. Garrard, 1965.
    Biography of the discoverer of Florida in 1513 (1460-
    1521). (I)
33 Bolton, Ivy. Father Junipero Serra. Ill. by Robert
    Burns. Julian Messner, 1952. Story of the cour-
    ageous, loving Franciscan padre from Madeira,
    Spain, who established nine missions from San Diego
    to San Francisco along the Camino Real (traveling
    mostly on foot) in 1712 and 1713. (YA)
34 Clarke, Ann Nolan. Father Kino, Priest to the Pimas.
    Ill. by H. Lawrence Hoffman. Farrar, Straus
    Vision Books, 1963. This biography of the Jesuit
    priest (1644-1711), a good friend of the Indians, will
    be of special interest to those who have a chance to
    visit the ruins of Tumacacori Mission and the still-

working Mission of St. Xavier de Bac, near Tucson,
Arizona. (YA)

34a Coleman, Eleanor S. The Cross and the Sword of
Cortez. Jacket by Lazlo Kubinyi. Simon and
Schuster. The story of Cortez' conquest of
Mexico as fictionally narrated by a young Spaniard
who had preceded Cortez to Mexico, and having
learned the language, offered his services as an in-
terpreter to Cortez, with the help of the Indian girl,
Malinche. As far as possible the actual words of
Cortez, Montezuma and others are used in the story.
(YA)

35 Dines, Glen. Golden Cities, Golden Ships: Early
Spanish Explorers of California. Ill. by the author.
McGraw-Hill, 1968. The story of Cabrillo and Fer-
relo, discoverers of the bay at San Diego; Vizcaino,
discoverer of Monterey Bay; Gaspar de Portola, San
Francisco Bay; and Juan Manuel de Ayala, who first
charted San Francisco Bay. (I and YA)

36 Duncombe, Frances Riker. The Quetzel Feather. Ill.
by W. T. Mars. Lothrop, Lee and Shepard, 1967.
A novel about a young Spaniard who ran away from
Cortez in Mexico to join in Alvarado's conquest of
Guatemala and how his attitude toward the conquerer
and the Indians changed. (YA)

36a Evernden, Margery. The Golden Trail. Ill. by Lynd
Ward. Random, 1952. The story of a young Mexican boy who, in 1775, followed Captain Anza on his
long hazardous trek to where he founded San Francisco in 1776, based on the diary of one Fray Pedro,
the chaplain and historian of the expedition. (I and
YA)

37 Howard, Cecil. Pizarro and the Conquest of Peru.
Handsomely illustrated. A Horizon Caravel Book.
American Heritage, 1968. The truly fabulous story
of Pizarro's conquest of Peru in 1532.

38 Johnson, William. Captain Cortez Conquers Mexico.
Ill. by José Cisneris. Random House, Landmark,
1960. Written in story form, the conquest is seen
through the eyes of Escobar, Cortez' right hand man,
a young page. (I)

39 Jones, Evan. Protector of the Indians: Bartolomé de
Las Casas. Ill. by George Fulton. Thomas Nelson
and Sons, 1958. The story of a Spaniard (1476-
1566), first a conquistador in Haiti who, after coming to believe that Indians had souls, spent most of his
long life trying to persuade the Spanish soldiers and

Church leaders that this was so and to prove that the
Christian faith, in its highest sense, was more powerful than Spanish swords. (YA)

40 Lampman, Evelyn Sibley. Temple of the Sun. Ill. by
Lili Rethi. Doubleday, 1964. Subtitled "A Boy
Fights for Montezuma," this is a fictional account of
the conquest of the Aztecs by Cortez in 1519, a good
story about the conquistadores based on sound research, with a glossary of Mexican names. (I and
YA)

41 Lobdell, Helen. Golden Conquest. Ill. by Seymour
Fleishman. Houghton Mifflin, 1953. The story of
Cortez' expedition, based on The Conquest of Mexico
by Prescott. (I)

42 Meredith, Robert and Smith, E. Brooks. Riding With
Coronado. Ill. by Leonard Everett Fisher. Little
Brown, 1964. Adapted and edited, this is Pedro de
Castenadas' eyewitness account of the exploration of
the southwest in an unsuccessful search for the Seven
Cities of Cibola. A list of the principal historical
persons of the narrative glossary, maps and two of
Coronado's letters. (YA)

43 Mirsky, Jeannette. Balboa, Discoverer of the Pacific.
Ill. by Hans Guggenheim. Harper and Row, 1964.
An exceptionally comprehensive biography of Vasco
Núñez de Balboa (1475-1517) who founded the first
successful settlement on the American mainland as
well as discovering the Pacific Ocean. The "Order
of Events" at the end outlines the story, while the
"Dramatis Personae" helps immensely to keep straight
the relationships of Spaniards and Indians.

44 Montgomery, Elizabeth Rider. Hernando DeSoto. Ill.
by Henry Gillette Garrard, 1964. A biography (1500-
1542) with an exceptionally good map on the end
covers, showing just where DeSoto landed in 1539,
where he defeated Tuscaloosa, where he first saw the
Mississippi River, and where he probably died in
1542. (I)

45 O'Dell, Scott. The King's Fifth. Ill. and maps by
Samuel Bryant. Houghton Mifflin, 1966. A novel of
the conquistadors and their lust for gold, the story
framed by the notes of a young cartographer, written
in his prison cell in Vera Cruz. (I and YA)

46 Riesenberg, Felix, Jr. Balboa, Swordsman and Conquistador. Ill. by Fedor Rojankovsky. Random
House, Landmark, 1956. A pleasantly fictionalized
biography of Balboa (1513-19) dependent upon the

author's imagination where there are no written
records, especially as to his early life.   (I)

47 Steele, William O. The Wilderness Tattoo: A Narrative of Juan Ortiz. Ill. with old prints. Harcourt
Brace Jovanovich, 1972. An engrossing story of
Juan Ortiz, a young Spaniard and his adventures with
the Timucua Indians in Florida in the early years of
the 16th century, also his later experiences as an in-
terpreter for DeSoto in his expedition of 1539-41.
The story moves swiftly between eight informative
"interludes" and one can, if one wishes, follow the
story line first and then go back to the informative
passages.   (I and YA)

48 Sterne, Emma Gelders. Vasco Núñez de Balboa. Ill.
by Leonard Everett Fisher. Alfred A. Knopf, 1961.
A carefully researched and personal biography of the
man who, on September 25, 1513, discovered the
Pacific Ocean from a peak on Darien. (Keats was
mistaken when he wrote of "stout Cortez" making
this discovery.)   (I and YA)

49 _____. Balboa, Finder of the Pacific. Ill. by
William Stobbs. Morrow Junior Books, 1956. A
thrilling story of the discovery of the Pacific in 1513
and the courage and honesty of the discoverer who
became the victim of greedy and dishonest men
(Pizarro for one).   (I)

50 Syme, Ronald. DeSoto, Finder of the Mississippi. Ill.
by William Stobbs. William Morrow, 1957. After
acquiring great wealth in Peru with Pizarro, DeSoto
returned to Spain, but then, hearing of Ponce de
Leon's discovery of Florida, at his own expense he
got together an expedition to explore it. From
Florida he went on through present Georgia and Carolina, then south to Alabama and Louisiana, finally
crossing the Mississippi and into Arkansas. After
his death in 1542 (he was born in 1500) the remnants
of his expedition ended up in Mexico in 1543.   (I)

50a _____. First Man to Cross America, The Story of
Cabeza deVaca. Ill. by William Stobbs. Morrow
Junior Books, 1961. The crossing from the Texas
coast to the west coast of Mexico was led by Cabeza
deVaca (1476-1566) and took eight harrowing years
from 1529-37. The other three survivors of the
Narvaez expedition--Castillo, Dorantes, and the big
Negro slave, Estaban--would surely never have survived to reach Mexico if it had not been for Cabeza
deVaca's humane treatment of their Indian captors,

for he was an exceptional Spaniard in his belief that
the natives were human beings.   (I)

51 _____ . Francisco Coronado and the Seven Cities of
Gold. Ill. by William Stobbs. Morrow Junior Books,
1965. Francisco Vásquez de Coronado (1510-1554?)
(in some libraries you'll find him under V for Vas-
quez) did not really believe in the existence of the
Seven Cities but was sent to search for them by the
Spanish governor of Mexico in 1540. Instead of gold
he found the fertile plains of Texas and valley of the
Missouri, but failed to recognize their value.   (I)

52 _____ . Cortez of Mexico. Ill. by William Stobbs.
William Morrow, 1951. A biography (1485-1547) of
the conqueror of Mexico in 1519 and the story of his
adventures leading up to it, the glories of Montezuma's kingdom, and finally, the sad end of the conqueror's life.   (I)

53 _____ . The Man Who Discovered the Amazon. Ill.
by William Stobbs. William Morrow, 1958. The
exciting story of the eight-month voyage of a group
of Spaniards and Indians, from its source to the
mouth of the Amazon in 1841, led by a young man,
Francisco de Orellana. The dangers throughout the
journey were climaxed by a confrontation with the
ferocious Conori women and, after escaping from
them, the great Atlantic Ocean itself which they had
to essay in their battered ships built on the banks of
the river.   (I and YA)

54 _____ . Francisco Pizarro, Finder of Peru. Ill. by
William Stobbs. William Morrow, 1963. A story of
hideous suffering and almost superhuman endurance
in the search for and treacherous conquest of Peru
(in 1532) and its fabulous treasures.   (I)

55 _____ . Quesada of Colombia. Ill. by William Stobbs.
Morrow Junior Books, 1966. A biography of Gonzalo
Jiménez de Quesada (1497-1579), a Spanish lawyer who
became an explorer, and after desperate encounters
with hostile Indians and other jungle perils, founded
the (present) city of Bogota in (present-day) Colombia
which he called New Granada, in the 1530s.   (I)

56 Wise, Winifred. Fray Junipero Serra and the California Conquest. Ill. with photographs and prints of
missions. Jacket by Jean Krulis. Scribner's, 1967.
A biography of the Spanish missionary (1713-84), based
on his own writings and the works of his contempor-
aries, and the story of his establishment of the chain
of missions along the California coast. The appendix

includes "Dramatis Personae" (a list of 23 who
played important parts in the conquest by the Church;)
a "Babble of Tongues" (a few words of Indian dialects
which the Spanish found useful); "California Mission
Chain" (a list of missions and their founding dates),
"Adorning the Wilderness" (a list of Church needs
compiled by Serra); "For the Record" (Serra's accounts for 1774); and "Mission Housekeeping" (articles
needed to set up a mission). Also a bibliography and
Index. (A)

57 Wojciechowska, Maia (Rodman). Odyssey of Courage;
The Story of Alvar Núñez Cabeza de Vaca. Ill. by
Alvin Smith. Atheneum, 1965. A biography of the
Spanish explorer (1490-1557) who tried to bring freedom and peace to the native Americans wherever he
went. Part One of the book covers Cabeza's epic
journey, mostly by land, from Florida to Mexico.
Part II takes him to South America and finally back
to Spain where false reports made him out to be a
traitor. (YA)

THE ENGLISH (Hudson)

58 Carmer, Carl. Henry Hudson. Ill. by John Cosgrave
II. Garrard, 1960. A Discovery Book. The story
of the English navigator (1562-1611) who discovered
the Hudson River for the Dutch in 1609, and Hudson
Bay for the English in 1611 and was left there to die by
the mutinous sailors of the "Discovery." (1562-1611)
(E)

59 Rachlis, Eugene. The Voyages of Henry Hudson. Ill.
by H. B. Vestal. Random House, Landmark, 1962.
Henry Hudson, born in 1552, was 55 years old before
he began the voyages mapped in this book, and it
was 1609 when he discovered the Hudson River for
the Dutch and 1611, Hudson Bay for the English.
(1552-1611) (I and YA)

60 Syme, Ronald. Henry Hudson. Ill. by William Stobbs.
Morrow Junior Books, 1955. A biography with ex-
cerpts from Hudson's own diaries and a map (1562-
1611). (I)

THE FRENCH

61 Allen, Merritt Parmalee. The Wilderness Way. Ill.
by Larry Toschik. David McKay, 1954. An

exciting story of the tremendous courage and persistence of La Salle and his aide, Tonti, and of the
fictitious adventures of a young Frenchman accompanying La Salle on his voyage to the mouth of the Mississippi. Told with verve and humor. (I and YA)

62 Buehr, Walter. The French Explorers in America.
Ill. by the author. G. P. Putnam's Sons, 1961.
Brief narratives about the principal French explorers
and settlers on the American continent. Emphasis on
Cartier, Champlain and La Salle but references to
Radisson, Verrazano, Marquette, Joliet and others.
(I)

63 Fuller, Iola. Gilded Torch. G. P. Putnam's Sons,
1957. A long novel about twin brothers who ac-
company La Salle on his mission to obtain the Mississippi River lands for France under Louis XIV.
Parts I and II are set in France in the flamboyant
court at Versailles, but the main body of the book is
Part III in which are related the harrowing and dis-
couraging adventures of La Salle and Tonti, the
problems of the Count de Frontenac, the interference
of the Jesuits and the troubles of the "Recolets,"
particularly Father Hennepin. (A)

64 Graham, Alberta Powell. La Salle, River Explorer.
Ill. by Avery Johnson. Abingdon Press, 1954. The
exciting story of the young French explorer who overcame savage Indians, hunger, extreme cold and even
treachery to claim the Louisiana territory for King
Louis XIV of France. He had many enemies and only
a few friends, but those were important, including,
among others, the Count de Frontenac, Tonti of the
Iron Hand, and, indeed, King Louis XIV. (I)

65 Norman, Charles. Orimha of the Mohawks. Ill. by
Johannes Troyer. Macmillan, 1961. The story of
Pierre Esprit Radisson's capture near Trois-Rivieres
in Canada and captivity by the Mohawks who adopted
him into their tribe, renamed him Orimha, and took
him to what is now New York State, ending with his
escape and return to his real family. The story
takes place in the 1650s but Radisson's life span was
from 1632 to 1710, and it was after his Mohawk captivity that he made important explorations. (YA)

66 North, Sterling. Captured by the Mohawks, and Other
Adventures of Pierre Radisson. Ill. by Victor Mays.
Houghton Mifflin, 1961. This story, based on Pierre
Radisson's own "Voyages" starts right in with his
capture by the Mohawks and adoption into the Mohawk

tribe and carries on with his attempt to escape, his
recapture, and his accompanying the Mohawks in their
war against the Eries. After his successful escape,
the story goes on to his explorations to the western
limits of Lake Superior, his visits to the Dakota
Sioux, his promotion of the beaver trade and discovery of the overland route to Hudson's Bay, ending
with the disappointments of his later years. (I and
YA)

67 Ridle, Julia Brown. Mohawk Gamble. Jacket and map
by the Etheredges. Harper and Row, 1963. An exciting novel about the early life of Pierre Radisson,
more a character study than a biography, according
to the author, and covering only the year he spent
after his recapture and torture by the Mohawks and
his plans and attempts to escape. Radisson later became largely responsible for the formation of the
Hudson Bay Company. (YA)

68 Syme, Ronald. Cartier, Finder of the St. Lawrence.
Ill. by William Stobbs. William Morrow, 1958.
The adventures of the good brave Frenchman (1491-
1557) who discovered the St. Lawrence River in
1553.

69   . Champlain of the St. Lawrence. Ill. by
William Stobbs. William Morrow, 1952. About
Champlain's explorations, settlements, and relations
with the Indians, from his 15th year to his death,
1585-1635. (I and YA)

70   . La Salle of the Mississippi. Ill. by William
Stobbs. William Morrow, 1953. Robert Cavalier de
La Salle was born in 1644 near the village of La Salle
in France. With Tonti of the Iron Hand he went to
the New World in 1666 and explored the Mississippi
but failed to establish the forts he had planned, before
his murder in 1687. A story of harrowing hardships
and courage. (I)

THE COLONIAL PERIOD (16th to 18th Centuries)

THE SOUTHERN COLONIES (16th and 17th Centuries)

71 Bothwell, Jean. Lady of Roanoke. Holt, Rinehart and
    Winston, 1965. An imaginative story of what might
    have happened to Raleigh's "lost colony" which was
    landed on Roanoke Island in 1587, and how little Vir-
    ginia Dare may have grown up, and how the colonists
    may have managed to exist without any further contact
    with England. A list of the colonists is included and
    an explanatory caste of the main characters, also an
    historical note and bibliography. (YA)
71a _____. Lost Colony. Ill. by Edward F. Cortese.
    Holt, Rinehart and Winston, 1953. A story of what
    could possibly have happened to the White-Dare
    Colony which completely vanished after 1587. There
    have been many theories but probably no one will
    ever know. (YA)
72 Campbell, Elizabeth A. The Carving on the Tree: A
    True Account of America's First Mystery--The Lost
    Colony of Roanoke Island. Ill. by William Bock.
    Little Brown, 1968. (E)
73 Johnston, Mary. To Have and To Hold. Houghton
    Mifflin, 1899. A wildly romantic thriller about the
    Jamestown settlement in the early 17th century when
    young women were imported from England to become
    wives for the men already there, and when the Indians
    were friendly one day and hostile the next. John
    Rolfe, husband of Pocahontas and her brother Nan-
    tauquas, are among some of the real characters in
    the novel.
74 Latham, Jean Lee. This Dear-Bought Land, by Jacob
    Landau. Harper, 1957. An absorbing fictional ac-
    count of Captain John Smith's adventures at James-
    town and his persistence in holding the colony for
    England in spite of scurvy, starvation, and hostile
    Indians. (I and YA)
75 Leighton, Margaret. The Sword and the Compass: The
    Farflung Adventures of Capt. John Smith. Ill. by
    James Leighton. Houghton Mifflin, 1951. A

22

biographical novel about the miraculous escapes, important explorations, and sad frustrations of this
English captain (1580-1631) whose life was once saved
by the Indian princess Pocahontas. (YA)

76 Lobdell, Helen. Captain Bacon's Rebellion. Jacket by
Henry C. Fitz. Macrae Smith, 1959. A novel in
which fictional Leigh Martinson, aged 16, takes part
in the rebellion of Nathaniel Bacon, in 1676, against
Jamestown's Governor Berkeley, appointed by King
Charles II of England. A very early chapter in
America's fight for independence. (YA)

77 Stevenson, Augusta. Virginia Dare, Mystery Girl. Ill.
by Harry Hanson Lees. Bobbs-Merrill, 1958. Childhood of Famous Americans Series. A purely fictional
story of the first white child, born of English parents,
in what is now the United States, in 1587. The true
story can never be known, but here is a supposition.
(E and I)

78 Wellman, Manly Wade.   Jamestown Adventures.
Ives Washburn, 1967. A story of Captain John
Smith's settlement at Jamestown, with both actual and
fictional characters and both real and imaginary
events, but all based on historical probability. (I)

THE SOUTHERN COLONIES (18th Century)

79 Best, Herbert. Carolina Gold. John Day, 1961. A
story of a certain Eliza Lucas, credited with the introduction of indigo into South Carolina, and how she
solved the problem of a treacherous foreman. (YA)

80 Blackburn, Joyce. James Edward Oglethorpe. Jacket
by Marvin Mattelson. J. B. Lippincott. A biography
of an early civil rights leader (1696-1785) who fought
against prison cruelty and slavery and in defense of
the poor; the founder of the Colony of Georgia in 1733
and a sympathizer with the American Revolutionists.
(YA and Up)

81 Coatsworth, Elizabeth. The Golden Horseshoe. Ill. by
Robert Lawson. Macmillan, 1935, revised by the
author, 1963. The adventures of a young Virginia
lady, half-Indian, who poses as a boy in order to go
on an expedition to the west. (I)

82 Faulkner, Nancy. A Stage for Rom. Ill. by Howard
Simon. Doubleday, 1962. A mystery story of the
18th-century theater in Williamsburg, in which twin
puppeteers, a boy and girl, search, more in fear than

hope, for their true parentage. (I)

83 McCall, Edith. <u>Log Fort Adventures</u>. Ill. by Carol
    Rogers. Childrens' Press, 1958. Included in this
    volume of true tales are the story of Jemima Boone's
    capture by and escape from the Indians; her father's
    (Daniel's) second escape from his Indian captors; and
    the story of how the women and girls helped save the
    Boonsborough Fort.

84 Orton, Helen Fuller. <u>A Lad of Old Williamsburg.</u>
    Photographs by Elinore Blaisdell. J. B. Lippincott,
    1938. A quiet little story of a boy's friendship with
    young George Washington, then aged 19, and of Wash-
    ington's courageous mission in behalf of Governor
    Dunwiddie in 1751. (I)

85 Parks, Aileen Wells. <u>James Oglethorpe, Young De-
    fender</u>. Ill. by Maurice Rawson. Bobbs-Merrill,
    1958-60. Childhood of Famous Americans Series.
    The story of the English childhood and youth of the
    man who founded the Colony of Georgia and settled
    Savannah in 1733, showing his early interest in prison
    reform and other human rights. (E)

86 Steele, William O. <u>Tomahawk Border</u>. Ill. by Vernon
    Wootin. Colonial Williamsburg, 1966 (Holt, Rine-
    hart and Winston). A 16-year-old in the Virginia
    Rangers has trouble in gaining the respect of his
    older companions as they defend the southwestern
    border of Virginia against the Indians. Exciting and
    humorous. (I and YA)

87 Watson, Sally. <u>The Hornet's Nest</u>, Holt, Rinehart
    and Winston, 1968. A story, rich in chuckly humor,
    about a Scottish pair, brother and sister, forced to
    flee to America because of their reckless words and
    actions against the British repression in Scotland,
    and about the hornet's nest they stir up in Colonial
    Williamsburg. A diagram of Williamsburg and a
    family tree of the relationships in the entertaining
    story. (I and YA)

THE NEW ENGLAND COLONIES (17th Century)

88 Albrecht, Lillie V. <u>Susanna's Candlestick.</u> Ill. by
    Lois Woehr. Hastings House, 1970. Susanna, in
    England, hears a gypsy's prophecy that she "faces
    a stormy sea and a long hard road, but a light to
    guide and shelter at the end." How this works out
    makes a well-plotted story of Puritan intolerance
    and Quaker faith.

89 Alderman, Clifford Lindsey. <u>The Devil's Shadow: The</u>
    <u>Story of Witchcraft in Massachusetts.</u> Ill. with maps
    and drawings. Julian Messner, 1967. A book as
    exciting as any work of fiction, about the mass hys-
    teria in Salem Village in 1692 (now Danvers) in which
    only those who confessed guilt were spared among the
    many accused of witchcraft. The leading character is
    Ann Putnam. An introduction to the subject of witch-
    craft in general and how it became a matter of im-
    portance in the 17th century is included. (YA)
90 Aldis, Dorothy. <u>Ride the Wild Waves.</u> Ill. by Robert
    Henneberger. Putnam, 1957. This story begins in
    England, at Tattershall Castle in 1628, as the Mas-
    sachusetts Bay colonizers lay their plans to emigrate
    and goes on to tell of their harrowing adventures at
    sea and sickness and death in Salem. Interwoven in
    this true story is that of an assumed "witch" who ac-
    companies the settlers as a nurse and servant. There
    is a list of the characters at the end with notes as to
    their fortunes after the arrival at Salem. (I)
91 Anderson, Bertha. <u>Tinker's Tim and the Witches.</u> Ill.
    by Lloyd Coe. Little Brown, 1951. A story about
    the days of witch hunting in Salem and the harm that
    was caused by fear and gossip. (E and I)
92 Anderson, Lonzo. Zeb. Ill. by Peter Burchard.
    Knopf, 1966. An absorbing story of a boy left alone,
    except for his dog, in the winter wilderness and how
    he builds a fire, finds food and shelter and survives
    the winter. (I and YA)
93 Bradbury, Bianca. <u>Goodness and Mercy Jenkins.</u> Ives
    Washburn, 1963. A novel of 1675 about a 16-year-
    old Puritan girl who is punished for not conforming
    to the rigid discipline of 17th-century New Haven, by
    being made to work unceasingly in the household of
    a harsh elder of the church, and how she set
    about to achieve freedom. (YA)
94 _____. <u>Sam and the Colonels.</u> Ill. by Charles Geer.
    Macrae Smith, 1966. A novel, based on day-by-day
    documentation, of the escape of two Puritan colonels
    from the agents of Charles II who tried to capture
    them and take them back to England for execution
    because of their part in the judgment of Charles I.
    (YA)
95 Bulla, Clyde Robert. <u>John Billington, Friend of Squanto.</u>
    Ill. by Peter Burchard. Thomas Y. Crowell, 1956.
    The story of a real boy in the Mayflower Company
    and how the Indian Squanto came to his aid when his

mischievous spirit got him into trouble.   (E and I)

96   Burt, Olive W.   John Alden, Young Puritan.   Ill. by
Vic Dowd.   Bobbs-Merrill, 1964.   Mainly the
story of John Alden's childhood and youth in
England and Holland.   A chronology of his life and
times (1599-1687), suggestions for further reading,
questions to look up, and projects relating to the
Mayflower Pilgrims complete the book.   (E and I)

97   Carleton, Barbee.   The Witches' Bridge.   Jacket by
Edward Gorey.   Holt, Rinehart and Winston, 1967.
A "present and past" mystery story in which a boy
tries to discover the secrets of old feuds dating
from the 17th century when his ancestors were exe-
cuted as witches.   A chart of the locale.   (I and
YA)

98   Chase, Virginia (Perkins).   The Knight of the Golden
Fleece; Twenty-first Son--Treasure Hunter--
Knight--Governor: A Biography of William Phips.
Ill. by Howard Simon.   Little Brown, 1959.   This
remarkable man was born in Maine in 1651 (he
died in 1695) but, with the support of Charles II
and James II, he became a treasure hunter and
brought back to England great riches from a sunken
Spanish galleon, for which accomplishment he was
knighted.   Appointed Governor of the Massachusetts
Bay Colony, he, through the influence of his wife,
Mary Spencer Phips, put an end to the Salem
witch hunts, in spite of the determination of Cotton
Mather to pursue them.   (YA)

99   Clapp, Patricia.   Constance: A Story of Early Plymouth.
Jacket by Sally Holliday.   Lothrop Lee and Shepard,
1968.   Essentially a love story about one of the
Mayflower Pilgrims, Constance Hopkins.   (YA)

100 Clarke, Mary Stetson.   The Iron Peacock.   Ill. by
Robert MacLean.   Viking, 1966.   A novel about a
young girl of the 1650s, indentured as a bond servant in the home of an Iron Master, head of the
"Company of Undertakers of the Iron Works in New
England."   This Iron Works, restored along with
the Iron Master's House, can be seen today in
Saugus, Massachusetts, also a house said to have
been the dwelling of the Scots captured at Dunbar
and sent to New England as indentured workmen.
Woven through an exciting plot, is a great deal of
information about these early iron works, the
Indians of the vicinity, and domestic details.   Most
of the characters are fictional though two important

ones are based on records of real people. (YA)

101 Coatsworth, Elizabeth. First Adventure. Ill. by
Ralph Ray. Macmillan, 1968. There really was
a Johnny Billington who came over on the Mayflower, he really did get lost, and he really was taken
in by the Indians. The author has expanded these
facts into a delightful story. (E)

102 Curren, Polly. Hear Ye of Boston. Ill. by Kurt
Werth. Lothrop Lee and Shepard, 1964. Very
young children will enjoy listening to this story as
they look at the pictures and those, just learning
to read, will develop an early taste for history.
(Picture and E)

103 Edwards, Cecile Pepin. Roger Williams, Defender of
Freedom. Ill. by Harve Stein. Abingdon, 1957.
Almost the whole first half of this biography takes
place in England where, under Archbishop Laud,
any dissension from the Church of England was
severely punished. Roger Williams (1603-1683)
also found suppression of religious freedom in New
England, and founded Rhode Island as a home for
all sects. (I)

104 Graves, Charles P. William Bradford. Ill. by Marvin
Besunder. Garrard, 1969. A biography of the
man (1590-1657) who, starting as an English orphan,
became a "Separatist" from the Church of England,
lived for ten years in Holland, sailed on the Mayflower in 1620, and became Governor of Plymouth.
(E and I)

105 Hall, Elvajean. Margaret Pumphrey's Pilgrim Stories.
Ill. by Jon Milsen. Rand McNally, 1962. Stories,
revised and expanded by Elvajean Hall, about real
people who came to the New World for various
reasons--all adventurous and courageous, though
often fearful. About one-third of the Mayflower
passengers were children, as can be seen by the
list of their names and probable ages at the end of
the book. The original stories were published by
Rand McNally more than 50 years ago. (I)

105a _____. Pilgrim Neighbors: More True Pilgrim
Stories. Ill. by Jon Nielsen. Rand McNally, 1964.
The struggles of the Pilgrims did not, by any means,
end with that happy first Thanksgiving feast. The
period covered by these dramatic stories lasts from
the fall of 1621 until the late summer of 1676,
after King Philip's War, with a brief epilogue about
the year of 1691. (I)

106 Hawthorne, Nathaniel. The Scarlet Letter. 1850. A
     small classic of Puritan intolerance. Various editions.
     (A)
107 Hays, Wilma Pitchford. Naughtly Little Pilgrim. Ill.
     by Marilyn Miller. Ives Washburn, 1969. The
     story of seven-year-old John Billington who got into
     all sorts of mischief on the Mayflower, and later
     got lost in the woods and was cared for by the
     Indian Squanto. (E)
108 _____. May Day for Samoset. Ill. by Marilyn
     Miller. Coward-McCann, 1968. A story about some
     settlers on an island off the Maine coast, who were
     not Puritans and who carried on the English custom
     of celebrating May Day. (E and I)
109 Jackson, Shirley. The Witchcraft of Salem Village. Ill.
     by Lili Rethi. Random Landmark, 1956. It all be-
     gan with a group of girls who had a club in Salem
     Village, Mass., in 1692 and gathered to hear Tituba,
     a slave from the West Indies, tell their fortunes and
     "bewitch" them with tales of Magic and superstition.
     (I and YA)
110 Lenski, Lois. Puritan Adventure. Ill. by the author.
     J. B. Lippincott, 1944. This attractively illustrated
     story gives a vivid impression of the grimness of
     Puritan life, even for the children, and tells of a
     merry young widow who arrives from Merry England
     bringing some jolly traditions and customs. (I)
111 Longfellow, Henry Wadsworth. The Courtship of Miles
     Standish. 1858. A long narrative poem about John
     Alden, Priscilla Mullins, and the unfortunate Captain
     Standish. (A)
111a MacGibbon, Jean. A Special Providence. Ill. by
     William Stobbs. Coward McCann, 1964. The first
     two thirds of the book are set in England and the last
     third at sea as the Mayflower sails for America.
     Interesting details of the preparations for the voyage,
     the construction and provisioning of the ship, and
     finally the voyage itself, as experienced by young
     Giles Hopkinson, based on the eye witness account
     of William Bradford. (I)
112 McGovern, Ann. If You Sailed on the Mayflower. Ill.
     by J. B. Handlesman. Four Winds, 1967. A highly
     original question and answer book about the Mayflower
     which might well be subtitled, "History for the Fun
     of It." (E)
113 Meadowcroft, Enid LaMonte. The First Year. Ill. by
     Grace Pauli. Thomas Y. Crowell, 1937-46. A

story about the Hopkins family who sailed on the
Mayflower and were among those who survived the
first hard winter in the New World. (E)

114 Molloy, Anne. The Years before the Mayflower. Ill.
by Richard Cuffari and with maps and old prints.
Hastings House, 1972. The story of William
Brewster and his company, their trials, frustrations,
and dissensions before finally setting sail on the
terribly overcrowded little Mayflower in 1620. (YA)

114a Peterson, Helen Stone. Roger Williams. Ill. by Ray
Burns. Garrard, 1968. Biography of the adventurous
and morally courageous man (1603-83) who believed
so strongly in religious freedom and the separation
of church and state that he founded Rhode Island in
1630, establishing there an example of that separation which was followed much later by the new United
States government. (I)

115 Petry, Ann. Tituba of Salem Village. Thomas Y.
Crowell, 1964. A novel about the negro slave de-
nounced as a witch during the Salem hysteria of
1692. (A)

116 Pilkington, Roger. I Sailed on the Mayflower: A
Boy's Discovery of the New World. Ill. by Douglas
Bisset. St. Martin's Press, 1966. A carefully
detailed and realistic story about the Pilgrims, first
in Holland and then in Massachusetts, their priva-
tions, suffering and courage, as narrated by Love,
the son of Elder Brewster. (I)

117 Smith, Bradford. William Bradford, Pilgrim Boy.
Ill. by Paul Busch. Bobbs-Merrill, 1953. Childhood of Famous Americans Series. William Bradford (1590-1657) spent most of his childhood and
youth in England so this book gives the English
background of the Scrooby Pilgrims, including much
about Elder Brewster the leader. Written by a
descendant of Brewster. (E)

118 Speare, Elizabeth George. The Witch of Blackbird
Pond. Jacket by Nicholas Angelo. Houghton Mifflin,
1958. A Newbery Prize book. A love story set in
the Connecticut Colony in 1687, the heroine a young
lady from Barbados whose gayety and verve ill fits
the Puritan ways. When the problem of witchcraft
enters into the story suspension mounts, nearly
to the last page. (YA)

119 Wood, James Playsted. The Admirable Cotton Mather.
Jacket by Joan Less. Seabury, 1971. Biography
of a much misunderstood Puritan preacher, prolific

writer and a man scientifically ahead of his time
(1663-1728). He is, unhappily, most often remembered for his part in the Salem witch hunts, but,
though he himself believed in witchcraft, he was
never one to accuse people of it without what he
considered solid evidence, and even then preferred
their conversion to their deaths. (YA)

120 Zeiner, Feenie (in consultation with George F. Willi-
son). The Pilgrims and Plymouth Colony. Ill.
with paintings, prints, drawings and maps of the
Period. American Heritage, 1961. A beautiful
book about the "saints and strangers" who came to
America in 1620, going into the history of the 17th-
century England from which they fled and showing
how they, in turn, were intolerant of later-comers.
(YA)

THE NEW ENGLAND COLONIES (18th Century)

121 Albrecht, Lillie. The Spinning Wheel Secret. Ill. by
Joan Balfour Payne. Hastings House, 1965. It
was considered a bad thing to be a tomboy in
Colonial Massachusetts, but eight-year-old Joan discovered (and so did others) after an Indian raid,
that boyish ways were very useful at times. She
also learned something else, but therein lies the
secret. (E and I)

122 Butters, Dorothy Gilman. Ten Leagues to Boston Town.
Macrae Smith, 1962. An entertaining novel about a
young lady and her 13-year-old brother traveling by
sleigh to Boston in 1750 and about their fantastic
adventures on the ten league trip. (I and YA)

123 Dalgliesh, Alice. The Courage of Sarah Noble. Ill.
by Leonard Weisgard. Charles Scribner's Sons,
1954. A story, based on fact, about a real eight-
year-old girl who, in 1707, went into the wilderness
to cook for her father until he could establish a
home for her mother and younger children, and also
about the early settlement of New Milford, Connecticut. (E)

124 Field, Rachel. Calico Bush. Wood engravings by
Allen Lewis. Macmillan, 1931-66. The story of a
French girl "bound out" in 1743, to a pioneer family
settling in dangerous Indian territory on the Maine
coast. A lyrical story worthy of its fine edition.
(I and YA)

125 Lenski, Lois. <u>Ocean-Born Mary.</u> Ill. by the author.
     J. B. Lippincott, 1939. A story of a little girl
     (based on a real character who lived to be 94) who
     was born on a pirate ship and thus became involved
     with the pirate captain who had spared her's and
     her mother's lives. Along with the story of Mary
     is a panoramic picture of life in a New England sea-
     port town (Londonderry, New Hampshire) in 1732 and
     an account of the settlers' rebellion against the
     "Pine Tree Law."
126 Mott, Michael. <u>Master Entrick: An Adventure--1754-
     1756.</u> Delacorte, 1965. A novel about an English
     lad kidnapped and taken to America to be sold as
     indentured servant. Escaping that fate, he is taken
     into an Indian tribe and finally becomes involved in
     the French and Indian war. (YA)
127 Smith, Fredrica Shumway. <u>Old Put: The Story of
     Major General Israel Putnam.</u> Ill. with photographs
     and contemporary prints. Rand McNally, 1967.
     A biography of the great military leader (1718-90)
     in the French and Indian Wars and also in the
     Revolution, with interesting military details and
     lively accounts of "Old Put's" courage and narrow
     escapes. (YA)
128 Speare, Elizabeth George. <u>The Prospering.</u> Houghton
     Mifflin, 1967. An adult novel by the author of "The
     Witch of Blackbird Pond" about the early years of
     Stockbridge, Massachusetts, 1737-52, as it grew
     from an Indian town to an English one; about the
     mission to the Indians and how the Indians were
     finally driven out. It is also about the conflict be-
     tween followers of Jonathan Edwards, with his belief
     in predestination, and those of John Sergeant who
     believed that God's grace was open to all. (A)
129 Thompson, Mary Wolfe. <u>Two in the Wilderness.</u> Ill.
     by William Plummer. David McKaye, 1967.
     Scholastic Book Services paperbound. Shortly before
     the Revolution, a 10-year-old boy and his 12-year-
     old sister manage by themselves in the wilderness of
     the New Hampshire Grants while their father makes
     the long journey back to Connecticut to fetch their
     mother and the younger children. For over six
     weeks they cope with wild animals and storms and
     protect the precious corn crop their father has plant-
     ed. (E)

THE MIDDLE COLONIES (17th Century)

130 Berry, Erick (Best). The Tinmaker Man of New Am-
     sterdam. Winston, 1941. A story of old New
     York in the time of Governor Stuyvesant, with music
     based on an old tune arranged by Nelson Sprackling.
     (E)

131 Daringer, Helen Fern. Country Cousin. Ill. by
     Stephani and Edward Godwin. Harcourt Brace, 1951.
     A slightly plotted period piece about an Endicott
     family, their clothes, parties and general goings-on
     in New York City in 1683. The third of a series.
     (I)

132 deAngeli, Marguerite. Elin's Amerika. Ill. by the
     author. Doubleday, Doran, 1941. A story about
     the early Swedish settlers in New Jersey, about
     1648, and one little girl in particular waiting anxious-
     ly for a ship from Sweden to bring her a playmate.
     Lovely illustrations and text about old Swedish cus-
     toms. (E and I)

133 deLeeuw, Adele. Peter Stuyvesant. Ill. by Vincent
     Colabella. Garrard, 1970. Biography of the first
     mayor of New Amsterdam (1592-1672) and largely
     about his difficulties with both the English and
     Dutch governments. (I)

134 Haviland, Virginia. William Penn, Founder and Friend.
     Ill. by Peter Burchard. Abingdon, 1952. Biography
     of Penn (1644-1718) mainly about his life in England
     and Ireland, but important here for the part about
     his founding of Pennsylvania and Philadelphia, the
     City of Brotherly Love. (E and I)

135 Lobel, Arnold. On the Day Peter Stuyvesant Sailed
     into Town. Ill. by the author. Harper and Row,
     1971. A book of delightful verse and pictures about
     the arrival of the Director-General at New Amster-
     dam in 1647 when he found the village in great dis-
     order. (E)

136 Malvern, Gladys. Wilderness Island. Jacket by
     Evelyn Copelman. Macrae Smith, 1961. A romance
     of New Amsterdam, 1628-45, in which the formerly
     good relations between Dutch and Indians are ruined
     by the killing of a friendly Indian and the acts of a
     tyrannical Dutch governor. (YA)

137 Peare, Catherine Owens. William Penn. Ill. by
     Henry C. Pitz. Holt, 1958. An adaptation of the
     author's definitive adult biography, Lippincott, 1957.
     (YA)

138 Syme, Ronald. William Penn: Founder of Pennsylvania.
     Ill. by Stobbs. William Morrow, 1966. Large print.
     (E and I)

THE MIDDLE COLONIES (18th Century)

139 Allen, Merritt Parmelee. The Flicker's Feather. Ill.
     by Tom O'Sullivan. Longmans Green, 1953. A story
     of Rogers' Rangers and the conflicts between them
     and the British Regulars in 1758-9, because of their
     different methods of warfare. Humor and a surprise
     ending. (YA)
140 Alter, Robert Edmond. Listen the Drum: A Novel of
     Washington's First Command. G. P. Putnam's,
     1963. A story based on thorough research, about
     George Washington's retreat from the French and
     Indians at Fort Necessity. Good map and reference
     list. (YA)
141 Best, Herbert. The Long Portage. Ill. by Erick
     Berry. Viking, 1948. A novel about the wagon
     road between Fort Edward and Fort William Henry,
     where the British, the Colonials, and Rogers'
     Rangers were all in constant danger of ambush by
     the Indians and French. A 17-year-old Englishman
     acts as scout and spy for Lord Howe. (I and YA)
142 Bobbé, Dorothie. The New World Journey of Anne
     MacVicar. Jacket by Anthony L. Gruerio. G. P.
     Putnam's Sons, 1971. Based on Anne's own book.
     "Memoirs of an American Lady," this story of her
     young years in Albany gives an illuminating view of
     the French and Indian Wars, the causes of the
     Revolution and the troubles besetting a loyalist family
     at that time. (I)
143 Brick, John. On the Old Frontier: A Tim Murphy Ad-
     venture. G. P. Putnam's Sons, 1966. A humorous
     tale of two reckless young woods runners in Pennsyl-
     vania who are determined to go to the Ohio country
     to trap and hunt but who frequently find themselves
     entrapped instead. (I)
144 Butler, Beverly. The Lion and the Otter. Dodd Mead,
     1957. A novel set in the period when the French
     and English were battling each other over the fort
     at Detroit, with Pontiac vacillating from side to
     side, causing confusion to a young French girl whose
     brother is a "coureur de bois" (trapper) with
     Pontiac's tribe, the young man she loves is an

English Lieutenant, and her father is violently
against both English and French. (YA)

145 Carmer, Carl. Rebellion at Quaker Hill: A Story of
the First Rent War. Ill. by Harve Stein. John C.
Winston, 1954. When the tenant farmers, called
"Levelers," revolted against their manor lords,
called patroons, in 1776, a gallant wife rode 160
miles to save their leader, William Prendergast,
from the gallows. (I and YA)

146 Coatsworth, Elizabeth. The Last Fort: A Story of the
French Voyageurs. Ill. by Edward Shenton. Holt,
Rinehart and Winston, 1952. A thrilling story of
the 1760s, about a boy's voyage from Quebec to the
Mississippi Valley, in search of land still under the
French flag. (YA)

147 Curren, Polly. Hear Ye of Philadelphia. Ill. by Kurt
Werth. Lothrop, Lee and Shepard, 1968. A story of
happenings in Philadelphia in the early days of the
country. (E and I)

148 de Angeli, Marguerite. Jared's Island. Ill. by the
author. Doubleday, 1947. A treasure hunt, life
with the Indians, and a growing appreciation of a
treasure better than gold are the main elements of
this story of a small boy's adventures around Barna-
gat Bay in 1760.   (I)

149 Edmonds, Walter D. The Matchlock Gun. Ill. by Paul
Lautz. Dodd Mead, 1941. A true exciting story
about a ten-year-old boy in New York State in 1757,
with lithographic drawings which will appeal to children not yet able to read. (E and I)

150 _____. They Had a Horse. Ill. by Douglas Gorsline. Dodd Mead, 1965. A poignant novella about
a very young couple, their most precious possession, a chair, and their need and deep desire for
a horse. (YA)

151 Gibbs, Alonzo. The Fields Breathe Sweet. Lothrop
Lee and Shepard, 1963. A love story of the early
Dutch Settlers on Long Island, in which an 18-year-
old maiden must chose between a persecuted,
fanatical Quaker and a light-hearted cobbler and also
consider her duty to her hard worked mother. (YA)

152 _____. A Man's Calling. Ill. by Cecile Rojer.
Lothrop Lee and Shepard, 1966. A strong novel
about a young half-breed's growth in self understanding and of the problems of her foster parents and
the young man she loves. She also grows to understand the need of a new, young country for law and

order, as she studies the methods of land surveying
and takes on "a man's calling." (YA)

153 Hall, Rosalys. Seven for St. Nicholas. Ill. by Kurt
Werth. J. B. Lippincott, 1958. A story, full of
humor and charming detail, about seven Dutch children who have been brought to the colony on Man-
hattan Island in the early 18th century and are fearful that St. Nicholas won't visit them there. The
second daughter, Maritje, especially misses old
Amsterdam and her grandparents and finds it hard
to adjust to the New World. (I)

154 Roberts, Kenneth. Northwest Passage. Doubleday,
1936. A novel, set mainly in New York State in
1757-9 having as its hero (though eventually a fallen
one), Major Robert Rogers and as its fictional
narrator, a young artist friend of Copley and Benjamin West. The plot deals with Rogers' expedition
against the Indians of St. Francis and his dreams
of finding a passage to the Pacific.

155 Singmaster, Elsie. I Heard of a River. Ill. by
Henry C. Pitz. Holt, Rinehart and Winston, 1948.
A novel about the German-Swiss Mennonites who
escaped from the desolated Palatinate of Germany,
and, at the invitation of William Penn, and after
many perils and hardships, settled in what is now
Lancaster County, Pennsylvania at the beginning of
the 1700s. (YA)

156 Welch, Ronald. Mohawk Valley. Ill. by William
Stobbs. Criterion, 1958. A novel about an aristocratic young Englishman who, having been sent down
from Cambridge for duelling, comes to America to
look after his father's fur-trading interests. His
education in woodsmanship and participation in the
Battles of Fort Ticonderoga and Quebec provide exciting action. (YA)

THE REVOLUTIONARY PERIOD

BIOGRAPHIES AND BIOGRAPHICAL NOVELS

157 Alderman, Clifford Lindsey. Samuel Adams, Son of
Liberty. Jacket by Robert Golster. Holt, Rine-
hard and Winston, 1961. Samuel Adams (1722-
1803) was a member of the class of 1740 at
Harvard, and there is interesting college material
here. Later, as one of the Sons of Liberty, he
may or may not have taken part in the shameful
rioting for which they were responsible, but he has
been called "The Chief Incendiary of the American
Revolution" and he was certainly a powerful propa-
gandist. (YA)

158 Alexander, Lloyd. The Flagship Hope: Aaron Lopez.
Ill. by Bernard Kingstein. Farrar Straus and
Cudahy, 1960. Jewish Publication Society. This
bibliography of one of the unsung Jewish heroes
(1752-81) of the American Revolution, covers the
period of Lopez' life from 1752, when he was a young
Marrano (a Jew who professed Christianity to save
his life and that of his wife) to his death in 1781.
(YA)

159 Bailey, Ralph Edgar. Guns over the Carolinas; The
Story of Nathaniel Greene. Maps by James Mac-
Donald, Frontispiece by Franz Alschuler. William
Morrow and Co., 1967. This biography of the man
second in command to George Washington (1742-86),
and the detailed maps accompanying it, give a co-
herent account of the Revolutionary War, particularly in the south where Greene, a master of the
tactics of strategic retreat, paves the way for
Cornwallis' surrender at Yorktown. (YA)

160 Bishop, Claire Huchet. Lafayette, French-American
Hero. Ill. by Maurice Brevannes. Garrard, 1960.
A Discovery Book. The story of some exciting adventures of Lafayette's early life, and of his important part in the American Revolution. (E)

161 Brown, Slater. Ethan Allen and the Green Mountain
Boys. Ill. by William C. Moyers. Random Land-

Mark, 1956.   Talk about violence!   That Green
Mountain gang were certainly a tough lot, as they
fought the feudal land-holding attempts of the
"Yorkers" to incorporate the New Hampshire Grants
(now Vermont) into their state of New York.   A
rousing story of Ethan's wild early life, his victory
at Ticonderoga and his capture and imprisonment by
the British.   (1738-89) (I)

162 Carmer, Elizabeth and Carl.   Francis Marion, Swamp
Fox of the Carolinas.   Ill. by William Plummer.
Garrard, 1962.   A Discovery Book.   A short biography (1732-95) with stories of his most famous
exploits.

163 Carter, Hodding.   The Marquis de Lafayette: Bright
Sword for Freedom.   Ill. by Mimi Korach.   Random, Landmark, 1958.   An exciting biography
(1757-1834) of the Frenchman who "ran away" to
help the American Colonists.   (I)

163a Coggins, Jack.   Boys in the Revolution.   Ill. by the
author.   Stackpole Books, 1967.   "Young Americans
tell their part in the War for Independence" and provide a splendid introduction to the subject of the
American Revolution with detailed drawings, a
chronology of the war and how the boys fitted into
it, and a guide to the illustrations.   Great research
material for writers about the period, young or
old.   (I and Up)

164 Coolidge, Olivia.   Tom Paine, Revolutionary.   Jacket
by Richard Cuffari.   Charles Scribner's Sons, 1969.
A serious study of a complex character (1737-1809)
whose support of the American and French Revolutions
and attacks on the religions of his day brought first
adulation, but later, loss of friends.   (YA)

165 Cousins, Margaret.   Ben Franklin of Old Philadelphia.
Ill. by Fritz Eichenberg.   Random House, 1952.
The story of a remarkable man--printer, inventor,
and statesman.   (I)

166 Daugherty, James.   Poor Richard.   Ill. with lithographs in two colors by the author.   Viking, 1941.
A well-written biography of Benjamin Franklin (1706-
1790) greatly enhanced by the illustrations and format of the book.   (I and YA)

167 d'Aulaire, Ingri and Edgar Parin.   Benjamin Franklin.
Ill. by the authors.   Doubleday, 1950.   Easy to
read but not "written down," and of course, brightly
illustrated.   (I)

168 deLeeuw, Adele.   George Rogers Clark, Frontier

Fighter.   Ill. by Russ Hoover.   Garrard, 1967.
A Discovery Book.   The story of Clark's conquest
of Illinois from the British and Indians.   (I)

169   Donovan, Frank.   The Brave Traitor: Benedict Arnold.
Ill. by Arthur Zaidenberg.   A. S. Barnes, 1961.   A
study of the man's character in war and peace, the
flaws and virtues in it and the frustrations which led
him into treachery.   (YA and Up)

170   Duncan, Lois.   Peggy.   Jacket by Colleen Browning.
Little Brown, 1970.   Its hard to believe that anyone
could be quite as heartless as young Peggy Shippen,
both before and after she married Benedict Arnold,
or that anyone could have been as merciless and
disloyal as Arnold himself, but this novel of the attempted betrayal of West Point shows them both in
a very bad light.   (YA)

171   Eaton, Jeanette.   That Lively Man: Ben Franklin.
Ill. by Henry C. Pitz.   William Morrow, 1948.
And a lively biography this is of one of the most
versatile characters in American history (1706-1790).
(I)

172   Gerson, Noel B.   Give Me Liberty: A Novel of Patrick
Henry.   Doubleday, 1966.   A biographical novel of a
great orator (1736-99) ("Give me liberty or give me
death"), but more than just that, this novel
points out Henry's service to the colony and state of
Virginia and to the newborn nation and its constitution.   (A)

173.   _____.   I'll Storm Hell.   Doubleday, 1967.   A biographical novel of "Mad Anthony Wayne" (1745-96)
with exciting accounts of his audacious military
strategy, with an afterword about the historical
basis.   Prominent in the novel are George Washington and Dr. Benjamin Rush.   (A)

174   _____.   The Swamp Fox, Francis Marion.   Doubleday, 1967.   An adult biographical novel about a man
(1732-95) who developed modern guerilla warfare
during the Revolution, from what he had learned
during the Cherokee War in the '60s.   (A)

175   Graham, Alberta Powell.   Lafayette, Friend of America.   Ill. by Ralph Ray.   Abingdon, 1952.   A biography, emphasizing Lafayette's services to the
Americans.   (E)

176   Green, Margaret.   Radical of the Revolution: Samuel
Adams.   Jacket by Anthony d'Admo.   Julian Messner,
1971.   This biography raises the interesting question
of the usefulness of violence in achieving one's ends.

Sam Adams (1722-1803) as a Son of Liberty, must
have believed it necessary. (YA)

177 Holbrook, Stewart. America's Ethan Allen. Ill. by
Lynd Ward. Houghton Mifflin, 1949. Biography of
the leader of Green Mountain Boys (1738-89) hero
of the victory at Fort Ticonderoga. (I and YA)

178 _____. The Swamp Fox of the Revolution. Ill. by
Ernest Richardson. Random Landmark, 1959. The
story of Francis Marion and his guerrilla tactics
against the British, as commander of a brigade of
South Carolinians. (I)

179 Kelly, Regina Z. Paul Revere, Colonial Craftsman.
Ill. by Harvey Kidder. Houghton Mifflin, 1963.
A biographical novel in which the author corrects
some of Longfellow's version of Revere's famous
ride. Footnotes and an author's note add special
interest for anyone planning to visit Boston. (I and
YA)

180 Lawson, Robert. Mr. Revere and I. Ill. by the author. Little Brown, 1953. This, along with other
books by Lawson, are "history on a lark"--just pure
fun. "An Account of Certain Episodes in the Career
of Paul Revere as revealed by his Horse, Sche-
herazade, late pride of Her Royal Majestie's 14th
Regiment of Foot." (I)

181 Lomask, Milton. Beauty and the Traitor: The Story
of Mrs. Benedict Arnold. Macrae Smith, 1967. A
novel about the treachery of Benedict Arnold and
his wife, Peggy Shippen Arnold, who encouraged him
in his treason. (YA)

182 Longfellow, Henry Wadsworth. Paul Revere's Ride.
Ill. by Paul Galdone. Thomas Y. Crowell, 1963.
A most attractive presentation of the well-known
poem. (All ages)

183 McKown, Robin. Thomas Paine. Jacket by Joseph
Cellini. G. P. Putnam's Sons, 1962. This excellent biography (1737-1809) dwells mainly on Paine's
American experiences but also tells of his English
youth and his French adventures, and, wherever he
might be, his humanitarianism. (YA)

184 Martini, Teri. Patrick Henry Patriot. Ill. by Robert
Jacobson. Westminster Press, 1972. A short
biography of the colorful orator (1736-99) who inspired the Virginia House of Burgesses with his
ringing words, "Give me Liberty or Give me
Death!". (I)

185 Merriam, Eve. The Story of Ben Franklin. Ill. by
by Brinton Turkle. Four Winds, 1965. An easy to

read, short biography with a time-line and afterword placing Franklin in relation to other historical
figures and events. (E and I)

186 Millender, Dharathula H. Crispus Attucks, Boy of
Valor. Ill. by Gray Morrow. Bobbs-Merrill,
1965. Mainly about the boyhood and youth of the
black boy, brought up as a slave, who found freedom at sea as a whaler and was the first of four
young men killed in the Boston Massacre in 1770,
considered the first engagement of the American
Revolution. (E and I)

187 Nolan, Jeannette Covert. Benedict Arnold, Traitor to
His Country. Julian Messner, 1956. A fictional
biography showing Arnold's original aim in life and
how it developed into treason.

188 O'Connor, Richard. The Common Sense of Tom Paine.
Ill. by Richard Cuffari. McGraw-Hill, 1969. Biography of the author of "Common Sense" and other books
which aided in the formation of the United States.
(1737-1809) (YA)

189 Pace, Mildred Mastin. Early American: The Story
of Paul Revere. Ill. by Henry S. Gillette. Charles
Scribner's Sons, 1940. In story form, this is a
portrait of the man (1735-1818) who was a silversmith, patriot, soldier, bell maker, and inventor of
a method of rolling copper. (I)

190 Sanderlin, George. Benjamin Franklin as Others Saw
Him. Ill. with photographs of paintings and prints.
Coward McCann and Geoghegan, 1971. The concise
biography at the beginning of this unique book ends
thus: "Inventor of the first republic of modern
times, skilled craftsman, renowned scientist, dis-
tinguished citizen, and master of the arts of his
century, Benjamin Franklin is one American writer
who brings honor not only to his country but to all
mankind." The following anthology of opinions of eminent men, however, shows that he was not so
highly considered by all. (YA and Up)

191 Saxon, Gladys. Paul Revere. Ill. by Jo Kotula and
jacket painting by Barren Storey. Follett, 1965.
A Beginning Social Studies Book. A picture book
story of Paul Revere's famous ride. (E)

192 Stevenson, Augusta. Anthony Wayne, Daring Boy. Ill.
by Gray Morrow. Bobbs-Merrill, 1948-62.
Childhood of Famous Americans Series. Showing
that even as a boy, Anthony Wayne was fairly
"mad." (E and I)

193 Sutton, Felix. Sons of Liberty. Ill. by Bill Barss.
       Map of the Thirteen Colonies by Barry Martin.
       Julian Messner, 1969. Short biographies of the
       following: Samuel Adams, John Hancock, Patrick
       Henry, Paul Revere, and Joseph Warren. (I)
194 Todd, A. L. Richard Montgomery, Rebel of 1775.
       Ill. and maps by Leonard Vosburgh. David McKay,
       1966. A solid, factual book about the 1775 expedi-
       tion into Quebec in which Montgomery (1736-75) took
       St. Johns and Montreal but was killed in the unsuc-
       cessful attempt to take Quebec. His conversion
       from English citizen to Continental rebel is described
       and his responsibility for securing the colonies
       against attack from the north is shown to be a de-
       cisive factor in the Revolution. A monument to him
       can still be seen in New York City where Broadway
       meets Fulton, Church and Vesey Streets. (YA and
       Up)
195 Wagner, Frederick. Patriot's Choice: The Story of
       John Hancock. Ill. with photographs of paintings and en-
       gravings. Dodd Mead, 1964. This biography of the
       wealthy merchant (1737-93) whose name appears first
       on the Declaration of Independence, provides a
       pleasantly readable and authoritative history of the
       causes and results of the American Revolution. (YA)

REVOLUTION IN THE NORTH

196 Albrecht, Lillie. The Grist Mill Secret. Ill. by
       Lloyd Coe. Hastings House, 1962. A story about a
       young Massachusetts girl entrusted by her father
       with a vitally important secret concerned with the
       Committee of Safety and the Minute Men; also a
       story of the intolerance and suspicion which develop
       in violent times. (I)
197 Beers, Lorna. The Crystal Cornerstone. Jacket and
       Frontispiece by Eleanor Mill. Harper and Brothers,
       1953. The story of a 16-year-old soldier serving
       under Washington and his growing understanding of
       the evils of war, but also the necessity of fighting
       for freedom. (YA)
198 Benchley, Nathaniel. Sam the Minuteman. Ill. by
       Arnold Lobel. Harper and Row, 1969. An I Can
       Read History Book. And for those who can't yet
       read, the story is made very clear by the enjoyable
       pictures of the events at Lexington, the beginning

of the Revolution. (Picture and E)

199 Berry, Erick (Best). Hay-Foot, Straw-Foot. Ill. by
the author. Viking, 1954. A humorous imaginary
account of how the words of "Yankee Doodle" might
have been composed and set to the music of an old
marching song. (I)

200 _____. Horses for the General. Jacket by Milo
Winter. Macmillan, 1956. An entertaining story of
a boy, too young and short to enlist in the army,
who with his dog finds ways to help the Continental
Army after meeting a courageous girl and her beloved horse. (I)

201 _____. Sybil Ludington's Ride. Ill. by the author.
Viking, 1951. A story about two real sisters, one
of whom, Sybil, made a famous ride, two years
after Paul Revere's, commemorated now by historical markers on Highway 216 near Danbury,
Conn. (I)

202 Boutwell, Edna. Daughter of Liberty. Ill. by Wendy
Watson. World, 1967. A story of the Revolution
built around a doll, sent over from England in the
Dartmouth of Boston Teaparty fame, and still on
view in the Old State House in Boston. (E and I)

203 Cheney, Cora. The Incredible Deborah: A Story
Based on the Life of Deborah Sampson. Ill. with
plates and a photograph of Deborah. Charles
Scribner's Sons, 1967. A biographical novel about
an amazing young lady who, in masculine garb, served
for almost two years in the Continental Army without revealing her sex. The Afterword gives the factual basis for the exciting story. (I and YA)

204 Clenard, Dorothy L. and Dorothy D. Newby. The
Hidey Hole. Ill. by Albert Orbaan. Duell Sloan
and Pearce, 1960. A lively contemporary mystery
story about the disappearance of a lady ancestor
in 1777 and the question of where she hid her
treasures. Interesting material about Washington
in Princeton. (I)

205 Dalgliesh, Alice. The 4th of July Story. Ill. by
Marie Nonnast. Charles Scribner's Sons, 1972.
A pictured history. (E)

206 deLeeuw, Cateau. Fear in the Forest. Ill. by L.
Vosburgh. Thomas Nelson, 1960. Story of a boy
who has an overwhelming fear of Indians because,
during the Revolution, they killed his father and
burned his home. In spite of this fear, however,

he accepts a job in a pack horse train, carrying
supplies to the string of forts in Ohio, being built
by General "Mad" Anthony Wayne. (I)

207   Dick, Trella Lamson. Flag in Hiding. Ill. by Don
Bolognese. Abelard Schuman, 1959. A suspenseful
story of a brother and sister living in the Tory-
dominated Hudson Valley at the time (1776) when
Burgoyne was coming down the Hudson, and St. Leger
coming up to meet him, loosing hordes of savage
Indians. (I)

208   Duncan, John M. Down the Mast Road. McGraw-Hill,
1956. Story about a 15-year-old boy who goes
"masting" for a tall pine tree and the dangers en-
countered in getting it to the sea, in 1775. (I)

209.   _____. Twelve Days 'til Trenton. McGraw-Hill,
1958. An exciting fictional account of Washington's
crossing of the Delaware. (I)

210   Edmonds, Walter D. Drums Along the Mohawk. Little
Brown, 1936. An epic novel of the warfare in the
Mohawk Valley from 1776 to 1784, the perserverance
and courage of the scattered farmers against British
regulars, green-coated Tories and painted Indians.
(A)

211   _____. Gordon's Clearing. From Seven American
Stories. Ill. by William Sants Bock. Little Brown,
1970. An absorbing novel about a young man, with
his little brother, and a girl, with her paralyzed
father, escaping from vengeful Tories and Indians
in upper New York State in 1777, and how quickly
the two young people grew up in their dependence
on each other. (I and YA)

211a Finlayson, Ann. Rebecca's War. Ill. by Sherry
Streeter. Frederick Warne, 1972. Rebecca Ran-
some, age 14, finds herself mistress of her house
and uneasy possessor of a vital secret, when Cornwallis marches into Philadelphia, and British officers
are billeted in her home. (I and YA)

212   Forbes, Esther. Johnny Tremain: A Story of Boston
in Revolt. Ill. by Lynd Ward. Houghton Mifflin,
1943. A Newbery Prize novel (also published in
paperback) whose hero, a young silversmith, injures
his hand and finds new employment with a Whig
newspaper. The plot builds up to the Battle of Lex-
ington and Concord. (I and YA)

213   Forman, James. The Cow Neck Rebels. With endpaper
maps. Farrar Straus and Giroux, 1969. An unusual
story of the Battle of Long Island in which two

brothers learn the realities of war as their Highland
Grandfather had learned them in the Battle of
Culloden, back in Scotland in 1745. Exceptionally
interesting characterizations and descriptions of nature. A fine anti-war novel. (YA and Up)

214 Fritz, Jean. Early Thunder. Ill. by Lynd Ward.
Coward-McCann, 1967. A novel of 1775 in which a
14-year-old boy plays an important role in turning
back the British near Salem, Mass. as he tries to
solve the conflict in his own heart and mind between
loyalty to the King or to his new country. (I and
YA)

215 Green, Diana Huss. The Lonely War of William Pinto.
Jacket by Don Bolognese, Little Brown, 1968. An
outstanding novel based on the actual characters of
the Pinto father and sons of New Haven, Conn. The
inner struggle of the youngest son, William, a paci-
fist, loyalist and Jew, results in a tragic conflict
with his father. (YA and Up)

216 Hall, Marjory. A Hatful of Gold. Westminster Press,
1964. A novel built upon the legend of Molly
Pitcher and the very few facts about her, culminating in the Battle of Monmouth. (YA)

217 _____. See the Red Sky. Westminster Press,
1963. A novel based on the real heroine, Sybil
Ludington, whose horse, Star, carried her on a ride
commemorated by historical markers and a statue
of the 16-year-old girl and the horse in Carmel,
New York. Author's note. (YA)

218 _____. The Seventh Star. Jacket by Clay Baker.
Westminster, 1969. A novel based on a legend
about the first American flag carried on the Ranger
of which John Paul Jones was captain, in 1777.
The main characters are fictional, but much of the
story is also based on records in Portsmouth, New
Hampshire, and an author's note at the end identifies the historical ones. The story of the quilting
of the flag may be verified by a visit to the Straw-
berry Bank Restoration in Portsmouth. (I and YA)

219 Hays, Wilma Pitchford. Fourth of July Raid. Ill. by
Peter Burchard. Coward McCann, 1959. An exciting story based on fact, about the British invasion
of New Haven, Conn., in 1779, their burning of
houses and the defiance of Joseph Tuttle. The
Morris house, burned at that time, was rebuilt in
1780 and is preserved as an historic landmark. (I)

220 Holberg, Ruth Langland. The Girl in the Witch

House. Ill. by Lloyd Coe. Hastings House, 1966.
A quiet little story about quiet people living in Cape
Anne, Mass., in 1775 and only slightly disturbed by
the Revolution (one brother fighting on the Rebel
side). Good description of daily life in that time
and place. (I)

221 Hopkinson, Francis. The Battle of the Kegs. Ill. by
Paul Galdone. Thomas Y. Crowell, 1964. A
brightly illustrated ballad about an actual incident
which enraged the British and boosted the morale
of the rebels. (Picture and E)

222 Hungerford, Edward Buell. Forge for Heroes. Ill.
by Bill Meeker. Wilcox and Follett, 1952. A
Valley Forge story (good title) of a young wagoner
who, in delivering axe-heads to General Washington,
finds himself involved in the sufferings, dangers,
and espionage in the camp. (YA)

223 Jones, Peter. Rebel in the Night. Jacket by Stan
Hunter. Dial, 1971. A rather grim novel of the
horror as well as the glory of the Revolution, its
"dark underside," and the varied motives that led
men to fight. (YA)

224 Leighton, Margaret. Who Rides By? Ill. by Joshua
Tolford. Farrar Straus and Cudahy, 1955. A
romance of the Revolution, set in New London and
Newport and having to do with the French allies,
particularly Ferson, the Swedish gallant with the
French forces. (YA)

225 Lowry, Janette Sebring. Six Silver Spoons. Ill. by
Robert Quackenbush. Harper and Row, 1971. An
I Can Read History Book. Both pictures and
words bring the Paul Revere story to the earliest
readers. (E)

226 Mason, F. Van Wyck. The Winter at Valley Forge.
Ill. by Harper Johnson. Random Landmark, 1953.
By the use of a few fictional characters, Mr.
Mason creates a good story of "the times that try
mens' souls" and gives the reader a feeling of
almost having experienced that terrible winter of
cold, hunger, disease and discouragement. (I and
YA)

227 Mayer, Jane. Betsy Ross and the Flag. Ill. by
Grace Pauli. Random Landmark, 1952. A story
which may be partly legendary as far as Betsy is
concerned but is factual about flags in general and
the stars and stripes in particular. (I)

228 Meadowcroft, Enid La Monte. Silver for General

<u>Washington.</u>   Ill. by Lee Ames.   Thomas Y.
<u>Crowell,</u> 1944-57.   A stirring story of the courage
of children and older civilians as well as the soldiers during the harrowing winter of 1777 and '78.
(I)

229   Miers, Earl Schenck.   <u>Yankee Doodle Dandy.</u>   Ill. by
Anthony D'Adamo.   <u>Rand McNally, 1963.</u>   Here is
the whole story of the Revolutionary War, dramatically told and well mapped, bringing to life the
major and some of the minor participants in the
action.   (I and YA)

230   Nelson, May.   <u>The Redbirds Are Flying.</u>   Ill. by
Carl Kidwell.   Criterion, 1963.   An exciting story
of a 14-year-old farmer's son and his Indian friend
who stumble upon some Tory spies, based on a
somewhat neglected bit of revolutionary history, the
"Paul Revere of New Jersey" episode.   (I)

231   Orton, Helen Fuller.   <u>Hoof-Beats of Freedom.</u>   Ill. by
Charles de Feo.   J. B. Lippincott, 1936.   Maps
of Long Island and New York City at the time of
the Revolution make this story of a young courier
for George Washington extremely real, especially
for children who live in those areas.   (I)

232   Palmer, Joan E.   <u>The Red Petticoat.</u>   Ill. by W. T.
Mars.   Lothrop Lee and Shepard, 1969.   The author
has built an exciting tale on the basis of historical
accounts of the Battle of Ridgefield, Conn., in
which there are several mentions of a certain red
petticoat.   (I)

233   Patterson, Emma L.   <u>The World Turned Upside Down.</u>
Jacket by Millard McGee.   Longmans Green, 1953.
Novel about a Dutch farmhand living beside King's
Ferry, and how the war came to him instead of his
going to the war.   His deep sense of loyalty to the
Tory "lord of the manor" creates a difficult decision for him to make--whether to support the
English King or the colonists.   To add to his
problem, his sense of honor interferes with his
devotion to the lady of the manor.   Good and unusual Revolutionary setting and characters.   (YA)

234   Phelan, Mary Kay.   <u>Four Days in Philadelphia 1776.</u>
Ill. by Charles W. Walker.   Thomas Y. Crowell,
1967.   This book recreates the four days of high
tension which culminated in the adoption of the
Declaration of Independence.   The signers come
vividly to life in their perplexities and concern for
the exact wording of the document.   (I and YA)

235 _____ . Midnight Alarm. Ill. by Leonard Vosburgh.
      Thomas Y. Crowell, 1968. The story of Paul
      Revere's Ride. (I)
236 Pope, Elizabeth Marie. The Sherwood Ring. Ill. by
      Evaline Ness. Houghton Mifflin, 1958. A skillful
      weaving of the revolutionary past with the 20th cen-
      tury in a well plotted novel about a young girl living
      with her crotchety antiquarian uncle on his haunted
      ancestral estate. (YA)
237 Roberts, Kenneth. Rabble in Arms: A Chronicle of
      Arundel and the Burgoyne Invasion. Doubleday Doran,
      1933. A sequel to the novel "Arundel" [see 897],
      with many of the same leading characters, fictional
      and real, and Benedict Arnold as the hero. Humor
      and realism combined; introduces some western
      Indian tribes. (A)
238 Stevenson, Augusta. Molly Pitcher, Girl Patriot. Ill.
      by Gene Garriott. Bobbs-Merrill, 1952-60. Child-
      hood of Famous Americans Series. Mary Ludwig
      Hays earned the name of Molly Pitcher because of
      the story of her carrying water to the wounded at the
      Battle of Monmouth in 1778. (E)
239 Sutton, Felix. We Were There at the Battle of Lexing-
      ton and Concord. Historical consultant, Earl Schenck
      Miers. Ill. by H. B. Vestal. Grosset and Dunlap,
      1958. A good story centering on "the shot heard
      round the world." (I)
240 Toepfer, Ray Grant. The White Cockade. Jacket by
      John Van Orden Chilton, 1966. An action-packed
      novel, with some real and some fictional characters,
      and a young scout as the hero, the plot culminating
      in the Battle of Minisink, July 22, 1779, with a
      diagram of the territory. (YA)
241 Viereck, Philip. Independence Must be Won. Ill. by
      Ellen Viereck. John Day, 1964. A vivid reconstruc-
      tion of the British attack, under Burgoyne, on Fort
      Ticonderoga and Fort Mt. Independence across from
      it as experienced by a fictional lad taking supplies to
      the Continental troops in the forts. The action of
      the story is clearly defined by maps and drawings,
      and there are diagrams of cannon, rifles and rifle
      equipment. The "Author's Note" on his research is
      of special interest. (I and YA)
242 Webb, Christopher. Matt Tyler's Chronicle. Funk and
      Wagnalls, 1958. The adventures, on land and sea,
      of a young Continental soldier in the Pennsylvania
      Rifles, and his acquaintance with woodsmen, pirates,

spies, redcoats and George Washington. (YA)

243   Wibberley, Leonard. John Treegate's Musket. Farrar
      Straus and Cudahy, 1959. A novel full of surprising
      adventures, beginning with the famous snowball
      fight, said to have sparked the Revolution, and
      ending with the Battle of Bunker Hill. Sam Adams
      an important figure in the story [see 244]. (YA)

244   _____. Peter Treegate's War. Farrar, Straus
      and Cudahy, 1960. A sequel to "John Treegate's
      Musket," covering the Battle of Breed's Hill, the
      crossing of the Delaware, Burgoyne's surrender.
      The plot concerns the conflict of a Peter Treegate,
      the foster son of a Scottish clansman who only
      wants revenge against the British for his losses in
      the Battle of Drummossie Muir in 1845 and does
      not care a tittle for the American cause--and the
      real son of an American patriot who had fought
      with the British on the Plains of Abraham. [See
      also entry 1349, 272, and 1367]. (YA)

245   Wise, William. Myer Myers, Silversmith of Old New
      York. Ill. by Leonard Everett Fisher. Farrar
      Straus and Giroux, 1958. Covenant Books. Written
      more like a novel than a biography (1723-95) and
      from a religious viewpoint, this book is particularly
      interesting for its account of the part played by the
      Jews in the American Revolution and of how they
      too were divided in their allegiance to England and
      the Colonies. (I)

246   Wriston, Hildreth T. A Yankee Musket. Ill. by Jo
      Polseno. Abingdon, 1959. A story of the war in
      the Vermont frontier country after the British had
      retaken Fort Ticonderoga. Two boys--a Yankee
      and a Tory--are caught up in the midst of fighting
      and learn that there are two sides to every war.
      (I)

247   Zawadsky, Patience. The Mystery of the Old Musket.
      Ill. by Frank Aloise. G. P. Putnam's Sons, 1967.
      A thriller of a mystery and spy story, set in the
      present but concerning Revolutionary times, about
      two boys and their grandfather seeking to restore
      their ancestor's good name and to discover the
      hiding place of a family fortune. (I)

REVOLUTION IN THE SOUTH

248   Allen, Merritt Parmeles. Battle Lanterns. Ill. by
      Ralph Ray Jr. David McKay, 1949. A novel of
      "Marion's Men" in which a lad of 17, after escaping
      from pirates and a year of slavery on an island in
      the West Indies, becomes an idolizing follower of
      Francis Marion, the Swamp Fox, who is sympathetical-
      ly portrayed. Through constant bloody action, the
      story shows the horrors of war and both the decency
      and brutality of men on both sides of the conflict.
      (YA)

249   Caudill, Rebecca. Tree of Freedom. Ill. by Dorothy
      Bayley Morse. Viking, 1947. A story, with beauti-
      ful nature details and good colloquial dialogue, of
      the Venables family, settling in Kentucky with land
      grant problems. Their courage and persistence in
      building a home-place and their part in the Revolu-
      tion make an inspiring tale. (YA)

250   Clagett, John. Gunpowder for Boonesborough. Jacket
      by Douglas Gorsline. Bobbs-Merrill, 1965. A
      Philadelphia boy, sent to join his parents in Boones-
      borough, Kentucky in 1776, joins "Gibson's Lambs, "
      Virginia militiamen, but because of a blue and white
      kerchief the Lambs consider him a traitor and throw
      him out in New Orleans where they are loading gun-
      powder for the Boonesborough fort. David takes
      wild risks to prove his Colonial loyalty. (I and YA)

251   Constiner, Merle. The Rebel Courier and the Redcoat.
      Jacket by Charles Waterhouse. Meredith, 1968.
      A 16-year-old Academy student in Charlotte, North
      Carolina, suddenly finds himself in possession of an
      important message from General Washington in the
      North to General Gates, Commander of the army in
      the South. Getting through both British and Colonial
      sentries, he becomes an observer of the Battle of
      King's Mountain. (I and YA)

252   Emery, Anne. Jennie Lee, Patriot. Westminster,
      1966. A young Charleston lady has friends, relatives,
      and beaux on both sides of the conflict between
      England and America, and only as the war nears its
      end, chooses her side. (YA)

253   Fox, Mary Virginia. Treasure of the Revolution. Ill.
      by Cary. Abingdon, 1961. Two children, boy and
      girl, are entrusted with a large amount of gold for
      the Colonial army as they are fleeing from Phila-
      delphia to go to their relatives in Virginia. The

girl's ingenuity comes to the fore more than once.
Thomas Jefferson (Uncle Tom to them) plays a part
in the story and Tom Paine appears briefly.   (I)

254   Gray, Elizabeth Janet.   Meggy MacIntosh: A Highland
Girl in the Carolina Colony.   Jacket by Marguerite
de Angeli.   Viking, 1930-58.   A novel of a young
Scottish girl who runs away to Carolina in search
of the famous Flora MacDonald and finds the High-
landers there in a losing fight against the American
patriots.   (YA)

255   Green, Robert James.   Patriot Silver.   Ill. by Lorence
F. Bjorklund.   St. Martin's, 1961.   A boy, dis-
guised as a trader and Loyalist, goes into British
East Florida to obtain information for Francis
Marion in Georgia and is captured by Seminole Indians and taken to British West Florida.   A little
known, and particularly bloody, aspect of the Revolutionary War.   (I and YA)

256   Hall, Marjory.   Another Kind of Courage.   Jacket by
Al Fiorantino.   Westminster, 1967.   Built partly
upon fact and partly legend, a novel about two
women, one the strong Nancy Hart ("War Woman")
and her daughter Sukey, "a fearful girl" but with
her own brand of courage.   The setting is Georgia.
(YA)

257   Havighurst, Walter.   Proud Prisoner.   Ill. by Leonard
Vosburgh.   Colonial Williamsburg (Holt Rinehart and
Winston), 1964. A story about a greatly maligned
(according to the author) man, Governor Henry
Hamilton of Detroit, called by the Americans "the
hair buyer," who was captured by them and suffered
great hardships in the jail at Williamsburg.   (YA
and Up)

258   Hays, Wilma Pitchford.   The French Are Coming.   Ill.
by Leonard Weisgard.   Colonial Williamsburg (Holt
Rinehart and Winston), 1965.   Maps and a prologue
set the historical and geographical scenes of action
for this story of a boy of 14, living in Yorktown
until forced by the troops of Cornwallis to take
refuge in Williamsburg.   Suspense is built on the
awaited arrival of the French fleet and the outcome
of the naval battle between it and the British fleet.
(I)

259   _____.   The Scarlet Badge.   Ill. by Peter Burchard.
Holt, Rinehart and Winston.   Colonial Williamsburg,
1963.   The trials of a young Loyalist boy at the beginning of the Revolution when Virginia declared her

independence from England. (I and YA)

260 Lawrence, Isabelle. Drumbeats in Williamsburg. Ill
     by Manning deV. Lee. Rand McNally, 1965. A
     sequel to "A Spy in Williamsburg [see 1501], about
     a 12-year-old who tries to "help" General Lafayette
     and Washington and prove to himself that he has
     courage. (I)

261 Meadowcroft, Enid La Monte. Holding the Fort with
     Daniel Boone. Ill. by Lloyd Coe. Thomas Y.
     Crowell, 1958. The story of the siege of the
     Boonesborough fort in Kentucky by the Indians, and
     prior to that, the kidnapping of Jemima Boone and
     her rescue. (I)

262 Monjo, F. N. Indian Summer. Ill. by Anita Lobel.
     Harper and Row, 1968. An I Can Read History
     Book. An unusually exciting book for elementary
     readers and charmingly and informatively illus-
     trated. (E)

263 Mundy, V. M. Brave Journey. Jacket by William
     McCaffery. Prentice-Hall, 1958. A little-known
     incident of 1780 is the basis for this story about
     the march of Scottish-American women, children,
     and aged folks through 200 miles of mountain forests
     to the safety of patriot settlements after their
     menfolk have taken to the hills for guerrilla fight-
     ing against Generals Clinton and Cornwallis. (YA)

264 Savage, Josephine. Daughter of Delaware. John Day,
     1964. An unusual Revolutionary story as the action
     takes place mainly in France where a 16-year-old
     American girl becomes well acquainted with many
     historical figures--Silas Dean, Benjamin Franklin,
     Beaumarchais, Marie Antoinette are some. The
     heroine plays a part in persuading the French to
     aid the Colonists. (YA)

265 Scott, Eric. Down the Rivers Westward Ho! Mere-
     dith, 1967. A true story, with some fictional
     characters, of the voyage of 200 pioneers from
     Fort Patrick Henry to Big Salt Lick, Tennessee.
     The diary of Colonel John Donelson, on which the
     story is based, is included at the back of the
     book, and a map of the 1000-mile trek at the be-
     ginning. (YA)

266 Steele, William O. The Year of the Bloody Sevens.
     Ill. by Charles Beck. Harcourt Brace and World,
     1963. The incredible journey of an 11-year-old
     boy seeking his father in "Kentuck" and obsessed
     with guilt because he did not go to the rescue from

the Indians of two men who had let him travel with
them.   (I and YA)

267 Thane, Elswyth. Dawn's Early Light. New abridged
edition. Condensation by Ann Finlayson. Jacket by
Paul Frame. Hawthorne Books, 1971. A love
story set in Williamsburg, Virginia, during the
Revolutionary War. The unabridged novel is the
first of a series of seven Williamsburg novels.
(YA)

268 Toepfer, Ray Grant. Liberty and Corporal Kincaid.
Chilton, 1968. A novel about Tarleton's dragoons
in 1781 and a 17-year-old corporal in Captain Jack
Jouett's militia which was out to check Cornwallis'
troops, climaxed by Jouett's heroic ride that saved
Jefferson and the Virginia legislature from capture
by the British.   (YA)

269 Wellman, Manly Wade. Battle For King's Mountain.
Ives Washburn, 1962. A sequel to "Rifles at Ramsour's Mill" about a scout belonging to Major William Chronicle's Scouts, by the name of Zake
Harper (fictional). A story of how the battle was
actually fought, with details of weather and locale.
(I)

270 _____. Clash on the Catawba. Ives Washburn,
1962. A sequel to "Battle for King's Mountain"
with more about Zake Harper and his friends and
enemies. A war story from start to finish about
Morgan's raiders, beset by Tarleton and Cornwallis who greatly outnumbered them.   (YA)

271 _____. Rifles at Ramsour's Mill. Ives Washburn,
1961. A story of divisions as to their loyalties
between friends and neighbors living near the south
fork of the Catawba in 1780. The young hero is on
the Continental side.   (I)

272 Wibberley, Leonard. Treegate's Raiders. Farrar,
Straus and Cudahy, 1962. The fourth of the Treegate Revolutionary series [see 243, 244, 1349, and
the fifth, 1362] in which Peter Treegate participates
in the battles of King's Mountain, Cowpens, and
Yorktown.   (YA)

THE NEW NATION (1783 to 1815)

THE OPENING OF THE WILDERNESS

273 Allen, Merritt Parmelee. East of Astoria. Ill. by
Millard McGee. Longmans Green, 1956. A novel
about an intrepid Scot who, during the conflict between the English Fur Company and the newly
formed Astor Company, led a small party from
Oregon to St. Louis, a long trek (1810-12) against
almost unsurmountable perils. A mysterious scent
is part of the plot, its source not revealed to the
very end of the story. (YA)

274 Andrist, Ralph K. To the Pacific with Lewis and
Clark. Consultant: Edwin R. Bingham. Ill. with
paintings, letters, sketches, maps and modern
photographs. American Heritage, 1967. The story
of the 7700 mile trek to the mouth of the Columbia
River in Oregon in 1804-6. (I and YA)

275 Averill, Esther. Daniel Boone. Ill. by Feodor Rojankovsky. First published in Paris in 1931. New enlarged edition. Harper and Bros., 1945. A picture
book story of the great hunter which older children
may enjoy reading to younger brothers and sisters.
(E and I)

276 Avery, Lynn. Cappy and the River. Ill. by Albert
Orbaan. Duell, Sloan and Pearce, 1960. A story
of a smart boy and equally smart dog on the river
route to Cincinnati in 1798. (I)

277 Bakeless, John. The Adventures of Lewis and Clark.
Ill. by Bea Holmes. Houghton Mifflin, 1962. The
exciting, authentic, enjoyably readable story of the
daring and successful expedition from the Mississippi
to the Pacific by Meriwether Lewis and William
Clark from 1803 to their return in 1806. (I and YA)

278 Brown, John Mason. Daniel Boone: The Opening of
the Wilderness. Ill. by Lee J. Ames. Random
Landmark, 1952. A stirring account of the adventurous life (1734-1820) of the great hunter and
frontiersman and the exploration and settlement of
Kentucky, the state which claims him. (I)

279 Carse, Robert. Go Away Home. W. W. Norton,
     1964. A novel about a boy who, in rescuing his
     dog, loses his family en route from Connecticut
     to the Western Reserve in Ohio, and in the com-
     pany of a blind piper, attempts to rejoin them.
     (YA)

280 Caudill, Rebecca. The Far-Off Land. Ill. by Brinton
     Turkle. Viking, 1964. A novel about the trek of
     pioneers from Fort Patrick Henry to the French Lick
     in Tennessee with a well-drawn map, and in that
     context, a love story and a Moravian girl's de-
     termination to refrain from killing Indians even in
     revenge. (YA)

281 Colver, Anne. Bread-and-Butter Journey. Ill. by
     Garth Williams. Holt, Rinehart and Winston, 1970.
     A beautiful story of human courage, drawn from the
     author's own family history, about a small group of
     people, led by a 15-year-old boy, traveling with
     pack horses across the mountains of Pennsylvania to
     a new home where the fathers awaited them.   (I)

282 Daugherty, James. Daniel Boone. Ill. by the author
     with original lithographs in color. Newbery Medal.
     Viking, 1939. A biography of Boone (1734-1820).
     (I)

283 _____ . Trappers and Traders of the Far West.
     Ill. by the author. Random, 1952. These stories
     are all part of the main story of John Jacob Astor's
     dream of controlling the fur trade of the world.
     The first section of the book is about the ill-fated
     voyage of the Tonquin around the Horn to the mouth
     of the Columbia, September 6, 1810 to June 4, 1811.
     The second is about the overland journey, July 5,
     1810 to February 15, 1812. The third section is on
     the return east, June 29, 1812 to April 30, 1813, and
     the fourth is called "The Dream Fades--Farewell
     Astoria, August 4, 1812." (I and YA)

284 Eifert, Virginia S. George Shannon, Young Explorer
     With Lewis and Clark. Ill. by Manning deV. Lee. Dodd
     Mead, 1963. A story of the Lewis and Clark ex-
     pedition (1804-6) as experienced by its youngest mem-
     ber, Shannon, who joined it at 16. The information
     given here about Sacajawea's later years seems to
     be subject to dispute. (I and YA)

285 Fast, Howard. The Tall Hunter. Ill. by Rafaello
     Busoni. Harper and Bros., 1942. A short poetic
     novel about a young hunter seeking revenge for the
     theft by Indians, of his young wife, and how a

meeting with Johnny Appleseed changed his heart
and viewpoint. (I and YA)

286 Fritz, Jean. The Cabin Faced West. Ill. by Feodor
Rajonkovsky. Coward-McCann, 1958. A short
book, based on a real incident, about a 10-year-
old girl feeling very much alone in western Pennsylvania in 1784 and wishing she could go back
east--until she has a surprising visitor. (I)

287 Hays, Wilma Pitchford. The Meriwether Lewis
Mystery. Ill. with maps, photographs and line
drawings-jacket by Andrew Snyder. Westminster,
1971. The story of Lewis (1774-1809), the inspiration given him by Jefferson, the lack of co-
operation by Madison, and the mystery of his early,
sudden death. (I and YA)

388 Lenski, Lois. A-Going to the Westward. Ill. by the
author. J. B. Lippincott, 1937. A story of the
travels of a Connecticut family to the Western Reserve of Ohio, as experienced particularly by 11-
year-old Betsy, interwoven with folk songs and
chapter headings from "Pilgrim's Progress." (I)

289 McMeekin, Isabel McLennan. Journey Cake. Ill. by
Nicholas Panesis. Julian Messner, 1942. A
wilderness trail story of a valiant free Negro
woman taking a motherless family to Kentucky to
find their father. (I)

290 Mantel, S. G. Explorer with a Dream: John Ledyard.
Jacket by Frank Kramer. Julian Messner, 1969.
The extremely adventurous life of this world-
traveler from New England (1751-1789), who tried
to find a land route across the North American
continent in order to develop the fur trade, provides his biographer with fascinating details of
Captain Cook's last voyage and Siberia and Russia
in the time of Catherine the Great. He was an
early anthropologist as well as explorer. (YA)

291 Martin, Patricia Miles. Daniel Boone. Ill. by Glen
Dines. G. P. Putnam's Sons, 1965. A See and
Read Beginning to Read Biography. A good first
book about this popular historical figure (1734-
1820). (E)

292 Meadowcraft, Enid La Monte. By Wagon and Flatboat.
Ill. by Ninon MacKnight. Thomas Y. Crowell,
1938. The story of a family move in 1789, first by
Conestoga Wagon and later by flatboat, from Pennsylvania to an Ohio town soon to be named Cincinnati. Dangers beset them all the way and there is

much historical detail incorporated into the action.
(I)

293 Robinson, Barbara. Trace Through the Forest. Jacket
by Jane Oliver. Lothrop Lee and Shepard, 1965.
Jim Fraley, 14, is the only boy to go with Colonel
Zane and 11 men to cut a trace through the forest
of the Ohio Territory to Chillocothe Town so that
settlers can move west. A lucky daredevil he, but
almost as clever a woodsman as the Shawnee Indian
who befriends him. The story also shows the enmity between Indian tribes preventing them from
uniting with Tecumseh against the White settlers.
(I and YA)

294 Steele, William O. The Far Frontier. Ill. by Paul
Galdone. Harcourt Brace and World, 1959. All of
Steele's books are excitingly plotted but each also
carries a deeper meaning than simply the perils of
frontier life. In this story a boy is "bound out" to
an absent-minded naturalist, so there is much nature
lore as well as adventures with the cruel Chica-
mauga Indians, but underneath all, the boy's growing
appreciation of "larnin'." (I)

295 _____. The Lone Hunt. Ill. by Paul Galdone. Harcourt, Brace and World, 1956. A relatively short
book, with an exciting plot and humorous vernacular,
about an 11-year-old boy and the price he pays for
running away to shoot "his" buffalo. (I)

296 _____. Wilderness Journey. Ill. by Paul Galdone.
Harcourt, Brace and World, 1953. A story full of
humor and adventures about a timid, sickly boy on
the dangerous Wilderness Trail to the French Lick.
(I and YA)

297 Stevenson, Augusta. Daniel Boone, Boy Hunter. Ill.
by Paul Laune. Bobbs-Merrill, 1943. The exciting
youth of the great hunter (1734-1820). (E)

298 _____. Zeb Pike, Boy Traveler. Ill. by Paul
Laune. Bobbs-Merrill, 1953. The story of the
boyhood of the man who discovered the peak named
for him but who never climbed it. (1779-1813)
He joined the army at the age of fifteen and, when
still very young, was chosen to lead two important
expeditions into the Louisiana Territory. (I)

299 Webb, Christopher. The River of Pee Dee Jack.
Funk and Wagnalls, 1962. An adventure story of
the first water with some mighty humorous characters, fur traders in search of the river that leads
to the Pacific and attempting to return to sell their
pelts. (I and YA)

300 White, Stewart Edward. Daniel Boone, Wilderness
       Scout. Ill. by James Daugherty. Doubleday, 1922.
       An extremely exciting and informative story of the
       dangerous life of Daniel Boone (1734-1820) and a
       fine delineation of the period of his long life, de-
       scribing the ethics and character of Indians and
       frontiersmen, the good and evil in both. (I and YA)
301 Wibberley, Leonard. Zebulon Pike, Soldier and Ex-
       plorer. Jacket and maps by Stan Campbell. Funk
       and Wagnalls, 1961. A biography (1779-1813) showing
       Pike's importance in explorations of the Mississippi,
       establishing forts, pacifying Indians and his part in
       the War of 1812. (YA)

PEOPLE AND PLACES

302 Banks, Stockton Y. Washington Adventure. Ill. by
       Henry Pitz. Whittlesey House, McGraw-Hill,
       1950. A good adventure and detective story in
       which a young boy, in searching for his older
       brother, discovers a land swindler and attempts to
       catch him. The setting is Washington, D.C. where
       the White House is in the process of being built
       (1800) and readied for John Adams, the first Presi-
       dent to occupy it. (I)
303 Bulla, Clyde Robert. White Bird. Ill. by Leonard
       Weisgard. Thomas Y. Crowell, 1966. A tender
       story of a lonely bitter old man and the boy he
       rescued as a baby and whom he tried to hold,
       isolating him from life and love. (I)
304 Clark, Mary Stetson. The Limner's Daughter.
       Viking, 1967. A novel about the daughter of an
       impoverished despondent painter accused of having
       had Tory sympathies during the Revolution. The
       girl rebuilds the family fortunes and bravely faces
       the unjust accusation about her father. Historical-
       ly, the story has much to do with the Middlesex
       Canal between Boston and Lowell. A foreword
       identifies historical characters. (YA)
305 Colver, Anne. Theodosia, Daughter of Aaron Burr.
       Holt, Rinehart and Winston, 1941-62. A biograph-
       ical novel of Burr, from his devoted daughter's
       viewpoint. (YA)
306 Crouse, Anna Erkine and Russell. Alexander Hamil-
       ton and Aaron Burr: Their Lives, Their Times,
       Their Duel. Ill. by Walter Buehr. Random,

World Landmark, 1958. A double biography, with
especially interesting material about the late 18th
and early 19th centuries--the beginnings of bossism
and machine politics, for example. (I and YA)

307 deLeeuw, Cateau. Give Me Your Hand. Little Brown,
1960. A story of pioneer farming in Ohio in the
early 19th century and the responsibilities of a 17-
year-old girl, mothering five younger brothers and
sisters, and tempted by a handsome young easterner
to leave the hardships of the country. (YA)

308 Desmond, Alice Curtis. Alexander Hamilton's Wife.
Ill. with photographs, and drawings by the author.
Dodd Mead, 1952. A biographical novel of Betsy
Schuyler Hamilton which portrays Alexander in the
adoring and forgiving eyes of his wife who outlived
him by 50 years. The Afterword gives a guide to
the various settings of the novel in Albany and New
York. (A)

309 _____. Bewitching Betsy Bonaparte. Ill. with
photographs. Dodd Mead, 1958. A biographical
novel of a very ambitious Baltimore girl who married Jerome Bonaparte, Napoleon's youngest
brother, dreaming of someday becoming a queen.
No one can say that she didn't try. (A)

310 Edmonds, Walter D. Seven American Stories. Ill. by
William Sauts Bock. Little Brown, 1970. The five
novels for young people in this book are listed
separately elsewhere, but the two short stories are
not. They are: "Water Never Hurt a Man," an
Erie Canal story, and "Uncle Ben's Whale" (how to
live inside a whale). (I and YA)

311 Emery, Anne. Carey's Fortune. Jacket by Clifford
Schule. Westminster, 1969. A novel of love and
politics in which a 17-year-old Annapolis belle,
threatened by the persistence of a man she does not
love, has to await events before she can be sure of
marriage to the one she does. He is a young newspaper man and the events which make marriage uncertain hinge on the many ballots which put Jefferson into the White House instead of Aaron Burr.
(YA)

312 Fall, Thomas. Goat Boy of Brooklyn. Ill. by
Fermin Rocker. Dial, 1968. The story of a 13-
year-old goatherd and his little sister aiding their
father's escape from Debtor's Prison in New York
City in 1800. Interesting material on the urban
problems of the early 19th century. (I)

313 Foster, John. Southern Frontiersman: The Story of
     Sam Dale. Morrow, 1967. Biography of a rough,
     tough Indian fighter (1772-1841) with stories of his
     narrow escapes from death in the Battles of New
     Orleans and the Great Canoe, and his account of
     Tecumseh's fiery speech urging the Creeks to an-
     nihilate the White Man. A book replete with violence
     and bloodshed and man's inhumanity to man on the
     southern frontier in the early 19th century. (I and
     YA)

314 Grubb, Davis. The Golden Sickle. Ill. by Leonard
     Vosburgh. World, 1968. A top-notch atmospheric
     mystery in the manner of Stevenson or Daphne Du
     Maurier, about a 12-year-old lad and a blind girl
     involved together in a search for stolen treasure,
     revenge and truth. The "Golden Sickle" is an inn,
     full of secret passageways and hollow walls. (YA)

315 Havighurst, Marion Boyd. Strange Island. Jacket and
     map by Peter Burchard. World, 1957. A novel
     in which the young governess of the little Blenner-
     hasset boys, gets caught up in the Burr conspiracy
     to take over Mexico and the southwest as an inde-
     pendent country, plans being laid on Blennerhasset
     Island in the Ohio River, in 1806. (YA)

316 Henry, Marguerite. Justin Morgan Had a Horse.
     Grosset and Dunlap, 1945. A story of the origins
     of the little Vermont work horse called a "Morgan
     Horse" based on authoritative sources. (I)

317 Hobart, Lois. The Patriot's Lady: The Life of Sarah
     Livingston Jay. Jacket painting and ill. by Doris
     Stolberg. Funk and Wagnalls, 1960. A biographical
     novel of the wife of John Jay, President of the
     Continental Congress, Minister to Spain in 1779,
     aide to Benjamin Franklin at peace conferences in
     Paris, foreign secretary for the United States, first
     Chief Justice of the new nation under Washington,
     diplomatic envoy to Britain, and Governor of N.Y.
     State. It can easily be judged that his wife's life,
     too, was worthy of a biography. (YA)

318 Kimball, Gwen. The Puzzle of the Lost Dauphin.
     Duell Sloans and Pearce, 1964. Framed by an ex-
     citing contemporary plot, this mystery story is
     built upon the possibility, or legend, that the son of
     Marie Antoinette and Louis XVI was actually brought
     to America in the early 19th century and that he be-
     came an Indian missionary living near DePere,
     Wisconsin, and renamed Eleazer Williams. Such a

person did exist and claimed to be the Dauphin.
(YA)

319 Knight, Ralph. The Burr-Hamilton Duel. Ill. with
photographs and contemporary prints. Franklin
Watts, 1968. Stories of both lives before the
duel and Burr's life thereafter. Burr (1756-1836)
and Hamilton (1757-1804). (YA)

320 Lenski, Lois. Bound Girl of Cobble Hill. Ill. by the
author. J. B. Lippincott, 1938. Based on old
records this is an authentic picture of life in Connecticut in 1789 as lived by an unfortunate seven-
year-old orphan "bound out" to a seemingly heartless stepuncle. (I and YA)

321 Meigs, Cornelia. The Covered Bridge. Ill. by Marguerite de Angeli. Macmillan, 1936-60. A story
of farm life in Vermont in 1800 where a little city
girl learns of winter hardships and beauty and the
Vermont character, as typified by Ethan Allen, who
plays an important part in the story. (I)

322 Orrmont, Arthur. The Amazing Alexander Hamilton.
Julian Messner, 1964. A story of Hamilton's mili-
tary and political careers and authorship of the
Federalist Papers (1757-1804). (Ya and Up)

323 Steele, William O. Trail Through Danger. Ill. by
Charlie Beck. Harcourt Brace and World, 1965.
An 11-year-old boy, hired to do chores, goes on a
buffalo hunt in the Carolinas with the flint-hearted
skin hunter who hired him, a nearly blind old man,
and three other men, one mean, one a "good guy" and
one, dimwitted. Though fearful of hostile Indians,
buffalo, hunger and storm, he is even more fearful
of life back home where he is known as a son of a
traitor who has helped the Cherokees murder white
people. (I)

324. _____. Winter Danger. Ill. by Paul Galdone.
Harcourt, Brace and World, 1954. Eleven-year-
old Caje's father is a "woodsy," a loner, determined
not to be dependent on anyone or have anyone dependent on him, but a desperately hard winter
teaches Caje that people need each other. Excitement, humor and a good plot. (I)

325 Tucker, Caroline. John Marshall. Jacket by Frank
Aloise. Farrar, Straus and Cudahy, 1962. A
biography (1755-1835) of the fourth Chief Justice
of the United States whose strict constructionism has
had a strong and lasting influence. There were
many other aspects of his life which bring in

historical events such as the winter with Washington
at Valley Forge, the treason of Benedict Arnold,
the near-war with France in 1797/8 and the trial
of Aaron Burr. An author's note brings in other
important court cases, including the Dartmouth College case. (YA)

326 Voight, Virginia Frances. The Girl from Johnnycake
Hill. Ill. by William A. McCaffery. Prentice-
Hall, 1961. A novel of two valiant women, mother
and daughter, who travel from New Haven to the
northwestern corner of Connecticut to live with the
mother's brother. His death before their arrival
leaves them with a wilderness farm to manage and
a hostile neighbor, determined to get their land
away from them. (YA)

327 Williamson, Joanne. The Glorious Conspiracy. Alfred
A. Knopf, 1961. A novel beginning in England in
the early days of the industrial revolution but in
which the main action takes place in the political
and newspaper world of New York and is about the
conflict between the Federalists and the Republicans.
(YA)

328 Wise, William. Alexander Hamilton. G. P. Putnam's
Sons, 1963. A serious biography of the man (1757-
1804) who strived so hard and successfully for a
strong central government and constitution at a time
when the 13 states were very loosely federated.
(YA and Up)

329 Wright, Alice. The Seed Is Blown. Ill. by Joan Berg.
Rand McNally, 1965. The map on pages 194/5 was
drawn by Rufus Putnam in 1804, and should be used
for reference throughout the story of this little
family of a brother and two sisters, who, losing
their father on their way from Pennsylvania to Kentucky, never gave up searching for him. Good material on the early settlement of Ohio, treaties with
the Indians, and establishment of "donation sites."
The exciting plot is based on a legend of an Indian
called Silverheels. (YA)

THE LAND WAR OF 1812

[The Naval warfare will be found in Part II under Sailing
Ships...]

330 Burgoyne, Leon E. Ensign Ronan, A Story of Fort
Dearborn. Frontispiece by Dirk Gringhuis. John

C. Winston, 1955. A novel in which most of the
characters were real persons--Antoine Guilmette,
Black Partridge, Sauganash and others. Even the
main character has been briefly recorded as "a
somewhat stubborn and headstrong but an extremely
brave young man." (YA)

331 Carmer, Carl. A Flag for the Fort. Ill. by Elizabeth Carmer. Junior Literary Guild. Julian
Messner, 1952. A story about a 13-year-old girl
who worked on the very flag that inspired "The Star
Spangled Banner"--based on historical facts about
the siege of Fort McHenry. (I)

332 Grant, Bruce. The Star-Spangled Rooster. Ill. by
W. T. Mars. World, 1961. A first-rate yarn
based on a true incident recorded from the time of
the bombardment of Fort McHenry. (E and I)

333 Hall, Marjory. Drumbeat on the Shore. Westminster,
1965. A skillful combination of fact and fancy,
woven into a novel of young love, set in Scituate,
Massachusetts during the War of 1812, with a
genealogical chart of the Bates family. (YA)

334 Hays, Wilma Pitchford. The Open Gate. Ill. by
Carolyn Cather Tierney. Coward McCann, 1970.
It is amazing how much history comes through
clearly in this simple charming story of a little
French-Creole girl in New Orleans, and the boy
next door behind the locked gate. The action all
takes place during the decisive Battle of New Orleans in 1815. (E and I)

335 Howard, Elizabeth. Candle in the Night. William
Morrow, 1952. A love story set in Detroit at the
time of its surrender to the English. (YA)

336 Nesbitt, Rosemary S. The Great Rope. Ill. by
Douglas Gorsline. Lothrop Lee and Shepard, 1968.
A story with historical basis, of a boy's bravery and
ingenuity during the war of 1812, near Oswego, New
York. (I)

337 Swanson, Neil H. and Anne Sherbourne. The Star-
Spangled Banner. Ill. by Norman Guthrie. John C.
Winston, 1958. A story of a boy watching, with
Francis Scott Key, the burning fort still flying the
15 stars and 15 stripes. (I)

338 Wallace, Willard. Jonathon Dearborn: A Novel of the
War of 1812. Little Brown, 1967. Full of perilous
adventures of a young law student who ships as a
privateer, but of interest also for its inclusion of
material on the political aspect of this war and the

intense anti-war and anti-administration feelings of
the times.   (A)

339   Wolfert, Jerry.   Brother of the Wind: A Story of the
Niagara Frontier.   Jacket by Charles Geer.   Day,
1960.   A young keelboatman undergoes spine-chill-
ing adventures on the Niagara River near the Falls,
and also becomes involved in the struggle between
Buffalo (burned in 1813) and nearby Black Rock for
the position of main shipping port at the western
end of Erie Canal.   (YA)

WESTWARD HO!

340   Adams, Samuel Hopkins. Wagons to the Wilderness.
Ill. by Norman Guthrie Rudolph. John C. Winston,
1954. A corker of a story told in the vernacular
of the time and place, about a lad of fourteen who
joins a train of traders to Santa Fe--the beginning
of the Santa Fe Trail. (I)

341   Allen, Merritt Parmelee. Make Way for the Brave:
The Oregon Quest. Ill. by Kreigh Collins. David
McKay, 1950. A novel constructed on Nathaniel
Wyeth's expedition to Oregon in 1832 in which a
young orphan boy meets and works with such characters as Jim Bridger, the Sublette brothers and
other intrepid mountain men and shares their encounters with the Indians. (YA)

342   . The Silver Wolf. Ill. by Allan Thomas.
David McKay, 1951. A novel about a group of
traders, going from Missouri to Santa Fe, in which
a young easterner teams up with young Kit Carson,
the plot centering on the question of foul play when
Judd discovers the death of his brother, who had
preceded him, and acquires a little silver figure of
a wolf found in his dead brother's money belt. (YA)

343   . The Spirit of the Eagle. Ill. by Avery
Johnson. Longmans Green, 1947. This novel follows "Western Star" (below) in time and is based on
the expedition of Captain Conneville of the U.S.
Army in which he attempted to learn as much as
possible about the country and Indian tribes, though
ostensibly a fur trader. (YA)

344   . The Sun Trail. Ill. by Lee Townsend.
Longmans Green, 1943. A novel based on the maps
and journals of Jedediah Smith who unlocked the door
to California. (YA)

345   . Western Star: A Story of Jim Bridger.
David McKay, 1941. A novel about the heroic ex-
ploits of the Rocky Mountain Company--Ashley,
Henry, Thomas Fitzpatrick, Etienne Provot, Robert

Campbell, the Soublette Brothers, Jed Smith, and
a score of others. (YA)

346 Allen, T. D. Doctor, Lawyer, Merchant, Chief.
Jacket by Tom Hall. Westminster, 1965. A biographical novel of John McLoughlin and the opening
of the Northwest, the struggle between the British
and Americans for domination of the Oregon country, Indian problems, and the ruthlessness of the
Hudson's Bay Company and, indeed of American
trappers as well. (YA)

347 Berry, Don. Mountain Men: The Trappers of the
Great Fur Trading Era. Ill. by Glen Dines.
Macmillan, 1966. Vividly written and illustrated,
this book is neither fiction nor biography but
stimulating background for stories about the era,
with suggestions for further reading on the subject.
(I)

348 Blassingame, Wyatt and Richard Glendinning. Men
Who Opened the West. Ill. by Frank Aloise.
G. P. Putnam's Sons, 1966. A comprehensive book,
beginning with the Spanish conquistadors and ending
with the heyday of the cattlemen which ended around
1874. (YA)

349 Burt, Olive. Brigham Young. Jacket by Lorence
Bjorklund. Julian Messner, 1956. The story of
the indomitable Mormon Apostle (1791-1877) and
leader of his people to Utah after they had been
driven out of Ohio, Missouri and Illinois; an organizer of exceptional ability and a man of constant
faith in the destiny of the Mormons. (YA)

350   . Wind Before the Dawn. Jacket by Lee
Smith. John Day, 1964. A novel with a factual
basis about a young Mormon "Sister" who traveled
to "Zion" (Salt Lake City) with three children in
her charge, after the Mormons had been driven out
of Illinois. (YA)

351 Carr, Mary Jane. Children of the Covered Wagon.
Ill. by Bob Kuhn. Thomas Y. Crowell, 1934. A
classic story of the Oregon Trail, its history incorporated in the action of the story of a seven-
year-old boy's experiences in a wagon train. (I)

352   . Young Mac of Fort Vancouver. Ill. by
Richard Holberg. Thomas Y. Crowell, 1940. A
fine combination of fact and fiction about a boy,
three-fourths white and one-fourth Indian, who is
sent to Fort Vancouver to be in the care of D.
John McLaughlin, the chief factor of The Hudson

Bay Company there. A thrilling climax. (I and YA)

353 Cranston, Paul. To Heaven on Horseback. Julian
     Messner, 1952. Biographical novel of the Whitmans,
     Marcus and Narcissa. especially the latter, one of
     the first white women to cross the Rockies. (A)

354 Dick, Trella Lamson. Valiant Vanguard. Ill. by Don
     Bolognese. Abelard-Schuman, 1960. The story of
     a family who migrate to the Oregon Territory in
     1846 and settle near the Whitman Mission to clear
     land and raise wheat. The father's determination
     "not to mess in Indian affairs" proves unworkable
     as the family becomes involved with an old Cayuse
     woman. (I and YA)

355 Dines, Glen. Long Knife: The Story of the Fighting
     U.S. Cavalry of the 1860 Frontier. Ill. by the
     author. Macmillan, 1961. (I)

356 Eaton, Jeanette. Narcissa Whitman, Pioneer of Ore-
     gon. Ill. by Woodi Ishmael. Harcourt, Brace and
     World, 1941. A good narrative biography of the
     wife (1808-47) of Dr. Marcus Whitman and her en-
     during courage and cheerfulness on the long hard
     journey into unfriendly Indian territory. (YA)

357 Evansen, Virginia B. Nancy Kelsey. Jacket and ill.
     by Paul Lautz. David McKay, 1965. A novel
     based on the real Nancy Kelsey who at 17 (in 1841)
     with a baby in her arms, was the first pioneer
     woman to enter directly into California by land, with
     the Bartelson-Bidwell Party. (YA)

358 _____. Sierra Summit. Ill. by Allan Thomas.
     David McKay, 1967. A novel based on the experi-
     ences of the Stephens-Murphy-Townsend Party, con-
     sisting of 26 men, 8 women, and 17 children, as
     they brought the first wagons over the Sierra Nevada
     in 1844. The final fate of a 17-year-old member
     of the party holds the reader in suspense to the end.
     (YA)

359 Felton, Harold. Jim Beckwourth, Negro Mountain Man.
     Ill. with photographs, prints of the period and maps
     by James MacDonald. Dodd Mead, 1966. A bi-
     ography of an almost legendary man (1798-1866),
     based largely on his own autobiography as dictated
     to a newspaper man, Thomas D. Bonner, in 1854
     or 5. Incredible as some of his adventures may
     seem they were certainly possible in the early days
     of the west. (YA)

360 Fox, Edward. Hunger Valley. Doubleday, 1965. A
     tense, realistic novel about the survival of a group

of children led by a 15-year-old girl after their
parents have died or been massacred by Black Feet
in a mountain valley in the winter of 1850. (YA)

361 Garst, Shannon. Joe Meek, Man of the West. Ill. by
Albert Orbaan. Julian Messner, 1954. Biography
of a mountain man (1810-74), perhaps not quite as
well known as some others--Davy Crockett, Kit
Carson, for example--but whose western adventures
vie with anyone's for thrills. He played an important part in the settlement of the Oregon territory. (YA)

362 _____. Kit Carson, Trail Blazer and Scout. Ill.
by Harry Daugherty. Julian Messner, 1942.
Biography, and especially good reading (1809-68)
because of the feeling it gives the reader of the at-
mosphere of early west, the way mountain men
talked, and their hairbreadth escapes from violent
deaths; especially showing Kit's native intelligence
and understanding of the Indians: "He spoke with a
straight tongue." His home in Santa Fe can still
be visited. (I and YA)

363 Grey, Katharine. Rolling Wheels. Frontispiece by
Frank Schoonover. Little Brown, 1932. One of
the best of covered wagon stories, a full-length
account of the Lambert family's long trek from
Indiana to California in 1846 when the U.S. was at
war with Mexico, a trip which included a meeting
with the ill-fated Donner party. (I and YA)

364 Guthrie, A. B. The Big Sky. An Edition for Younger
Readers. Ill. by Jacob Landau. Houghton Mifflin,
1950. Older ones may also prefer this edition to
the original for the revision is largely in the matter
of length (and it is still long enough to thoroughly
involve the reader in the western world of a small
group of buffalo hunters). A strong realistic novel
of the northern Mississippi country in 1830-43.
(YA and Up)

365 Harte, Bret. Stories of the Early West with a foreword
by Walter Van Tilburg Clark. Platt and Munk,
1964. The first one of these stories, "Luck of
Roaring Camp," was written in 1868. (A)

366 Henry, Will (Henry Allen). Sons of the Western Frontier. Jacket by Leonard Vosburgh. Chilton, 1966.
Eleven tales of the old west and some of its younger heroes and villains, all tough, realistic yarns,
taken in good part from the author's historical
novels. (YA)

367   Higgins, Marguerite. Jessie Benton Frémont. Ill. by
      B. Holmes. Houghton Mifflin, 1962. Biography of
      the wife of the Pathfinder, John Frémont, an intrepid
      woman with unceasing faith in her husband. (YA)
368   Johnson, Annabel and Edgar. Wilderness Bride. Harper
      and Row, 1962. A romance of the Mormon's trek
      from Nauvoo to Salt Lake in which a girl of 15 and
      a troubled English youth (whose widowed mother has
      married a Mormon as his number three wife) are
      betrothed and finally come to understand each other
      and the strange religion which brought them together.
      (YA)
369   Jordan, Polly Carver and Lucy Post Frisbee. Brigham
      Young: Covered Wagon Boy. Ill. by Gray Morrow.
      Bobbs-Merrill, 1962. Childhood of Famous Ameri-
      cans Series. The Boyhood of the (later) leader of
      the Mormons to Salt Lake (1801-77).
370   Lampman, Evelyn Sibley. Princess of Vancouver.
      Jacket and map by Douglas Gorsline. Doubleday,
      1962. A long rich novel about the daughter of Dr.
      John McLoughlin, chief factor of the Hudson Bay's
      trading post on the Columbia River, and his part-
      Indian wife--about French voyageurs and their Indian
      wives, many Indian tribes of the northwest, and
      the coming of Yankee traders and settlers and
      Protestant missionaries to the Oregon territory,
      1824-38. The "Author's Note" at the end carries on
      the story of McLoughlin and how he eventually be-
      came an American citizen. (YA)
371   _____. Wheels West: The Story of Tabitha Brown.
      Ill. by Gil Walker. Doubleday, 1965. A true story
      about a real woman. And what a woman! Grandma
      Brown, at 66 and lame, made the long gruelling
      trip over the Oregon Trail in 1846, and when she
      arrived, set out to support herself and make money.
      Spunky, and full of merry tales, she had a vivid
      imagination which foresaw many future inventions.
      (I and YA)
372   Latham, Frank. Jed Smith. Ill. by William Hutchin-
      son. Garrard, 1968. A Discovery Book. A short
      biography of the short but full life (1799-1831) of
      one of the first men to cross the Sierra Nevadas
      from west to east and to travel by land from south-
      ern California to the Columbia River. (E and I)
373   Lathrop, West. Keep the Wagons Moving. Ill. by
      Douglas Duer. Random, 1949. A novel of ad-
      venture and suspense about an 18-year-old and his

younger brother making their way to Oregon through
dangers from wild weather, swollen rivers, desert,
Indians, outlaws, and near the end, extreme loneliness. (YA)

374 Luce, Willard and Celia. Jim Bridger. Ill. by George
I. Parrish, Jr., 1966. Garrard, 1966. A Discovery Book. Biography of the great frontiersman
(1804-81) who discovered the Great Salt Lake, built
Fort Bridger, trapped beaver, guided wagon trains,
and acted as a scout for the U.S. Army. (E and I)

375 McCall, Edith. Wagons over the Mountains. Ill. by
Carol Rogers. Childrens' Press, 1961. The history of the wagon trains to the west, 1821-69, with
stories about Marcus Whitman, John Bidwell, and
"Billy Cody" (Buffalo Bill) as a boy. (I)

376 Meader, Stephen W. Buffalo and Beaver. Ill. by
Charles Beck. Harcourt, Brace and World, 1960.
A novel of the adventures of the mountain men,
mainly the son of one, Jeff Barlow, who is also an
artist. Details of wilderness life, Indian tribes,
and wild life are so skillfully woven into the action,
and the dialogue is interesting for its admixture of
French patois. (YA)

377 _____. Keep 'em Rolling. Ill. by Al Savitt.
Harcourt, Brace and World, 1967. A sequel (which,
however, stands alone) to "Buffalo and Beaver" in
which the artistic mountain man, Jeff Barlow, is
reintroduced, an older man now, in the days of
wagon trains. (YA)

378 Moody, Ralph. Kit Carson and the Wild Frontier.
Ill. by Stanley W. Galli. Random, 1955. A good
solid, biography (1809-68) with a fine clear map,
showing the routes Kit traveled and the main loca-
tions of events in the story. (YA)

379 Morrow, Honoré. On to Oregon. Ill. by Edward
Shenton. William Morrow, 1946. The story of a
13-year-old boy who, after his parents both die on
the early part of the Oregon Trail, leads his
younger brother and sisters (one, a new-born baby)
from Fort Bridger to the Whitman Mission, a trek
of 1000 miles of hazardous travel. (I and YA)

380 Moseley, Elizabeth R. Davy Crockett: Hero of the
Wild Frontier. Ill. by Thomas Beecham. Garrard,
1967. A Discovery Book. A short biography
(1786-1836) of the man whose tall stories are more
often remembered than his own exciting life story.
He was killed in the Battle of the Alamo.

381 Nielsen, Virginia. The Road to the Valley. Ill. by Vana
     Earle. David McKay, 1961. A novel about a young
     girl who after the death of her father assumes the
     responsibility for leading her mother and young
     brother on the long trek from Missouri to Utah as
     members of a wagon train of Mormons and antago-
     nistic Missourians. (YA)

382 Parkman, Francis. The Oregon Trail, 1846, with an
     introduction by Harry Sinclair Drago. Ill. with
     biographical illustrations and pictures of the setting
     of the book. Great Illustrated Classic Edition,
     Dodd Mead, 1964. (A)

383 Place, Marian T. Marcus and Narcissa Whitman.
     Ill. by Gerald McCann. Garrard, 1967. The
     dramatic experiences of this medical missionary
     and his wife who helped blaze a trail for wagons
     to travel to Oregon in the 1840s. (E)

384 Randall, Ruth Painter. I, Jessie. Ill. with photo-
     graphs. Little Brown, 1963. A biographical novel
     of Jessie Benton Frémont, daughter of Senator
     Thomas Hart Benton and devoted wife of John Fré-
     mont, explorer, soldier, and political leader. (YA)

385 Scott, Paul and Beryl. Eliza and the Indian War Pony.
     Ill. by Don Bolognese. Lothrop, Lee and Shepard,
     1961. The story, based on her own "Memoirs of
     the West," of Eliza Spaulding whose missionary
     parents went with the Whitmans to serve the Nez
     Percé Indians in Oregon. When the Whitmans and
     others were massacred by the Cayuse Indians, little
     Eliza's ability to talk the Nez Percé language came
     to her rescue. (I)

386 Smith, Fredrica Shumway. Frémont: Soldier, Ex-
     plorer, Statesman. Ill. with photographs and maps.
     Rand McNally, 1966. A clear, factual biography
     (1813-90), particularly useful for its maps. (A)

387 Stevenson, Augusta. Kit Carson, Boy Trapper. Ill.
     by Robert Doremus. Bobbs-Merrill, 1945-62.
     Childhood Famous Americans Series. The story of
     Kit's youth and preparations for the work he was
     to do as a man. He was born in Kentucky in 1909,
     but his family moved to Missouri when he was a
     boy, and later his family home was in Santa Fe,
     New Mexico. His real home was in the saddle.
     (E and I)

388 Stone, Irving. Immortal Wife. Doubleday, 1944. A
     biographical novel of Jessie Benton Frémont and
     her support and understanding of her husband,

John Charles Frémont, their lives together and apart,
in exploring, pioneering, gold mining, and politics.
(A)

389   Watson, Sally. Poor Felicity. Ill. by Leo Summers.
Doubleday, 1961. A story about a young Virginia
girl and a boy from Illinois, pioneering in the
Oregon Territory at the time of the founding of
Seattle, 1852. Humorous and informative. (I)

390   Yates, Elizabeth. Carolina's Courage. Ill. by Nora
S. Unwin. E. P. Dutton, 1964. An outstanding
covered wagon story in which a little girl carries
her dearest possession, a doll named Lyddy Lou,
almost all the way from New Hampshire to Nebraska. Good detail of preparations for such a
trip and the sacrifices made by women and children
of their most cherished possessions. (I)

PEOPLE AND PLACES--East of the Mississippi

391   Aldis, Dorothy. Lucky Year. Ill. by John Dukes
McKee. Rand McNally, 1951. What an amusing
mixture the author concocted here--hogs (over a
thousand of them), a Pork Palace where they are
slaughtered, a steamboat race, and--Jenny Lind.
And what's most remarkable, it is a true story,
set in Madison, Indiana in 1851. (I)

392   Bulla, Clyde Robert. The Ghost of Windy Hill. Ill.
by Don Bolognese. Thomas Y. Crowell, 1968.
The story of a family who are asked to live for a
month at Windy Hill in order to find out whether it
is really haunted, as the owner's wife suspects.
Strange things do happen which make for a good
mystery story. (E and I)

393   Butler, Beverly. Feather in the Wind. Dodd Mead,
1965. A novel, beginning during the Black Hawk
War in Wisconsin in 1832, in which a young woman
finally learns that no one is entirely independent.
(YA)

393a   _____. Song of the Voyageurs. Dodd Mead, 1956.
A charming story of 1830 in Wisconsin, about family relationships in a French-Canadian household, and
the difficult choice faced by a young eastern girl--
a handsome Philadelphian? Or a half-Indian, half-
Frenchman? Historical figures are Solomon Juneau
and his wife and the story reaches its climax in
Milwaukee.

394   Carse, Robert. Fire in the Night. Jacket by Ray
      Houlihan. W. W. Norton, 1965. A good yarn for
      young New Yorkers as all the action takes place on
      the New York waterfront or in the harbor. The
      plot hinges on stolen designs for a new China Clip-
      per, and the attempts of a 13-year-old and his pals
      to catch the thief.
394a Ceder, Georgiana Dorcas. Winter Without Salt. Ill.
      by Charles Walker. Morrow Junior Books, 1962.
      A short story about the importance of salt to the
      early settlers of Kentucky and about the common
      humanity of Indians and white men. (I)
395   Chastain, Madye Lee. Emmy Keeps Her Promise.
      Ill. by the author. Harcourt, Brace and World,
      1956. A pleasurable period piece about two sisters,
      living in New York in the 1850s; the older one's de-
      termination to pay back a loan and her sister's equal
      determination to see her sister find the "Right man."
      (I)
396   _____. Plippen's Palace. Ill. by the author. Har-
      court, Brace and World, 1961. A story about a
      group of people both erratic and kind, set in New
      York City in the 1850s, and occasionally bringing in
      friends from other books by this author: also the
      story is interspersed with verses. (I)
397   Clark, Mary Stetson. The Glass Phoenix. Jacket by
      Laurel Brown. Viking, 1967. A novel about the
      formula for golden-ruby glass being acquired in a
      strange way by a 16-year-old boy working in the
      Sandwich Glass Factory in 1827. The author, as in
      other of her books, has built a good fictional plot
      upon a sound factual foundation as explained in the
      Afterword.
398   Coatsworth, Elizabeth. The Peddler's Cart. Ill. by
      Zhenya Gay. Macmillan, 1956. A rattling good
      story of an 11-year-old boy who goes on a peddling
      trip with his father in New York State in 1857,
      meeting with a series of exciting adventures, and
      learning what a great good man his father is. (I)
398a Coblentz, Catherine Cate. The Blue Cat of Castle
      Town. Ill. by Janice Holland. David McKay, 1949.
      There was a river that sang to a kitten, and the
      kitten, as she grew to be a cat (a blue one, mind
      you), carried the song to the people who offered her
      a home and inspired them to perfect their crafts
      of weaving, pewter work, carpentering and carpet
      making in Vermont in the 1830s. A uniquely charm-

ing story. (I and YA)

399 Constiner, Merle. Meeting at the Merry Fifer. W. W.
Norton, 1966. Hugh, an orphan of 15, on his way
to seek his fortune in Cincinnati, is befriended by
an indentured boy running away from a cruel master.
Hugh changes places with him in order to give him
time to escape, and so runs into a great deal of
danger. (I)

400 Derleth, August. Wind over Wisconsin. Scribner's,
1938. A novel about the early French settlers
near Portage, Sac Prairie and Madison, Wisconsin
and about Blackhawk's defeat. (A)

401 Drury, Maxine. George and the Long Rifle. Ill. by
Harve Stein. Longmans Green, 1957. Poor
blundering George goes with his understanding older
brother Silas to Ohio to take up land in 1819. But
the fever strikes Silas and George is thrown on his
own. (I)

402 Dunham, Montrew. Oliver Wendell Holmes Jr., Boy
of Justice. Ill. by Jerry Robinson. Bobbs-Merrill,
1961. Childhood of Famous Americans Series. A
delightful story of the childhood of one of our most
famous jurists (1841-1935). (E and I)

403 Edmonds, Walter. Tom Whipple (In "Seven American
Stories" by Edmonds.) This short, amusing story
was taken and expanded from one found in an old
book by Lydia Maria Child, about a Yankee lad who
decided to see the world. The settings are New
York State and Russia. (I)

404 _____. Two Logs Crossing: John Haskell's Story.
Ill. by Tibor Gergely. Dodd Mead, 1943. A moving
story about a 16-year-old who goes trapping to support his mother and younger brother and sisters and
to pay back a debt and the amount staked him by a
wise old judge. In his lonely work he learns that
there is no easy way to independence. Beautiful
nature pictures in text and drawings. (I)

405 Friermood, Elizabeth Hamilton. The Wild Donahues.
Doubleday, 1963. A "Gothic" novel, set in northern
Indiana, in horse-racing country, in the 1850s; the
main character, a 17-year-old lady who certainly
doesn't use very good sense. Of course if she did
there wouldn't be any story. (YA)

406 Frisby, Margaret. Annie Lee and the Wooden Skates.
Ill. by Darrell Wiskur. Oxford Press, 1942, revised edition, 1969. (Regensteiner) An entertaining story about the children of Robert E. Lee,

particularly eight-year-old Annie, the "in-between."
(I)

407 Gibbs, Alonzo. The Least Likely One. Lothrop, Lee
     and Shepard, 1964. A novel of a 17-year-old's
     search for understanding of his father and for self-
     discovery. True characters included are Stephen
     Foster, Ole Bull and the journalist James Gordon
     Bennett. (YA)

408 Graham, Shirley. Jean Baptiste Pointe DeSable,
     Founder of Chicago. Julian Messner, 1953. A
     biography of the man [sometimes found in libraries
     under the name "Pointe de Sable"] (1745?-1818) about
     whom not a great deal is known. The author has
     done a great deal of research to supply enough facts
     to write a good story of a remarkable man from
     Haiti who found the site for Chicago in 1772 and
     called it "the place I choose." (YA)

409 Gray, Elizabeth Janet. Jane Hope. Macmillan, 1933-
     61. A period piece about a harum-scarum 12-year-
     old developing into a mature 16-year-old in Chapel
     Hill, North Carolina just before the Civil War.
     (YA)

410 Grote, William. Fiddle, Flute and the River. Jacket
     by Charles Geer. Meredith, 1967. A humorous
     story of two boys trying to get to New Orleans on
     the Mississippi. (I and YA)

411 Havighurst, Walter and Marion. Song of the Pines:
     A Story of Norwegian Lumbering in Wisconsin.
     Ill. by Richard Floethe. Holt, Rinehart, and
     Winston. (11th printing, 1968). A 16-year-old
     boy in Norway hears of the wonders of America
     from a little pied piper of a man from Wisconsin,
     and with the help of other emigrants he finally
     reaches Wisconsin and finds a career in making
     cant hooks for lumbering. (I and YA)

412 Howard, Elizabeth. Peddler's Girl. Jacket by Louis
     Darling. William Morrow, 1951. A young lady,
     properly brought up in Detroit after her mother's
     death, takes to the road with her younger brother
     and peddler uncle. She soon finds herself faced
     with a choice of loves and life. (I and YA)

413 Johnson, Annabel and Edgar. The Burning Glass.
     Harper and Row, 1966. A strong novel of a con-
     sumptive 15-year-old who feels himself a drag on
     his trader father and brother and leaves them to
     go off with an old mountain man who refuses to
     kill Indians but is bent on revenge towards another

beaver hunter. Boy and man are captured by Crow
Indians and from then on, the tension mounts. (YA)

414 Lawson, Marian. Solomon Juneau Voyageur. Ill. by
Robert Hallock. Thomas Y. Crowell, 1960. Biography of the French-Canadian voyageur (1793-1856)
and the story of the founding of Milwaukee in 1846
as a consolidated city. (I and YA)

415 Lenski, Lois. Phebe Fairchild: Her Book. Ill. by
the author. J. B. Lippincott, 1936. A story about
a little girl's year with her country cousins, while
her parents are at sea, and how she cherishes her
Mother Goose book. It is a singing book of nursery
rhymes and hymns, and pleasant picture of country
life in Connecticut in 1830. (I)

416 McNeer, May. Stranger in the Pines. Ill. by Lynd
Ward. Houghton Mifflin, 1971. A fairly long, serious novel about a young apprentice who has run
away from his master, and, indeed, his past, and,
with a strong sense of guilt, takes refuge in the
Pine Barrens of Southern New Jersey. (YA)

417 Mason, Miriam. Susannah, the Pioneer Cow. Ill. by
Maud-Miska Petersham. Macmillan, 1941-56. The
adventures of a cow traveling from Virginia to
Indiana with her owners who led her behind their
covered wagon. (E)

418 Meader, Stephen W. Boy with a Pack. Ill. by Edward
Shenton. Harcourt, Brace and World, 1939. An
adventure story of a young peddler, traveling by
foot and Erie Canal boat from his home in New
Hampshire to Ohio, encountering wild animals,
slave catchers, horse thieves and other "varmints"
but also some kindly folk, gentle Quakers, and a
most attractive young lady. (I and YA)

419 _____. The Fish Hawk's Nest. Ill. by Edward
Shenton. Harcourt, Brace. A detective story
about smugglers, set in Cape May County, New
Jersey, in which a boy stumbles on the first clue
and then follows the case to the finish. (I and YA)

420 Musgrave, Florence. Merrie's Miracle. Ill. by Mary
Stevens. Hastings House, 1962. A story showing
what life was like for a young girl going on 16, in
the Western Reserve of Ohio in the 1830s, a place
largely settled by well educated people from Connecticut and so quite different from most frontier
settlements. (I)

421 Nolan, Jeannette Covert. The Little Giant: Stephen
A. Douglas. Julian Messner, 1964. Biography of

a political warrior (1813-61) who, as senator, supported the growth of railroads, the war with Mexico, the Missouri Compromise, and popular sovereign-
ty.   In spite of their deep differences, after Lincoln
defeated him in the 1860 race for the Presidency,
Douglas immediately offered his services to Lincoln
and staunchly supported him.   (I and YA)

422   Peterson, Helen Stone. Henry Clay, Leader in Congress.
Ill. by Vic Dowd. Garrard, 1964. A Discovery Book.
A biography of the man (1777-1852) who became the
youngest U. S. senator when at the age of 29 he was sent
to fill an unexpired term for a year. He was also
Speaker of the Kentucky House, Speaker of the U. S.
House, Secretary of State and finally a U. S. Senator
again. He fostered the famous Missouri Compromise
and the Compromise of 1850. (E and I)

423   Stephens, Peter John. The Perrely Plight: A Mystery at
Sturbridge. Ill. by R. D. Rice. Atheneum, 1965.
A good mystery story, set in Sturbridge, Mass. in
1836 in which a boy of 12 finds himself curiously
involved in a family feud, a farm burning and a
matter of a stolen hoard of money.   Interesting
character developments.   (I and YA)

424   West, Jessamyn. Except for Me and Thee. Harcourt,
Brace and World, 1949 (Avon, 1970). This gentle
family saga of a Quaker family is a sequel to "The
Friendly Persuasion" but can be read quite
separately. Though set in the period before, during and after the Civil War, many of the family's
problems seem like those of a hundred years later
--pacifism vs. activism and civil disobedience,
the "generation gap" and the reluctance of the
elders to change their way of life. (A)

425   _____ . The Friendly Persuasion. Harcourt,
Brace and World, 1970. A collection of gently
humorous short stories about the Quaker Birdwell
family in Indiana in the mid 19th century. (A)

426   Wilkie, Katherine E. The Man Who Wouldn't Give Up:
Henry Clay. Jacket by Stephen Voorhies. Julian
Messner, 1961. Biography of the man often called
the "Great Compromiser" (1777-1852) and, as
such, a very controversial figure in American politics in the first half of the 19th century; a man
four times disappointed in his attempts to be President and who never gave up the fight to preserve
the Union. (YA)

427   Witten, Herbert. Escape from the Shawnee. Ill. by

Lorence F. Bjorklund. Follett, 1958. A story of
a man and boy caught by the Shawnees while out
scouting for new settlers for Kentucky, and how
they managed to escape and survive during their
long trek back on the trail, in heavy winter weather,
the man suffering from a gunshot wound in the
thigh, and the 11-year-old boy having to care for
him.   (I)

428   Worth, Kathryn. They Loved to Laugh. Ill. by Marguerite DeAngeli. Doubleday, 1942. A gently nur-
tured Virginia girl, orphaned in her mid-teens, is
adopted into a hardworking, rambunctious family in
North Carolina, consisting of four teasing boys and
an unwelcoming daughter. Her adjustment to this
new life makes a charming and entertaining novel.
(YA)

PEOPLE AND PLACES--West of the Mississippi

429   Byars, Betsy. Trouble River. Ill. by Rocco Negri.
Viking, 1969. A humorous, exciting story of a
12-year-old boy, his dog, and his feisty grandmother escaping from the Indians on a raft he had
made himself.   (I)

430   Coatsworth, Elizabeth. The Sod House. Ill. by
Manning deV. Lee. Macmillan, 1954. A story of
the dangers and hardships besetting a German
family who, on a loan from the New England Emi-
grant Aid Society, move from Boston to Kansas at
the time when the abolitionists were trying to settle
anti-slavery families on that much fought-over
Border State.   (E and I)

431   MacDonald, Lucile and Ross, Zola H.   The Courting
of Ann Maria. Jacket by Leonard Vosburgh.
Thomas Nelson, 1958. A pioneer love story, set
in the Oregon Territory after the 54-40 treaty with
England in 1846. In 1850 the American government
passed a Land Donation Act, giving a bachelor 320
acres of land and twice that much to a married
man. Does the dashing Gabriel La Plante want
Ann Maria's hand for herself or for the extra
acres? And what about Hugh Conway, the gentle-
manly Britisher? With all sorts of tensions between
the American settlers and the Hudson's Bay people,
it's anyone's guess as to which suitor will succeed.
(YA)

432 May, Charles Paul. Stranger in the Storm. Ill. by
     Victor Ambrus. Abelard Schuman, 1972. Two
     little girls find themselves alone in the Iowa farm-
     house of one, in the midst of the "Great Blizzard
     of 1850" with almost no food except for the milk of
     two cows (if they can get to the barn to milk them).
     And worse yet, there are two men with guns coming
     around off and on, in search of a runaway slave.
     (I)
433 Noble, Iris. Courage in Her Hands. Julian Messner,
     1967. A novel about a young lady from Boston, at
     the Russian Fort Ross in Northern California in the
     early part of the 19th century, growing in courage
     as she faces physical hardships, Indian hostility,
     and finally a decision about marriage. The "Au-
     thor's Note" identifies one true character, a young
     Russian named Zachar Chichinov, who wrote an
     account of his stay at Fort Ross, "Adventures in
     California." (YA)
434 O'Dell, Scott. Island of the Blue Dolphins. Jacket by
     Evaline Ness. Houghton Mifflin, 1960; a remark-
     able story, based on historical records, of a young
     girl "Robinson Crusoe" alone for 18 years, on a
     rocky island off the coast of California, 1835 to '53.
     The island, now called the "island of San Nicholas,"
     is west of Santa Barbara. (I and YA)
435 Twin, Mark. The Adventures of Tom Sawyer and
     Huckleberry Finn. There are many good editions in-
     cluding paperbounds of these books written in 1876
     and 1884. All ages.
436 Woolridge, Rhoda. Hannah's Brave Year. Jacket by
     Robert Quackenbush. Bobbs-Merrill, 1964. A story
     of the Missouri frontier in the 1830s or so, and a 12-
     year-old girl holding her family together after the
     death of their parents from cholera, and fending off
     Indians and the mortgage holder. (I)
437 _____. That's the Way, Joshuway. Bobbs-Merrill,
     1965. A Missouri boy with dreams of going west,
     discovers that helping others make a home gives
     even greater satisfaction than adventuring in the
     wilderness. A story of the brighter side of pioneer-
     ing. (I)

TEXAS AND THE MEXICAN WAR

438 Alter, Robert Edmond. Two Sieges of the Alamo. Ill.
     by Albert Orbaan. G. P. Putnam's Sons, 1965. A

       novel of the defense of the fortified building against
the Mexicans, in 1835 and '36.   (YA)

439 Baker, Betty. The Dunderhead War. Harper and
      Row, 1967. A humorous novel about the Grand
      Army which, in its "dunderhead" way, took Santa
      Fe from the Mexicans in 1846 in the war that
      brought California into the Union, and about a
      German uncle who tries to bring law and order into
      that army. (YA)

440 Clark, Ann Nolan. Summer Is for Growing. Ill. by
      Agnes Tait. Farrar, Straus and Giroux, 1968.
      A story of a little girl's life on a hacienda in New
      Mexico at the time of transition from the Mexican
      to the American way of life, in 1851. (I)

441 Davis, Julia. Ride with the Eagle: The Expedition of
      the First Missouri in the War with Mexico, 1846.
      Maps by Paul Tremblay. Harcourt, Brace and
      World, 1962. A novel built on diaries of men
      who covered nearly 4000 miles to take Santa Fe
      and El Paso from the Mexicans in 1846. (YA)

442 Haynes, Nelma. Panther Lick Creek. Ill. by Wil-
      liam Moyers. Abingdon, 1970. A story of pio-
      neering in Peters' Colony (now Dallas), Texas, in
      which two boys have dangerous adventures with wild
      animals and Indians, learn how to tame wild horses
      and mules, and find joy and satisfaction in con-
      tributing to the settlement of a beautiful land.
      Horse lovers take note. (I)

443 Hoff, Carol. Johnny Texas. Ill. by Bob Meyers.
      Follett, 1950. The story begins with little Johann,
      fresh from Germany with his parents, in 1834, and
      through it are woven strands of early Texas his-
      tory. (I)

444 _____. Johnny Texas on the San Antonio Road. Ill.
      by Earl Sherwan. Follett, 1953. A sequel to
      "Johnny Texas" in which Johnny takes a load of
      corn on a 600 mile journey on the Old San Antonio
      Road and returns with the gold payment, constantly
      in great danger from an unscrupulous blackguard.
      (I)

445 Jackson, Helen Hunt. Ramona. Roberts Bros., 1884.
      A novel about a girl, half-Indian and half Spanish,
      in California shortly after the Mexican War, and
      the relations between Indians and Spanish at that
      time. (A)

446 Johnson, William. Sam Houston, The Tallest Texan.
      Ill. by William Reusswig. Random, 1953. An

exciting biography of the hero of San Jacinto (1793-
1863) who had grown up with Indians and fought
with "Old Hickory" and who became President of
the Texas Republic and later governor of, and
senator from, the Lone Star State.   (I and YA)

447   Latham, Jean Lee.   Retreat To Glory: The Story of
Sam Houston.   Jacket by John Martinez.   Harper
and Row, 1965.   A biographical novel of Houston
(1793-1863) who ran away to the Indians as a boy,
fought with Old Hickory as a young man, was the
hero of San Jacinto, and later a political leader
in and from Texas.   (YA)

448   _____ .   Sam Houston.   Gerrard, 1965.   A Discovery Book.   The story of the savior of Texas
at San Jacinto in April 1836, when his small
forces defeated the much larger forces of Mexican
Santa Ana.   (E and I)

449   Norton, André (Alice Mary).   Stand to Horses.
Jacket by Edwin Schmidt.   Harcourt, Brace and
World, 1956.   Exciting fiction, based on actual
journals and diaries kept by army officers and
scouts known as mountain men, who were stationed
at Santa Fé in the violent period between the
Mexican War and the War between the States. (YA)

450   Stevenson, Augusta.   Sam Houston, Boy Chieftain.
Ill. by Paul Laune.   Bobbs-Merrill, 1944-53.
Houston's boyhood was spent in a Cherokee village
where he lived in the Chief's house, became a brave,
and received the Indian name of Raven.   (E)

451   Vinton, Iris.   The Story of Robert E. Lee.   Ill. by
John Alan Maxwell.   Grosset and Dunlap, 1952.
A biography mainly concerned with Lee's boyhood,
youth and career as a West Pointer in Mexico and
Texas.   (I)

452   Warren, Robert Penn.   Remember the Alamo!.   Ill.
by William Moyers.   Random, 1958.   The futile
defense of the Alamo in 1836, in which fewer than
200 men died before the onslaught of Santa Ana's
thousands of Mexican soldiers, provides the climax
of this story of how Texas, first part of Mexico,
then an independent country, finally became the
28th state of the Union.   YA

GOLD IN CALIFORNIA

453   Bulla, Clyde Robert.   The Secret Valley.   Ill. by
Grace Paull.   Thomas Y. Crowell, 1949.   A

story for beginning readers, with 12 songs, music
and words, about a family in search of gold in
California. (E and I)

454   Burt, Olive. Jayhawker Johnny. Ill. by Albert
Orbaan. John Day, 1966. A story (with a factual
basis) of a family traveling to California on their
own except when following a group of "jayhawkers,"
young men goldseekers, and a wagon train of both
gold-seekers and pioneers. Both these groups
break up on the way, and thirst and starvation take
their toll, but Johnny, aged seven, and his mother,
keep going. (I)

455   Fleishman, Sid. By the Great Horn Spoon. Profusely
ill. by Eric von Schmidt. Little Brown, 1963. A
hilarious story about a boy and his English butler
out to seek a fortune in the gold fields of California
in 1849 for the laudable purpose of saving his aunt
from having to sell her house and all her posses-
ions. A laugh-out-loud book. (I and YA)

456   Lampman, Evelyn Sibley. The Bandit of Mok Hill.
Ill. by Marvin Friedman. Doubleday, 1969.
A story of northern California in 1851 and an
orphan boy who, having been befriended by a famous bandit, wishes to become part of his band.
However, his plans are foiled by a professor of
elocution who takes him to the gold fields intend-
ing to use him as a singer. A story of divided
loyalties and ambitions. (I)

457   Luce, Willard and Celia. Sutter's Fort--Empire on the
Sacramento. Ill. by Paul Frame. Garrard, 1969.
The rise and fall of Sutter's Empire in the 1840s,
of which the fort in Sacramento has been restored;
how Sutter ruled it and entertained there such
guests as Kit Carson and John Fremont, and defended it from enemies, human and animal, until the
Gold Rushers and the Mexican War caused its
downfall. (I)

458   White, Dale (Place). The Singing Boones. Ill. by
Dorothy Bayley Morse. Macmillan, 1957. A story
of a poor but valiant family setting out for the gold
fields of California in 1852, because of the father's
ambition to give his frail wife and six children the
goods he bought with gold. (YA)

EARLY TRANSPORTATION

459 Adams, Samuel Hopkins. Chingo Smith of the Erie
       Canal. Ill. by Leonard Vosburgh. Random, 1958.
       An action-packed story of the building of the Erie
       Canal and of a homeless waif whose dearest ambi-
       tion is to someday captain a boat on it. (I and YA)

460 _____ . The Pony Express. Ill. by Lee J. Ames.
       Random, 1950. A book of good stories about the
       daredevil riders of the Pony Express and their
       horses, based on what records the author could find.

461 Angell, Polly. Pat and the Iron Horse. Ill. by Clif-
       ford H. Shule. Aladdin Books, 1955. Young Pat
       Mulvaney leaves famine-stricken Ireland in 1846 to
       seek his fortune in America and make a home for
       his mother and her younger children. He gets
       work immediately in the building of the Erie Rail-
       road, and the story goes on to tell about the prob-
       lems of blasting for the road through rocky hills,
       the conflicts between Orangemen and other Irish,
       and between railroaders and Canalers, between Irish
       and German immigrants, and finally, between earlier
       settlers and newcomers. (YA)

462 Bailey, Ralph Edgar. Wagons Westward: The Story of
       Alexander Majors. Map by James McDonald. Jack-
       et and frontispiece by Richard Cuffari. William
       Morrow, 1969. More a story of early freight trans-
       portation than a biography of Majors (1814-1900),
       who was a freight pioneer and leader before the
       Golden Spike united the roads, and afterward too,
       in reaching places remote from the Union Pacific.
       It is also a story of passenger transportation by
       coach and Pony Express mail carriage, and a trib-
       ute to an exceptionally honest, daring and persistent
       hero. (I and YA)

463 Baker, Betty. Do Not Annoy the Indians. Ill. by
       Harold Goodwin. Macmillan, 1968. The story of
       three young easterners trying to run a stagecoach
       relay station in frontier Arizona, around 1858, with
       U.S. cavalrymen and overly friendly Indians getting
       in the way. The rules of the Butterfield Overland
       Mail Company include one: "Do not annoy the In-
       dians," and the "Author's Note" on stagecoach lines
       includes a copy of original instructions to the em-
       ployees of the Company. A fun-filled book. (I)

464 Best, Herbert. Watergate: A Story of the Irish on
       the Erie Canal. Ill. by Erick Berry. John C.

Winston, 1951. A humorous novel about a "drivin'
boy" on the Canal, strongly recommended to New
York Staters who live near it, regardless of age.
Contains a foreword about the building of the Erie
Canal. (YA and Up)

465   Bonham, Frank. Honor Bound. Jacket by Robert
      Bantram. Thomas Y. Crowell, 1963. An un-
      put-downable mystery novel of the first stagecoach
      to the west coast on the Great Overland Mail.
      Why is President Buchanan sending a bottle of
      Atlantic Ocean water and two weasles to the pro-
      slavery governor of California? Why must Cullen
      keep his eye constantly on a girl traveler who is
      always knitting (and very badly) a long scarf for
      the governor? And how does one decide between
      keeping his word to an individual or doing one's
      best for his country? YA

466   Bulla, Clyde Robert. Riding the Pony Express. Ill.
      by Grace Paull. Thomas Y. Crowell, 1948. A
      story of a young boy's first experience as a Pony
      Express rider, with four catchy songs composed by
      the author. (E)

467   Burt, Olive. Camel Express: A Story of the Jeff
      Davis Experiment. Ill. by Joseph C. Camana.
      John C. Winston, 1954. A most unusual story of
      a most unusual experiment, the importation of
      camels for desert warfare against the Indians in
      1856. (I and YA)

468   Calhoun, Mary. High Wind for Kansas. Ill. by
      W. T. Mars. William Morrow, 1965. There is
      lots of fun in this short book about a wagon with
      sails and the Overland Navigation Company--based,
      in part, on an actual incident in Westport, Mis-
      souri in 1853. (E and I)

469   Chandler, Edna Walker. Stagecoach Driver. Ill. by
      Jack Merryweather. Benefic Press, 1968. A Tom
      Logan story in which Tom acts as a stagecoach
      whip for Wells Fargo and earns enough money to
      buy his own ranch. (E)

470   Chastain, Madye Lee. Jerusha's Ghost. Ill. by the
      author. Harcourt, Brace and World, 1958. A
      light, entertaining little period piece whose only
      connection with the subject of transportation is when
      four little girls, spending the summer together on
      Long Island, discover a balloonist experimenting in
      a nearby meadow. (I)

471   Fall, Thomas (Snow). Canalboat to Freedom. Ill. by

Joseph Cellini.   Dial, 1966.   (Dell Paperback,
1970).   The ostensible hero of this canalboat and
underground railroad story is an orphan sent to
America as an indentured worker for a canalboat
owner, but the true hero is the free Negro cook
on the boat.   (I and YA)

471a   Franchere, Ruth.   The Travels of Colin O'Dae.   Ill.
by Lorence Bjorklund.   Thomas Y. Crowell, 1966.
An amusing story of a traveling show and their experiences on the Illinois River.   (I)

472   Henry, Marguerite.   San Domingo, The Medicine Hat
Stallion.   Ill. by Robert Longhead.   Rand McNally,
1972.   A treasure of a book in every way, about a
teenager whose father is an embittered man and
takes out his frustrations in brutal treatment of his
son; about the stallion, San Domingo, the light of
the boy's life and his only comfort; about the Pony
Express and the coming of the telegraph line.   The
setting is the Wyoming territory in the 1850s.   (I
and YA)

473   Meader, Stephen W.   Jonathan Goes West.   Ill. by
Edward Shenton.   Harcourt, Brace and World,
1946.   The travels of a 16-year-old lad from Maine
to Illinois by schooner, rail, foot, and a booksell-
er's caravan.   (I)

473a   _____ .   Who Rides in the Dark?   Ill. by James
McDonald.   Harcourt, Brace and World, 1937.
A story of old stagecoach days, freight wagons,
passenger coaches, and highwaymen, about a boy
working as a stable boy at the "Fox and Stars" at
Deptford, New Hampshire, who finds adventure in
pursuit of a band of highwaymen.   (I and YA)

474   Orton, Helen Fuller.   The Treasure in the Little Trunk.
Ill. by Robert Ball.   J. B. Lippincott, 1932.   The
story of a 12-year-old girl traveling with her family
from Vermont, over the Mohawk Turnpike, to make a
new home in western New York State near the Erie
Canal, then under construction (1820s).   (I)

475   Spier, Peter.   The Erie Canal: Song with Illustrations.
[by the author].   Doubleday, 1970.   Historical notes
and music at the end.   (Picture and E)

476 Allen, Merritt Parmelee. Blow Bugles Blow. Ill. by
   Alan Moyler. Longmans Green, 1956. A novel
   about a farm boy serving under General Sheridan;
   about the Battle of the Wilderness, and the last
   desperate race with Lee's forces. (YA)

477 _____. Johnny Reb. Ill. by Ralph Ray Jr. David
   McKay, 1952. A splendid war novel, combining
   humor, realism and excitement and giving the
   southern side of the conflict, while still being fair
   to the north. (YA)

478 _____. The White Feather. Ill. by C. B. Fall.
   David McKay, 1944. An outstanding war novel, as
   always in this author's works--combining humor
   and realism with fairness to both sides--about a
   Kentucky mountain boy who joins Morgan's Raiders.
   (YA)

479 Anderson, Betty Baxter. Powder Monkey. Maps by
   Raphael Palacios. New York Graphic Society,
   1962. A story with a slight fictional plot, about
   the battles on and near the Mississippi River, with
   descriptions of the rivercraft used during the Civil
   War and the duties of a "powder monkey." (I and
   YA)

480 Benét, Stephen Vincent. John Brown's Body. Doubleday Doran, 1927. A book-length narrative poem of
   the Civil War, a Pulitzer Prize winner. (A)

481 Borland, Hal. The Amulet. J. B. Lippincott, 1957.
   A novel about a volunteer for the Confederacy who
   leaves Denver and the girl he was about to marry
   to fight in a war he doesn't understand, for reasons he doesn't understand but hopes, somehow, to
   discover. The Battle of Wilson's Creek provides
   an answer. (A)

482 Bradbury, Bianca. Flight into Spring. Ives Washburn, 1963. A light novel about a frivolous Maryland girl who marries a grim puritanical farmer
   from Connecticut and goes to live with his parents
   on a rugged farm. Though her family were

Northern sympathizers, her in-laws consider her a
"secesh" and disapprove of her intensely. (YA)

483 Brick, John. Yankees on the Run. Duell, Sloan and
Pearce, 1961. A story based upon factual incidents,
in which two young Yankees make their escape from
dreaded Andersonville Prison, near Macon, Georgia.
(YA)

484 Burchard, Peter. Jed. Ill. by the author. Coward
McCann, 1960. A fine short novel about a 16-year-
old Yankee soldier and a small rebel boy and his
dog. (I)

485 _____. North by Night. Ill. with maps by the author. Coward McCann, 1962. A thrilling novel
about the danger-frought escape of two Yankees from
a Confederate jail where they had been imprisoned
after the Federal charge on Fort Wagner. Based
on the war experiences of Mrs. Peter Burchard's
grandfather. (YA)

486 _____. Rat Hall. Ill. by the author. Coward
McCann, 1971. A short vivid story of a Yankee
escape from Libby Prison in Richmond, Virginia
in 1864, based on the actual escape of 100 prisoners
at that time. (I and YA)

487 Catton, Bruce. Banners at Shenandoah. Doubleday,
1955. A novel about a 17-year-old recruit from
Michigan who carried Sheridan's banner in the cavalry. (A)

488 _____. A Stillness at Appomattox. Doubleday,
1953. A history in reportorial style of the last
year of the Civil War. (A)

489 Coatsworth, Elizabeth. George and Red. Ill. by Paul
Gionanopoulos. Macmillan, 1946-69. Episodes in
the lives of two boys living near Niagara Falls, one
the son of a southern sympathizer, the other the son
of an abolitionist, a Lincoln man. The final episode
is connected with a little-known event in 1866, the
Irish Fenian expedition. (I)

490 Commager, Henry Steele. America's Robert E. Lee.
Ill. by Lynd Ward. Houghton Mifflin, 1951. A
biography of Lee (1807-70) in a well-written and
well-made book, giving considerable attention to his
part in the Mexican war and ending with his surrender at Appomatox. (I)

491 Crane, Stephen. The Red Badge of Courage (1895).
New American Library. A Signet Classic, edited
and with an introduction by R. W. Stallman. An
impressionistic novel about a young northern soldier

in the bloody Battle of Chancellorsville, written by
Crane when he was 24.   (A)

492   Crary, Margaret.   The Calico Ball.   Prentice-Hall,
1961.   A novel of the conflict between Indians and
Whites near Sioux City at the gateway of the Dakota
Territory in 1861/2, when most of the menfolk were
away fighting in the Civil War.   Ginger Bryant, a
14-year-old girl, is deeply concerned over the
wrongs each inflicts on the other, and uses her
understanding of the Indians to good avail.   (YA)

493   Cromie, Alice Hamilton.   A Tour Guide to the Civil
War.   Introduction by Bill Irvin.   Quadrangle,
1964.   Almost every reader will find, from this
book, some nearby landmark, museum, or battle--
ground site and learn about some of the lesser
known areas of conflict in the War Between the
States.   (A)

494   Daniels, Jonathan.   Mosby, Gray Ghost of the Con-
federacy.   Ill. by Albert Orbaan.   J. B. Lippincott.
Very much a military story about the guerrilla
fighter (1833-1916) who continued fighting even after
Appomatox and was never entirely "reconstructed."
(YA)

495   _____.   Robert E. Lee.   Ill. by Robert Frankenburg.   Houghton Mifflin, 1960.   A biography (1807-
70) focussing on Lee's military campaigns during
the Civil War.   (I and YA)

496   Daringer, Helen Fern.   Mary Montgomery, Rebel:
Ill. by Kate Seredy.   Harcourt, Brace, 1946.
A novel about a young girl in Atlanta before and
during the War.   (I and YA)

497   Davis, Julia.   Mount Up: A True Story of the Civil
War.   Ill. with photographs and a map.   Harcourt,
Brace and World, 1967.   Based on the reminiscences
of Major E. A. H. McDonald of the Confederate
Cavalry, this is as exciting a war story as any fictional one and shows the Virginians of the Confederacy as admirable and understandable.   (Ya and Up)

498   Dick, Trella Damson.   The Island on the Border.
Abelard-Schuman, 1963.   A story about a family
living on the peninsula of southern Missouri, between
the Confederate states of Arkansas and Tennessee,
taking refuge from rebel raiders on an island in the
Missouri River, while the father is away fighting for
the Union.   Their adventures include helping escaping
slaves and a northern spy and trying to forage for
food.   (I)

499 Edmonds, Walter D. Cadmus Henry. (See Seven
     American Stories). A humorous novel about a
     volunteer aide to Confederate General Magruder when
     General McClellan was beginning his peninsular cam-
     paign against Richmond and about his flight in a
     balloon to spy on the northern forces and his es-
     capades after the rope connecting him with the
     ground is accidentally severed. A good story of
     good people, northern and southern, black and white,
     briefly introducing Harriet Tubman. (I and YA)

500 Edwards, Sally. The Man Who Said No (James Louis
     Petigru). Coward McCann, 1970. Biography of a
     South Carolinian (1789-1863) who stood virtually
     alone in his community in his opposition to his
     state's secession from the Union, not only in 1860
     but long before, when South Carolina threatened to
     secede over the tariff. (YA)

501 Epstein, Samuel and Beryl. The Andrews Raid; or,
     The Great Locomotive Chase. Ill. by R. M.
     Powers. Coaard McCann, 1906. Whew! What a
     story! And a true one at that, of Yankees stealing
     a train, The General, right from under the noses
     of Confederate soldiers, and of a Confederate
     train, The Texas, in hot pursuit. One can hardly
     catch his breath reading it. (YA and Up)

502 Freeman, Douglas Southall. Lee of Virginia. Ill.
     with photographs. Charles Scribner's Sons, 1958.
     This one-volume biography (1807-70) was written by
     the Pulitzer Prize winning author of a four-volume
     biography and another prize winner, "Lee's Lieu-
     tenants," and was published after his death. This
     recommends it as first choice of young adult
     biographies of Lee. (YA)

503 Garthwaite, Marion. Holdup on Bootjack Hill. Ill. by
     Leo Summers. Doubleday, 1962. A California
     story of 1862 which has nothing to do with the war
     but shows that life went on regardless--this about
     an 11-year-old girl, a slightly older boy, and their
     Indian friend, Winky Loosefoot, who is charged with
     holding up a stage. (I)

504 Green, Margaret. President of the Confederacy:
     Jefferson Davis. Julian Messner, 1963. Biography
     (1808-89) of the man who became the scapegoat of a
     lost cause but who did accomplish marvels in build-
     ing a government and army under stress and against
     much opposition, even from southerners. (YA)

505 Hall, Anna Gertrude. Cyrus Holt and the Civil War.

Ill. by Dorothy Bayley Morse. Viking, 1964. A
unique Civil War story in its telling of the northern
home front in New York State during the four terrible years; how the war affected the lives of boys
too young to fight, and the mothers, wives, sweet-
hearts of those who went to battle. The matters of
enlistments, the draft, and "bounty-jumpers" enter
into the story, which is based on stories told by the
author's father and the diaries of her grandfather.
(I)

506 Hall, Marjory. Beneath Another Sun. Jacket by William Plummer. Westminster, 1970. What was it
like, for a young girl, to be a northerner, living
in Richmond, Virginia, during the Civil War?
Julia's father, leaving Connecticut to join the Confederate Army, asks his wife and daughters to come
south for the duration and there they are kindly but
coolly treated as "the enemy." The tragedy of the
War is poignantly illustrated in this novel, based on
facts and records but with, in the main, fictional
names. (YA)

507 _____. The Carved Wooden Ring. Jacket by Al
Fiorentino. Westminster, 1972. A novel about a
young Baltimore woman, frivolous and thoughtless,
as the war begins, and writing to beaux on both
sides of the conflict though entirely sympathetic
with the southern cause. As the war grows in in-
tensity and horror, she takes up nursing and also
becomes involved in espionage activities which result in her being banished to Richmond. As in the
book, Euphemia Mary Goldsborough was her real
name, and much of the story is based on her
diary. (YA)

508 Hancock, M. A. Menace on the Mountain. Ill. by
H. Tom Hall. Macrae Smith, 1968. This story,
told in mountain vernacular, is about the terrifying
bushwhackers (deserters from both southern and
northern armies and thorough blackguards), how
they laid waste the country in the foothills of the
Blue Ridge Mountains and took over the homeplace
of a boy named Jamie McIver, and what Jamie was
finally able to do about it. (I and YA)

509 Havighurst, Marion Boyd. The Sycamore Tree.
World, 1960. A novel about a young Ohio lady
with brothers serving conflicting armies, who
though an admirer of General Morgan, falls
in love with a northern soldier and grows in

understanding of the evils of slavery. (YA)

510 Hinkins, Virginia. Stonewall's Courier--The Story of
     Charles Randolph and General Jackson. Jacket by
     Ezra Jack Keats. McGraw-Hill, 1959. A story,
     based on fact, about a 16-year-old in the Confederate
     army. (I)

511 Hooper, Byrd. Beef For Beauregard. Ill. by Charles
     Geer. G. P. Putnam's Sons, 1959. A 16-year-old
     whose father won't let him enlist in the Confederate
     army, does his bit by leading a crew of young
     neighbors in rounding up eight "mossyhorns" (cows)
     and herding them to Louisiana to sell to the southern
     army--he hopes to General Beauregard himself.
     Written with humor and realism and the rhythm of
     Texas speech in the 1860s. (I and YA)

512 Hunt, Irene. Across Five Aprils. Cover painting and
     maps by Albert John Pucci. Follett, 1964. Winner
     of the 1964 Follett award, novel of a family torn
     by the war and the impact of this dissension upon a
     10-year-old boy who has to take on a man's role on
     the farm. Lincoln, Grant, Sherman, General George
     Thomas and Robert E. Lee figure in the story along
     with other military leaders, and contemporary atti-
     tudes are shown in the action of the novel. (YA)

513 Hunt, Mabel Leigh. Lucinda, a Little Girl of 1860.
     Ill. by Cameron Wright. J. B. Lippincott, 1934.
     A gentle, old-fashioned story, including the verses
     of many old songs of the period but dealing too
     with the serious realities of slavery and the Civil
     War (I).

514 Icenhower, Joseph B. The Scarlet Raider. Chilton,
     1961. A war story in which a 16-year-old
     joins Mosby's Raiders. (YA)

515 Kantor, MacKinlay. Gettysburg. Random Landmark,
     1952. A story of the battle and Lincoln's address
     afterward, written by a Civil War authority, sensitive
     to the real personalities involved in the conflict.
     (I)

516 Keith, Harold. Rifles for Watie. Thomas Y. Crowell,
     1957. A Newbery Prize novel, tough and realistic,
     about the little-known Western campaign of the
     Civil War, in which the Cherokee Indians fought on
     both sides, Stand Watie being the leader of the
     Cherokee Rebels. A young runaway from Kansas
     also takes part in both sides of the struggle and
     sees the evil of war and the nobility of some men,
     both Union and Confederate. (YA)

517 Lawson, John. The Spring Rider. Jacket by Richard
     Powers. Thomas Y. Crowell, 1968. A Civil War
     fantasy in which a country boy and his sister, who
     live near one of the battlefields, see the ghosts of
     a Yankee soldier from Maine, a southern colonel,
     Stonewall Jackson, and Abraham Lincoln. (YA)

518 Levy, Mimi Cooper. Corrie and the Yankee. Ill. by
     Ernest Crichlow. Viking, 1959. A tense, exciting
     story of a little Negro girl whose father is a scout
     for the Union army. The "quarters" of a southern
     plantation where she lives, is beset by "patrollers"
     after the escape of a young Yankee from a Con-
     federate prison. (I)

519 McGiffin, Lee. Swords, Stars and Bars. Ill. by
     Robert MacLean. E. P. Dutton, 1958. Eight ex-
     citing stories of Confederate cavalry heroes:
     Mosby, Butler, Forrest, Hampton, Morgan, Stuart,
     Wheeler and Shelby. (I and YA)

520 McNicol, Jacqueline Morrell. Ride for Old Glory.
     Ill. by Charles Walker. David McKay, 1964. A
     great Civil War novel in which a homeless boy of
     14 is "took in" by a rascal named Old Man Dolf,
     escapes to a circus, finds a friend from Shawneetown
     in southern Illinois, General James Wilson, becomes
     an army courier and observes the battle outside
     Nashville in which the Confederates, under General
     Hood, were defeated. The last chapter identifies the
     real characters in the plot, including a couple of
     horses, some circus performers, and Johnny him-
     self. (YA)

521 Malkus, Alida Sims. We Were There at the Battle of
     Gettysburg. Historical Consultant, Earl Schenck
     Miers. Ill. by Leonard Vosburgh. Grosset and
     Dunlap, 1955. A young Gettysburg boy watches the
     beginning of the great battle and then finds himself
     embroiled in the clashing confusion of the conflict,
     helping the wounded and carrying off the dead, until
     he is captured by Confederate soldiers. (I)

522 Meader, Stephen. The Muddy Road to Glory. Ill. by
     George Hughes. Harcourt, Brace and World, 1963.
     A realistic Civil War novel about a 16-year-old who
     joins the Twentieth Maine Regiment of the Army of
     the Potomac, fights in the battles of Spotsylvania,
     Cold Harbor and in the Wilderness skirmishes, is
     captured and sent to the prison camp on Belle Isle,
     near Richmond, and is finally back with his regi-
     ment at the time of Lee's surrender. (YA)

523   Mitchell, Margaret. Gone With the Wind. Macmillan,
      1936. A Pulitzer Prize novel, a panorama of the
      war and reconstruction in Georgia which has fas-
      cinated young and old readers for over 35 years and
      will probably continue to do so for the foreseeable
      future. Some of its characters (Scarlett O'Hara,
      Rhett Butler) have become almost legendary. (A)
524   Monjo, F. N. The Vicksburg Veteran. Ill. by Douglas
      Gorsline. Simon and Schuster, 1971. A story of
      the Vicksburg siege and victory by the Union army
      under General Grant whose 12-year-old son accom-
      panied him on the campaign, told as the son's
      account. (E and I)
525. Norton, André. (Alice Mary). Ride Proud, Rebel.
      Jacket by W. T. Mars. World, 1961. A novel
      about a Confederate soldier who had been with Mor-
      gan's raiders, and who after disastrous defeats
      fights his way to join General N. Bedford Forrest--
      based on unpublished sources. (YA)
526   Orbaan, Albert. Forked Lightning: The Story of
      General Philip Sheridan. Ill. by the author. Haw-
      thorne Books, 1964. A book which should appeal
      equally to horse lovers and Civil War buffs, it has
      two heroes, Sheridan (1832-88) and his horse, Rienzi.
      Good diagrams of crucial battles which they led.
      (I and YA)
527   Palmer, Bruce. Chancellorsville: Disaster in Victory.
      Macmillan, 1967. An account of the crucial battle
      with four tactical maps and historic photographs and
      engravings and a chronology of events, just the book
      for readers interested in military strategy.
      (YA and Up)
528   Randall, Ruth Painter. I, Varina! A Biography of
      Mrs. Jefferson Davis. Ill. with photographs. Little
      Brown, 1962. The story of a gently nurtured
      southern girl (1827-1906) who became First Lady of
      the Confederacy and whose courageous devotion to
      her husband in times of great adversity, must always
      be admired by northerners and southerners. (YA)
529   Rauch, Mabel Thompson. Vinnie and the Flag Tree.
      Duell, Sloan and Pearce, 1959. A novel of the Civil
      War in southern Illinois (present Carbondale), based
      on the author's family history. (YA)
530   Reeder, Red. Sheridan: The General Who Wasn't
      Afraid to Take a Chance. Ill. with photographs and
      maps. Duell, Sloan and Pearce, 1962. A biography,
      in story form (1832-88). (I and YA)

531 Seifert, Shirley. Look to the Rose. J. B. Lippincott,
    1960. A novel about a young Chicago lady, Eleanor
    Kinzie (the mother of Juliette Low, founder of the
    Girl Scouts), who marries a southerner, William
    Gordon, and goes to live in Georgia in the 1850s.
    The second part of the book deals with the Civil
    War battles in which young Gordon fights for the
    southern cause, and the third part concerns problems
    of the reconstruction period as they affect the mar-
    ried life of "Nelly" and "Willy." (A)

532 Shirreffs, Gordon D. The Mosquito Fleet--The Tin-
    clads at the Siege of Vicksburg. Jacket by Alice
    Gripman. Chilton, 1961. One adventure after
    another for two youths in the Mississippi River
    fleet: getting lost in the swamps of the Yazoo
    Valley, eluding rebel patrols as they struggle to
    find their way back, and finally finding themselves
    fighting on the wrong side at Vicksburg. (YA)

533 Sims, Lydel. Thaddeus Lowe, Uncle Sam's First
    Airman. Jacket by Frank Aloise. Putnam, 1964.
    The story of a daring young balloonist (1832-1913)
    who organized an Aeronautics Corps for the Union
    Army. (I and YA)

534 Smith, Bradford. Dan Webster, Union Boy. Ill. by
    Charles V. John. Bobbs-Merrill, 1954. Childhood
    of Famous Americans Series. The story of Daniel
    Webster's boyhood and youth, his going to Exeter
    and Dartmouth College (teaching between terms to
    make money), his love of oratory and his famous
    words, "Liberty and union, now and forever, one
    and inseparable." (E and I)

535 Steele, William D. The Perilous Road. Ill. by Paul
    Galdone. Harcourt, Brace and World, 1958. A
    story of a little boy who tries to be a spy for the
    Confederacy even though his brother is in the Union
    army and who learns about the realities of war.
    (I and YA)

536 Webb, Christopher. Mark Toyman's Inheritance.
    Funk and Wagnalls, 1960. 14-year-old Mark and his
    aunt travel by wagon to California where he works
    for the gold seekers in Sacramento. Later the Civil
    War takes him back east where he participates in
    the battles of Shiloh, Vicksburg and the Wilderness--
    realistically narrated in the first person. (YA)

537 Wellman, Manly. Rebel Mail Runner. Ill. by Stuy-
    vesant Van Veen. Holiday House, 1954. Confeder-
    ate Mail Runners get family correspondence through

enemy lines and are in constant danger of being
hanged as spies. (I and YA)

538 _____ . Ride Rebels. Jacket by William Ferguson.
Ives Washburn, 1959. A story about the exploits of
some of Jeb Stuart's cavalry scouts and their wide
variety of missions: spying and spy catching,
escape from imprisonment, and finding meat for the
Confederate army. (I and YA)

539 Werstein, Irving. The Many Faces of the Civil War.
Ill. with maps. Julian Messner, 1961. An excep-
tionally clear and completely absorbing story of the
Civil War, focussing on the generals of both sides.
(I and YA)

540 Whittier, John Greenleaf. Barbara Frietchie. Ill. by
Paul Galdone. Thomas Y. Crowell, 1965. A
beautifully illustrated edition of Whittier's poem
which pays tribute to the chivalry of the
Rebel army as well as to the courage and
patriotism of an old lady of Frederick, Maryland.
(Picture Book)

THE CLOSING FRONTIER (1865 to 1900)

BIOGRAPHIES

541 Apsler, Alfred. Northwest Pioneer: The Story of
Louis Fleishner. Ill. by Morton Garchik. Farrar
Straus and Cudahy, 1960. Jewish Publication Society of America. A Biography of a Bohemian Jewish boy who became a frontier trader and soldier in
the late 19th century, and, finally, a great bene-
factor of Portland, Oregon. (I)

542 Bailey, Ralph Edgar. Indian Fighter: The Story of
Nelson A. Miles. Jacket and frontispiece by Leslie
Goldstein, maps by James MacDonald. Morrow
Junior Books, 1965. The story of Miles' military
career beginning with the Civil War and ending with
the Spanish-American War, but dealing chiefly with
the Indian conflicts: campaigns against the Kiowas
and Comanches (1874), Sitting Bull (1877), Chief
Joseph of the Nez Percé (1877), the Apaches and
Geronimo (1886), and the Sioux (1890-91). (YA)

543 Cody, Col. William. The Adventures of Buffalo Bill.
Harper, 1904. This account, by Buffalo Bill himself, of Indian fighting and buffalo hunts, strains the
reader's credulity and is not to be read for literary
style; but it's fun to read, though shocking to our
current thinking about the treatment of minorities and
the ecology of the West. (I)

544 Collier, Edmund. The Story of Buffalo Bill. Ill. by
Nicholas Eggenhofer. Grosset and Dunlap, 1952.
The story of William Cody's adventurous life (1846-
1917), with emphasis on his western exploits--
buffalo hunting, Indian fighting, and the Pony Express. (I)

545 Erdman, Loula Grace. Many a Voyage. Dodd Mead,
1960. A biographical novel of Edmund G. Ross,
written from the viewpoint of his wife, Fanny. Ross
has come down in history mainly because of his
vote preventing the impeachment of President Johnson, but he was important in many other ways--as a

newspaper man in Sandusky (Ohio), Milwaukee, and
"bloody Kansas"; as a promoter of railroads, as a
Senator from Kansas, and as governor of the territory of New Mexico. (A)

546 Felton, Harold W. Nat Love, Negro Cowboy. Ill. by
David Hodges. Dodd Mead, 1969. The adventures
of the young Negro, born a slave in 1854, who became a legend as "Deadwood Dick" for his sharp
shooting, cattle roping and bronco riding, ending
his days sedately as a Pullman porter. Based on
his own book: "The Life and Adventures of Nat
Love; Better Known in the Cattle Country as Deadwood Dick. " (I)

547 Garst, Shannon (with Warren Garst). Wild Bill Hickok.
Julian Messner, 1952. Biography of James Butler Hickok (1837-76) who came by the nickname of
"Wild Bill" rightly as overland stage boss, Indian
fighter, Union scout, marshal of Hayes and Abilene,
and reluctant showman with Buffalo Bill's Wild West
show. Chronology of his short, thrill-packed life.
(YA)

548 Holbrook, Stewart H. Wild Bill Hickok Tames the West.
Ill. by Ernest Richardson. Random Landmark,
1952. For roughness and toughness it's hard to
beat this true story of James Hickok (1837-76),
commonly known as Wild Bill, and this book tells
the story with all the rootin' tootin', gunshootin' of
the West of the 1860s and '70s. (I)

549 Judson, Clara Ingram. Mr. Justice Holmes. Ill. by
Robert Todd. Follett, 1956. An exceptionally
readable biography of the great jurist (1841-1935),
with emphasis on his youth and middle years. (YA)

550 Leighton, Margaret. Bride of Glory: The Story of
Elizabeth Bacon Custer. Farrar, Straus and
Cudahy, 1962. A biographical novel of the daunt-
less wife of George Armstrong Custer (1842-1933)
and also of the general. (YA)

551 _____. The Story of General Custer. Ill. by
Nicholas Eggenhofer. Grosset and Dunlap, 1954.
In the front of the book is a pictorial chronology
of Custer's life (1839-76): his birth in New
Rumsley, Ohio, his West Point and Civil War
careers, his Indian fighting and court martial, and
finally his death in battle with the Sioux under
Crazy Horse. (I)

552 Randall, Ruth Painter. I, Elizabeth. Jacket by
Robert C. Lowe. Ill. with photographs. Little

Brown, 1966. A biography, told as an autobiography,
of Elizabeth Bacon Custer, who shared much of the
army life with her husband, General Custer, and
wrote and illustrated books about their lives together in later years. (YA)

553 Rennert, Vincent Paul. Western Outlaws. Ill. with
photographs. Jacket by Rosemary Wells. Crowell-
Collier, 1968. Journalistic accounts of the careers
of nine outlaws and their gangs: Wes Hardin, The
Jones-Yunger gang, Sam Bass, Billy the Kid, Black
Bart, Butch Cassidy, Rube Nurrows, the Dalton
Brothers, and Bill Carlisle. (YA)

554 Reynolds, Quentin. Custer's Last Stand. Ill. by
Frederick T. Chapman. Random Landmark, 1951.
A biography of General George Custer, with main
attention centering on his West Point training and
fighting. (I)

555 Stevenson, Augusta. George Custer, Boy of Action.
Ill. by Al Fiorentino. Bobbs-Merrill, 1963.
Childhood of Famous Americans Series. The author
seems to have tried her best to make General
Custer, boy and man, an estimable character, but he
still is revealed here as a spoiled brat and overly
ambitious general. (E)

556 _____. Buffalo Bill, Boy of the Plains. Ill. by
E. Joseph Dreany. Bobbs-Merrill, 1948. Childhood of Famous Americans Series. His real name
was William Cody, but this story of his boyhood
clearly shows how he came by his nickname.

557 Wilson, Ellen. Annie Oakley, Little Sure Shot. Ill.
by Vance Locke. Bobbs-Merrill, 1958. Childhood
of Famous Americans Series. Annie Moses was
the real name of the girl, known these days best,
perhaps, as the heroine of "Annie Get Your Gun."
Here is the story of her life (1860-1926) but mainly
of her childhood. (E and I)

WILD WESTERNS

558 Brown, Dee. Action at Beecher Island. Doubleday,
1967. Modern Library Paperback, 1970. The
story of the nine-day siege of Forsyth's Scouts by
Plains Indians in western Kansas in September of
1868, based on reports, diaries, letters, and accounts of Indian and white participants and presented
from varying viewpoints. (A)

559 _____ . Showdown at Little Big Horn. Jacket by
         Paul Frame. Ill. with photographs. Putnam's,
         1964. In continuous narrative form this is the
         story of Custer's last stand, based on reports,
         diaries, letters and testimony of soldiers, civilians
         and Indians involved in the action. (A)

560 _____ . Yellowhorse. Houghton Mifflin, 1956.
         Bantam, 1972. A novel, based on the story of the
         use of the balloon "Intrepid" in defending Fort Yel-
         lowhorse against an attack by Sioux Indians, as re-
         lated to Dee Brown by the principal actor, Tom
         Easterwood. (A)

561 Chandler, Edna Walker. Gold Nugget. Ill. by Jack
         Merryweather. Benefic Press, 1967. A story of
         Tom Logan (part of a series about Tom) going
         with his friends after gold in the Colorado Rockies.
         (E)

562 _____ . Gold Train. Ill. by Jack Merryweather.
         Benefic Press, 1969. How Tom Logan and his
         friends foil some train robbers. (E)

563 Erdman, Loula Grace. The Far Journey. Dodd Mead,
         1955. A novel about a gently raised young woman
         whose husband has his heart set on going west.
         Despite her mother's urging her to stay in Missouri
         until her husband can come for her, she decides she
         must join him in the wilds of Texas and sets out on
         the long journey in a covered wagon, with her five-
         year-old son and an alcoholic uncle. It proves to
         be more than a journey in distance and danger--in-
         deed, a journey in character building. (A)

564 Ford, Paul Leicester. The Great K. and A. Train
         Robbery. Dodd Mead, 1897. A light romance of
         the wild west at the end of the century, written with
         the grace and charm of the late 19th century humor.
         Worth a search. (A)

565 Gendron, Val. Powder and Hides. Ill. by Rus Ander-
         son. Longmans Green, 1954. This novel about one
         of the last great buffalo hunts in 1873, poses for
         the reader, as it does for Johnny Doane in the
         story, serious questions about the relations of white
         men and Indians, and the part played by the buffalo
         in those relations. (YA)

566 Grey, Zane. Riders of the Purple Sage. Great Wes-
         tern Edition, Grosset and Dunlap, n.d. The prose
         is as purple as the sage and the characters are
         stereotyped, but it should be read as a classic ex-
         ample of early "westerns." Grey wrote at least 60

such novels, and it must be said that he knew the
early west, having Indian blood and having lived the
rugged adventurous life about which he wrote.   (A)

567 Honig, Donald. Jed McLane and Storm Cloud. Ill. by
Al Savitt. McGraw-Hill, 1968. An amusing yarn
about a 15-year-old living at an army post and forever
getting into hot water.   (I)

568 _____. Jed McLane and the Stranger. Ill. by Al
Savitt. McGraw-Hill, 1969. A sequel to "Jed
McLane and Storm Cloud," packed with humor and
action, in which a fight with some renegade Sioux
has a salutary effect on the "stranger."   (I)

569 O'Brian, Jack. Valiant, Dog of the Timberlane. Ill.
by Kurt Weiss. John C. Winston, 1935. The
story of the part played by a dog in the war between
sheep and cattle ranchers in the 1890s.   (I and YA)

570 Russell, Donald. Adam Bradford, Cowboy. Ill. by
Max Rauft. Benefic Press, 1970. A story about a
young cowboy finding that he can learn a great deal
from a Spanish-American lad. Interesting illustrations of rope braiding.   (E)

571 White, Dale (Place). The Johnny Cake Mine. Ill. by
Richard Bennett. Viking, 1954. An excellent story
of silver mining in Montana Territory in 1870 with
two young cousins working their claims against the
hazards of heavy snow, leaking mine shafts, claim
jumping, shootings and robbery.   (YA)

572 _____. Thunder in His Moccasins. This story of
a boy buffalo hunter in the Cimmaron country in
1874, is amusing because of his bravado, but dis-
tressing as it tells how white men slaughtered the
buffalo and the Comanche.   (I)

573 Wister, Owen. The Virginian, 1902. Macmillan.
One of the classic westerns in which the famous
line, "When you call me that, smile" appeared for
the first time. Pretty long-winded though.   (A)

574 Wormser, Richard. The Black Mustanger. Ill. by
Don Bolognese. Morrow Junior Books, 1971. It's
hard to believe how deep and long-lasting was the
bitterness between North and South after the Civil
War, or even that Yankees hesitated to work or
eat side by side with a "darky." The action of this
novel has to do with the catching and branding of
wild prairie mustangs, but the theme is the hu-
manity beneath white, red and black skins.   (I and
YA)

575 _____. Ride a Northbound Horse. Ill. by Charles

Geer. Morrow Junior Books, 1964. A good story
of the life of cattle drovers in the 1870s, in which
a boy has his own beautiful mare stolen from him,
and takes an old gray in her place thus making
himself a horse thief in danger of being hanged. (I)

576 Wyatt, Geraldine. Wronghand. Ill. by Kurt Werth.
Longmans Green, 1949. A 16-year-old whose
father was killed in the Civil War, takes on a man's
responsibilities in driving a herd of cattle up the
Chisholm trail, facing danger from buffalos, wolves,
Comanches, Cheyennes, and dissension among other
herders. (I)

PERIOD AND REGIONAL STORIES

577 Archer, Marian Fuller. There Is a Happy Land. Ill.
by David Cunningham. Albert Whitman, 1963. A
story, based on pioneer diaries, letter and recollections and with a most unexpected climax, about
a young Norwegian girl who joins her parents in
their Wisconsin Farm, near Oshkosh in 1866, having
learned much about farming in Norway. (I)

578 Armstrong, William. Sounder. Ill. by James Barkley.
Harper and Row, 1969. A poignant story of a black
sharecropper and his noble dog and his son, who
suffers for both man and dog and gives them both
his love. (I and YA)

579 Bailey, Jean. Cherokee Bill, Oklahoma Pacer. Ill. by
Pers Crowell. Abingdon-Cokesbury, 1952. A
horse story about the race to stake claims on the
Cherokee Strip. (I)

580 Baker, Elizabeth. Fire in the Wind. Ill. by Robert
MccLean. Houghton Mifflin, 1961. The 11-year-
old son of a Chicago detective, in 1871, tries
some detecting on his own, in order to free a friend
from suspicion in a case of stolen papers and a
stolen horse. The climax of the story is the Great
Chicago Fire. (I)

581 Beatty, Patricia. Bonanza Girl. Ill. by Liz Dauber.
William Morrow, 1962. A humorous period piece
built on true happenings in the Coeur d'Alenes in
the 1880s, but with fictional characters. (I and YA)

582 _____. The Lady from Black Hawk. Ill. by Robert
Frankenburg. McGraw-Hill, 1967. A novel about
three youngsters attempting to find a stepmother in
the rip-snortin' mining town of Eagle City in Idaho

Territory. Calamity Jane enters the plot and a
man who claims to be the original of "Huck Finn."
An author's note provides the background for the
book. (I and YA)

583 _____. A Long Way to Whiskey Creek. Jacket and
frontispiece by Frank Altschuler. Morrow Junior
Books, 1971. Two "unalike" boys head for Whiskey
Creek, Texas, in 1879, to bring back the body of
one's older brother "who got himself shot," Their
adventures en route are highly entertaining as is the
Texas-flavored dialogue. (I and YA)

584 _____. The Nickel-Plated Beauty. Ill. by Liz
Dauber. William Morrow, 1964. A delightful period piece, set in the Washington Territory in 1886,
about seven children who work hard to buy their
Mother a badly needed new stove. (I)

585 _____. O the Red Rose Tree. Ill. by Liz Dauber.
Morrow, 1972. A nostalgically humorous story of
1893 Oregon, about a 13-year-old and her friends
and an old quilt-maker from Kentucky. The title
applies to a quilt pattern, in case you're wondering.
(I and YA)

586 _____. The Queen's Own Grove. Ill. by Liz
Dauber. William Morrow, 1966. The story of an
English family who come, for reasons of the father's
health, to Riverside, California, and how the children help their elders to adapt to American ways and
how the father helps the California orange growers.
(I)

587 Benchley, Nathaniel. Gone and Back. Jacket by Jay J.
Smith. A tragic novel, in spite of its humorous
style, of a boy's loss of confidence in his father,
the historical setting being that of the Great Land
Rush for homesteads on the Cherokee Strip of
Oklahoma in 1879. (YA and Up)

588 Bishop, Curtis. Stout Rider. Ill. by M. J. Davis.
Steck Company, 1953. A true story, fictionalized
only to make it more readable, of a 10-year-old
Texas boy who rode more than 300 miles to save
his father's ranch from some crooked Englishmen
and the tough hombres they had hired. (I and YA)

589 Brink, Carol Pirie. Caddie Woodlawn: A Frontier
Story. Ill. by Kate Seredy. Macmillan, 1935.
A Newbery Medal Book. An intrepid 12-year-old
girl never lacks for excitement in western Wisconsin in the Civil War period. Not a Civil War story,
however, but one about the perils and pleasures of
frontier life. (I)

590 Burchard, Peter. Stranded: A Story of New York in
     1875. Ill. with photographs and a map of lower
     Manhattan in 1875. Coward McCann, 1967. A
     novel about gang warfare along the waterfront, lower
     Broadway, Coney Island, and back alleys and cel-
     lars of Water Street in 1875, the tough period of po-
     litical bossism in New York history. (YA and Up)

591 Cather, Willa. O Pioneers. Jacket by Anita Kahrl.
     Houghton Mifflin, 1913. A classic novel of foreign
     settlers in Nebraska around 1900--Bohemians,
     Swedish, French and Norwegians--the principal char-
     acter being a Norwegian girl whose love for the land
     is the dominant theme of the book. (A)

592 Clark, Walter Van Tilburg. The Ox-Bow Incident.
     With an Afterword by Walter Prescott Webb. Ran-
     dom House, A Signet Classic paperback. First
     published in 1940. A novel about a lynching in a
     Nevada town in 1885, showing how each man in-
     volved in the case suffers in his own peculiar way,
     knowing that justice is not being served.

593 Cook, Olive Rambo. Serilda's Star. Ill. by Helen
     Torrey. Longmans Green, 1959. A fine horse
     story with a good plot and interesting history of
     "thorough-breds." (I and YA)

594 Davis, Verne T. The Runaway Cattle. Ill. by Charles
     Geer. William Morrow Junior Books, 1965. You
     can scarcely believe all the consequences of what
     starts as a simple chase after a bull, a heifer, two
     cows and a farm dog, by two boys in western Michi-
     gan, along about 1890. It might not have been so
     exciting if the cattle hadn't been joined by a volun-
     teer mouse. (I)

595 _____. The Time of the Wolves. Ill. by Ezra Jack
     Keats. William Morrow, 1962. A tense story of
     two young boys, minding their father's cattle alone
     in the marshlands of Michigan in winter, in the
     1860s. (I)

596 deAngeli, Marguerite. Copper-Toed Boots. Ill. by
     the author with delicate lithographs. Doubleday,
     1938. A story of life in a small Michigan town
     (Lapeer) in the 1870s as lived by a little boy--of his
     escapades and good times. (E and I)

597 deJong, Dala. The House on Charlton Street. Ill. by
     Gilbert Riswold. A Scribner Mystery for Young
     People, 1962. A present and past (late 19th cen-
     tury) story of old letters, boarded up fireplaces,
     and a boy with a chip on his shoulder, combined

with some history of Greenwich Village in New
York City. (YA)

598 Duncombe, Frances Riker. Cassie's Village. Ill.
by W. T. Mars. Lothrop Lee and Shepard, 1965.
A story based on a real crisis in Westchester
County, New York, in the 1890s when the village
of Katonah was threatened with extinction because
of the plan to build a new and larger Croton Dam.
Our heroine is a little girl who can't bear the
thought of being separated from her friends and
whose ingenuity and detective work bear fruit.   (I)

599 Erdman, Loula Grace. The Wide Horizon, A Story
of the Texas Panhandle. Jacket by Elizabeth Ann
Erdman. Dodd Mead, 1956. A sequel to "The Wind
Blows Free," a family story somewhat on the order
of "Little Women." (I and YA)

600 _____. The Wind Blows Free. Dodd Mead, 1952.
A novel of the 1890s about a warm loving family
and how they adapt themselves to living in a lonely
dugout in the Texas panhandle, near Amarillo, after
moving from settled East Texas. A winner of the
American Girl, Dodd Mead Prize Competition.
(I and YA)

601 Estep, Irene. Pioneer Sodbuster. Ill. by Berthold
Tiedemann. Benefic Press, 1958. A slight story
but worthwhile for its maps and detailed illustrations of a covered wagon, a wagon ferry, etc.   (I)

602 Eunson, Dale. The Day They Gave Babies Away. Ill.
by Douglas Gorsline. Farrar, Straus and Giroux,
1946-70. A story, published three times in Cos-
mopolitan Magazine, and dramatized on radio and
television, about a 12-year-old boy trying to find
good homes for his five orphaned younger brothers
and sisters. A minor classic.   (I and Up)

603 Flory, Jane. Faraway Dream. Ill. by the author.
Houghton Mifflin, 1968. An entertaining story of
a spunky little orphan girl apprenticed to a milliner
and of her distant dream.

604 _____. Mist on the Mountain. Ill. by the author.
Houghton Mifflin, 1966. A sequel to "Peddler's
Summer" and a book with much more realism and
content than the other. Amanda Schoville is now
ten years old and, while continuing to enjoy life to
the full, is aware of its sorrows, as she helps her
mother "birthing a baby" and tries to help the feck-
less family of the "sinful" Essie. Interesting and
authentic details of western Pennsylvania of a

century ago. (I and YA)

605 _____. Peddler's Summer. Ill. by the author.
Houghton Mifflin, 1960. A story of an almost too-
good-to-be-true girl of nine who accompanies a peddler on his route in western Pennsylvania in 1871 in
order to demonstrate the new sewing machine and thus
make money for her widowed mother and seven sisters. (I)

606 _____. A Tune for the Towpath. Ill. by the author.
Houghton Mifflin, 1962. A story of the Delaware
Canal, the canallers who traveled on it, and, in
particular the daughter of a lock tender who looks
down her nose at "canallers." (I)

607 Friermood, Elizabeth Hamilton. One of Fred's Girls.
Jacket by Roger Hane. Doubleday, 1970. A romance of a pretty waitress from Indiana, working in
the Fred Harvey "eating place" in New Mexico Territory in 1891. (I and YA)

608 Hall, Lynn. Too Near the Sun. Ill. by Stefan Martin.
Follett, 1970. A novel about life in an Iowa com-
mune, in 1875, founded by a Frenchman, Etienne
Cabet. A 17-year-old girl, Armell Dupree, questions the philosophy of completely communal living,
with its total lack of individual freedom. (YA)

609 Holberg, Ruth and Richard. Oh Susannah. Ill. by the
authors. Doubleday, 1939. A charming little story
showing the difference between life on the Minnesota
frontier and that in more settled Vermont, in 1872.
(E and I)

610 Lawson, Robert. The Great Wheel. Ill. by the author.
Viking, 1957. A young Irish lad goes to Chicago
where he finds work on the construction of the great
wheel invented by George Washington Gale Ferris,
an important feature of the World's Columbian Exposition in 1893. Good engineering detail and
humorous dialogue. (I and YA)

611 Means, Florence Crannell. A Candle in the Mist.
Ill. by Marguerite de Angeli. Houghton Mifflin,
1931-59. The story of a young girl's trust in her
foster brother who has run away to live with the
Indians, under suspicious circumstances, and of the
courage of the whole family when forced to leave
their comfortable Wisconsin home to pioneer in
Minnesota, in 1871. (I and YA)

612 Miller, Helen Markley. The Long Valley. Jacket by
Tom Donne. Doubleday, 1961. A novel about a
young woman, dedicated to her impractical father

and her brother and younger sisters in their struggle for survival in a lonely cabin in one of Idaho's
coldest winters, with a love story woven through it.
(YA)

613 North, Sterling. The Wolfling: A Documentary Novel
     of the Eighteen-Seventies. Ill. by John Schoenherr.
     E. P. Dutton, 1969. Winner of the Dutton Animal
     Book Award. The story of a boy and his half-dog,
     half-wolf pet which he brought up from a whelp in
     southern Wisconsin (Lake Koshkonong). Inter-
     spersed through the story are biographical details
     of a great Swedish-American naturalist, Thure
     Kumlein (1819-88). The documentary notes at the
     end make good reading too. (I and Up)

614 Norton, André (Alice Mary). Rebel Spurs. Jacket by
     Peter Burchard. World, 1962. A sequel to the
     Civil War novel "Ride Proud, Rebel," this takes
     Drew Rennie, now 19, to the Santa Cruz valley in
     southern Arizona in 1866 in search of a father he's
     never seen. A good western horse story. (YA)

615 Nye, Harriet Kamm. Uncertain April. Dodd Mead,
     1958. A 17-year-old girl (18 by the end of the
     novel) tries to take her mother's place for her
     father and little sisters and serve as hostess in her
     father's summer hotel on a little Lake Superior is-
     land, near the Wisconsin mainland. Backwoods though
     it may have been, there is a rich French heritage in
     the family, of fine clothes and furnishings and man-
     ners, combined with an Indian heritage of respect
     for the land, threatened by timber-greedy newcomers.
     (YA)

616 Orton, Helen Fuller. The Secret of the Rosewood Box.
     Ill. by Robert Ball. J. B. Lippincott, 1937. It
     was a long here-and-there hunt for Grandmother's
     hat box which finally resulted in discovering its
     secret. (E and I)

617 Portis, Charles. True Grit. Jacket by Paul Davis.
     Simon and Schuster, 1968. A comic, original novel
     about a 14-year-old girl, sharp as a whip, who sets
     out to avenge the murder of her father. (A)

618 Rolvaag, D. E. Giants in the Earth: A Saga of the
     Prairie. Translated from the Norwegian by Lincoln
     Colcord and the author. Harper and Bros., 1927.
     (Harper and Row Paperback). A great, long novel
     about the Norwegian immigrants to the Dakota Ter-
     ritory during the 1870s and early '80s, how they
     braved the terrible hardships of winter and summer

and how they helped each other; and about the ef-
fects of the great prairie loneliness on women. An
introduction by Colcord tells how Rolvaag used his
own American experience as a basis for the novel.
(A)

619 Sawyer, Ruth. Roller Skates. Ill. by Valenti Angelo.
Viking, 1936 and 1964. A Yearling Book, Dell,
1970. An utterly delightful story of Old New York
in the 1890s, when Edward McDowell was a young
man. Louis Sherry was starting a candy store,
and Browdowski was a poor, unknown violinist. A
happy story, full of the joie de vivre of a 10-year-
old "temporary orphan" who makes friends with a
wide variety of people. Children--please share the
book with your grandparents. (I and Up)

620 Shields, Rita. Norah and the Cable Car. Ill. by
Richard Bennett. Longmans Green, 1960. A story
of a little girl who wants to win a prize to please
her grandfather after the cable cars of San Francisco replace the horse cars, one of which Grandpa
drove for years with his beloved team of old horses.
(I)

621 Smith, Fredrika Shumway. The Fire Dragon: A
Story of the Great Chicago Fire. Ill. by Ray Nay-
lor. Rand McNally, 1956. Along with the exciting
action of this story is the theme of how great dis-
asters point up men's interdependence. (I)

622 Strachan, Margaret Pitcairne. Mennonite Martha. Ill.
by Charles Geer. Ives Washburn, 1961. A story
of a little girl who dearly wants a pretty dress and
bonnet but whose Mennonite grandparents in 1884
frown on such vanities. (I)

623 Switzer, Gladys. Abigail Goes West. Jacket by Ezra
Jack Keats. William Morrow, 1963. A story for
sheer amusement, about a 17-year-old girl traveling, by train from Pennsylvania to California in the
1870s, and, having turned down a suitor before
leaving home, finds two more among her fellow
passengers. (YA)

624 Veglahn, Nancy. Follow the Golden Goose. Ill. by
Milton Johnson. Addison-Wesley, 1970. A novel
of Deadwood, South Dakota, in the Gold Rush of
1876, and of a boy whose life and ambitions are
oddly changed by, of all things, cats. (I and YA)

625 Voils, Jessie Wiley. Summer on the Salt Fork. Ill.
by Leonard Fosburgh. Meredith, 1969. A loving,
often quarrelsome, thoroughly normal family of two

parents and four children   go to the Indian Territory
for the summer so that their father can supervise a
newly bought herd of cattle.   Based on the experiences of the author's mother at the age of ten.   (I)

626   Wellman, Manley Wade.   The Great Riverboat Race:
The Story of the Natchez and the Robert E. Lee.
Jacket by William Ferguson.   Ives Washburn, 1965.
Partly fictionalized story of the 1870 great race up
the Mississippi between the two great river boats,
starting in New Orleans on June 30 and ending at
St. Louis on July 4.   The fictional hero is drawn
from an actual person, a young man of 19, inter-
ested in railroading and opposed to steamboats.
(YA)

627   White, Dale.   Hold Back the Hunter.   John Day, 1959.
A novel about a young man in 1870, an ardent admirer of Jim Bridger, who comes to realize that
the day of the mountain men has passed and that
the need for conservation of national resources has
begun, with a good map of the Yellowstone National
Park and a key to the events in the story.   (I and
YA)

628   _____.   The Wild-Horse Trap.   Ill. by Richard
Bennett.   Viking, 1955.   A mystery-adventure-horse-
racing story in which a 15-year-old, outlawed from
the territory because of a robbery his father is accused of committing, gets a job as a trainer with a
Kentucky horse breeder establishing the first racing
stable in Montana.   At the same time, the lad de-
termines to solve the mystery of his father's disappearance and to absolve him of guilt in the robbery.   (YA)

629   Whitney, Phyllis.   Creole Holiday.   Westminster,
1959.   A romance set in New Orleans at Mardi
Gras time, in which a young lady, half Yankee and
half Creole, has to chose between the stage and
marriage.   (YA)

630   Wilder, Laura Ingalls.   By the Shores of Silver Lake.   In
which Pa becomes a railroad man until he finds a homestead in Dakota and files a claim.   (I)

631   _____.   Farmer Boy.   Ill. by Garth Williams.
Harper and Bros., 1933.   The story of Almonzo
Wilder's boyhood in New York State in the 1870s.
(I)

632   _____.   The First Four Years.   Laura and Almonzo Wilder's first years together on a homestead
and tree claim in South Dakota territory.   Story was

found after Mrs. Wilder's death in 1957 and given
to Mr. MacBride to be published in 1971. (I and Up)

633 _____. Little House in the Big Woods. Ill. by
Garth Williams. Harper Brothers, 1932. The first
of the series of pioneer stories based on the author's
new life, in Wisconsin. (I)

634 _____. The Little House on the Prairie. In which
the Ingalls family moves to Indian country in Kansas
and builds a new home there. (I)

635 _____. Little Town on the Prairie. In which Laura
earns her teaching certificate. (I and YA)

636 _____. The Long Winter. About a hard winter in
the Dakota territory, forcing the family to move into town. (I)

637 _____. On the Banks of Plum Creek. In which
Laura and her family leave their Kansas home and
travel across Kansas, Missouri, and Iowa to settle,
first, in a sod house in Minnesota and then in a
"real house". (I)

638 _____. On the Way Home: The Diary of a Trip
from South Dakota to Mansfield, Missouri, in 1894,
with a setting by Rose Wilder Lane. Ill, with 18
photographs. Jacket by the Etheridges. Harper
and Row, 1962. Here we have the story as discovered in Mrs. Wilder's diary, found after her
death and as the memories of her daughter Rose
enrich it, of what happened after all the "Little
House" books. (YA)

639 _____. These Happy Golden Years. In which Laura
becomes engaged and married. (I and YA)

640 Williams, J. R. Oh Susanna! Ill. by Albert Orbaan.
G. P. Putnam's Sons, 1963. A novel of hardships
and romance of homesteading on the prairies in the
1860s. In Kansas. (YA)

641 Wissmann, Ruth. Katy Kelly of Cripple Creek. Ill.
by Dorothy Bayley Morse. Dodd Mead, 1968.
Katy's experiences with friends and enemies in a
gold mining town in Colorado in the 1890s. (I and
YA)

642 Yates, Elizabeth. Sarah Whicher's Story. Ill. by
Nora S. Unwin. E. P. Dutton, 1971. Based on a
chapter of the history of Warren, New Hampshire:
"How Sarah Whicher was Lost in the Woods, What
Happened and How They Hunted For Her." 1870.
(E and I)

THE FIRST QUARTER OF THE 20th CENTURY

PERIOD AND REGIONAL STORIES

643 Aldrich, Bess Streeter. A Lantern in Her Hand.
     Appleton, 1928. Grosset and Dunlap, 1956. A
     gentle, slow moving family saga with, at its center,
     a woman who had come to Nebraska in an oxcart in
     the mid-19th century and lived there for 20 years
     of the 20th. (A)

644 Andrus, Vera. Black River: A Wisconsin Story.
     Ill. by Irene Burns. Little Brown, 1967. A simple
     little period story of 1907, about the life of a family
     whose father runs a creamery and whose daughters
     have a genius for getting into mischief. (I)

645 Bachmann, Evelyn Trent. Tressa. Ill. by Lorence
     Bjorklund. Viking, 1966. A story of a "tenderfoot"
     girl of ten from an eastern city apartment, trying
     to adjust to the wide open space and storm hazards
     of West Texas, in the 1920s--a good picture of
     ranch life. (I)

646 Benezra, Barbara. Fire Dragon. Ill. by Franc and
     Constance Roggeri. Criterion, 1970. A book with
     two themes: the famous San Francisco earthquake
     of 1906 for one, and, for the other, the friendship
     and understanding developed between a couple of 18-
     year-old youths, one Chinese and one American, in
     the aftermath of the fire and the rebuilding of the
     city. (I)

647 Bissell, Richard. Julia Harrington. Ill. with re-
     productions of original advertisements, mail order
     catalogues and other period pieces. Little Brown,
     1969. A good book for family reading and looking,
     possibly of more interest to grandparents than to
     the young generation. (All Ages)

648 Bond, Gladys. On the Stranger's Mountain. Ill. by
     Derek Lucas. Abelard Schuman, 1969. The first
     part of this book is set in Pennsylvania in 1921 and
     is about the Pittsburgh steel workers and immigrant
     miners. In the latter half, a family, whose father
     has been killed in a mine accident, moves to a new

life with a new father, in Idaho.   (I)

649   Carlson, Natalie Savage. The Half Sisters. Ill. by
Thomas de Grazia. Harper and Row, 1970. A quiet
little story of a family of six daughters in Maryland, in 1915. Three are "the girls" of a first
marriage, and the other three are "the children."
Luvvie, aged 12, is about to graduate to the status
of "the girls'." (I)

650   _____. Luvvie and the Girls. Ill. by Thomas de
Grazia. Harper and Row, 1971. A sequel to
"The Half Sisters" about Luvvie's life in a Mary-
land convent school.   (I)

651   Cather, Willa. My Antonia. Ill. by W. T. Benda.
Houghton Mifflin, 1918-26-46. One of the Great
Books in American literature, the story of a Bohemian girl in Nebraska farm lands around the
turn of the century.   (A)

652   Christgau, Alice E. Runaway to Glory. Ill. by Leo
R. Summers. Young Scott, 1965. A compas-
sionate story of two who feel "left out," one because of age and one because of youth. The grandfather is an old Civil War veteran who still, in
Minnesota in 1905, likes to talk about his fighting
days under Sherman, and the other is a 12-year-
old boy. Together, however, they manage to show
courage and wits in a crisis.   (I)

653   Coatsworth, Elizabeth. Indian Mound Farm. Ill. by
Fermin Rocker. Macmillan, 1943-69. A short
book about an endearing little girl and her equally
endearing lame duck, a farm built on a high Indian
mound, and an Indian "hired man." (E and I)

654   Constant, Alberta Wilson. Those Miller Girls. Ill.
by Beth and Joe Krush. Thomas Y. Crowell,
1965. A thoroughly amusing story, set in a small
Kansas town in 1910, about two imaginative and
reckless motherless girls, 11 and 12, their professor father and his car, "The Great Smith." Other
early automobiles are brought into the story (the
Steamer, Franklin, etc.) as are other events of
the period, such as a Chatauqua speech by the
three-times defeated William Jennings Bryan. (I)

655   Coolidge, Olivia. Come By Here. Ill. by Milton
Johnson. Houghton Mifflin, 1970. A sad novel,
with a basis of truth, about a little black girl,
Minty Lou, in Baltimore in the early 1900s, how,
after losing her loving parents, she is shunted
about from one unwilling relative to another, half

starved, badly clothed and cruelly punished for
simply "being in the way." (YA)

656 deLeeuw, Adele. Blue Ribbons for Meg. Ill. by
"Mac" Schweitzer. Little Brown, 1950. A little
Boston girl goes to visit her cousins on a cavalry
post in South Dakota and must learn to adjust to a
new way of life. (I)

657 Erdman, Loula. The Good Land. Jacket by William
Barss. Dodd Mead, 1959. The third of a trilogy
about a family living in the Texas panhandle, following 1) "The Wind Blows Free" and 2) "The Wide
Horizon." This book carries the family into the
20th century, when the youngest daughter is "almost
fifteen." They are no longer pioneers but have
sympathy and understanding for those who are, the
immigrants from the east, victims of unscrupulous
land salesmen. (A)

658 Ferber, Edna. So Big. Doubleday, 1924. A Pulitzer
Prize winning novel about a young widowed truck
farmer, Selina DeJong and her son, Dirk, and their
later success in the restaurant business in Chicago.
(A)

659 Fisher, Dorothy Canfield. Understood Betsy (1917).
Ill. by Martha Alexander. Holt, Rinehart and
Winston, 1972. First published in 1917, this story
of an overly "understood" little girl transplanted to
a Vermont farm, has deservedly been revived in
attractive form. (E and I)

660 Fisher, Laura. Never Try Nathaniel. Jacket by
John Falter. Holt, Rinehart and Winston, 1968.
The trials of a 14-year-old boy living in Idaho at
the turn of the century. It is hard to believe in the
cruelty of the elders in the story, but all comes out
right in the end. (I)

661 Frazier, Neta Lohnes. Litte Rhody. Ill. by Henrietta
Jones Moon. A story about a "going-on-ten" girl
in northern Michigan at the turn of the century--a
good book for a 10-year-old to read to a younger
sister. McKay, 1953, 1966. (E and I)

662 Friermood, Elizabeth Hamilton. Ballad of Calamity
Creek. Jacket by Luciana Roselli. Doubleday,
1962. A light "love vs. career" novel about a
young Hoosier lady who goes to teach in the mountains of southeastern Kentucky and learns the
language and music of the mountain people. (YA)

663 _____. Doc Dudley's Daughter. Doubleday, 1965.
A "love vs. career" novel about a beginning

librarian, just out of high school, set against the
background of the Cuban campaign of the Spanish-
American War. (YA)

664 _____. Promises in the Attic. Jacket by Herman
B. Vestal. Doubleday, 1960. A novel about a high
school senior and her dreams of becoming an author,
and how the disastrous Dayton flood of 1913 provides
her with material for publication. (I and YA)

665 _____. Whispering Willows. Jacket by Don Almquist. Doubleday, 1964. A quiet novel of a friendship between a white girl and a black one in a small
town in Indiana in 1910/11, showing the beginnings of
Black pride and aspiration. (YA)

666 Gates, Doris. The Elderberry Bush. Ill. by Lilian
Obligado. Viking, 1967. A gentle little story of
the lives of two little girls in the early 1900s in
northern California. (I)

667 Hall, Elizabeth. Phoebe Snow. Ill. by Bea Holmes.
Houghton Mifflin, 1968. A most entertaining story
of a 14-year-old girl who tries to pass herself off
as a grown-up celebrity going to the Louisiana
Purchase Centennial Fair of 1904 in St. Louis. (I)

668 Heck, Bessie Holland. The Hopeful Years: A Book
about Millie. Ill. by Lorence Bjorklund. World,
1964. The third in the "Millie" series, in which
Millie, at 17 in 1917, is working her way through
high school in a small town near the Oklahoma
farm where her father has finally settled down.
The telephone (party line), the Model T Ford, and
electric lights are all exciting innovations and a
tornado and the entrance of the United States into
World War I are dramatic highlights of Millie's
momentous 17th year. (I and YA)

669 _____. Millie. Ill. by Mary Stevens. World,
1961. A post-pioneer period piece, set in the
Kramachi Mountains of Oklahoma in 1911--a time
of transition, when the importance of education was
beginning to be felt. Millie's father is a restless
man and moves every year, so Millie's schooling is
a "sometime thing." (I)

670 _____. The Year at Boggy. Ill. by Paul Frame.
World, 1966. In this sequel to "Millie," the 12-
year-old girl is finally able to finish a year of
school and pass from sixth grade with high hopes
that her father may be willing to stay put for one
or two more years, so that she can get through
eighth grade. (I)

671 Henry, Marguerite. <u>Brighty of the Grand Canyon.</u> Ill.
     by Wesley Dennis. Rand McNally, 1953. Newbery
     Medal winner. Take the Grand Canyon as the set-
     ting and a spirited little burro as the principal char-
     acter. Add a famous lion hunter, Uncle Jimmy
     Owen, and President Teddy Roosevelt and a dyed-
     in-the-wool villain, and the mysterious disappearance
     of an old prospector, and how can you miss? (I
     and YA)

672 Hosford, Jessie. <u>An Awful Name to Live Up To.</u> Ill.
     by Charles Geer. Meredith, 1969. The diary of a
     girl named Julia Ward Howe Hoffman makes delight-
     ful reading with its Nebraska prairie setting in 1901.
     Judy's life holds childish escapades, some real
     perils and sadness and much love. (I and YA)

673 _____. <u>You Bet Your Boots I Can.</u> Jacket by Ned
     Glattauer. Thomas Nelson, 1971. A sequel to
     "An Awful Name to Live Up to" in which Julia Ward
     Howe Hoffman continues her diary and grows thin
     and into her teens. A nostalgic book for grand-
     parents who shared that innocent place and time and
     an eye-opener for teens of today. (YA)

674 Lenski, Lois. <u>Strawberry Girl.</u> Ill. by the author.
     J. B. Lippincott, 1945. A fine regional story about
     the "Florida Crackers" in the early 1900s--their
     courage, their pugnacity, their flavorful speech
     with its old English idioms, their hardships and
     pleasures, written by one who visited them in their
     homes in the 1940s and made her sketches there.
     (I)

675 Long, Laura. <u>George Dewey, Vermont Boy.</u> Ill. by
     Harry H. Lees. Bobbs-Merrill, 1952. Childhood
     of Famous Americans Series. An entertaining
     biography of the hero (1837-1917) of Manila Bay in
     the Spanish American War of 1898, though his
     boyhood, which occupies most of the book was way
     back before the Civil War. (E)

676 McBride, Mary Margaret. <u>The Growing Up of Mary
     Elizabeth.</u> Ill. by Lorence Bjorklund. Dodd Mead,
     1966. A book of episodes in the simple, happy life
     of a 12-year-old girl living on a Missouri farm in
     1910. (I)

677 Meader, Stephen. <u>The Buckboard Stranger.</u> Ill. by
     Paul Calle. Harcourt, Brace and World, 1954. The
     mystery of the stranger's background provides the
     suspense of this story set in a small New Hampshire
     mill town in 1906. A good horse story too. (YA)

678 _____ . Red Horse Hill. Ill. by Lee Townsend.
    Harcourt, Brace and World, 1938. A story of a boy,
    his dog, snow horse racing, a horse thief, and life
    in general in a New Hampshire farming community
    when the auto was still a newcomer. (I and YA)

679 Miles, Miska. Uncle Fonzo's Ford. Ill. by Wendy
    Watson. Atlantic Little Brown, 1968. An amusing
    story of an uncle who usually does the wrong thing,
    but always does something, and of a family, living
    in Missouri in 1910, who know how to happily "make
    do" with whatever they happen to have. (E and I)

680 Miller, Helen Markley. Kirsti. Doubleday, 1964. An
    inspiring novel about a young Finnish girl, with her
    pioneering family in a primitive Idaho valley home
    in 1901 where much "sisu" (inner quality of strength
    like second wind) was needed to brave winter
    storms, near-starvation and childbirth. Good materi-
    al on the Finns in America and their proud heritage.
    There is also a tender love story. (YA)

681 Montgomery, Elizabeth Rider. When a Ton of Gold
    Reached Seattle. Ill. by Raymond Burns, and
    photographs. Garrard, 1968. The story of the city
    of Seattle during the Klondike Gold Rush, and what
    life was like there at that time and how Erastus
    Brainerd looked ahead. (I)

682 Musgrave, Florence. Marged: The Story of a Welsh
    Girl in America. Ill. by Arline K. Thomson.
    Farrar, Straus and Cudahy, 1956. A 1912 period
    piece about a newly settled Welsh family in the
    Pennsylvania country along the Ohio River, near
    Pittsburgh, and how 12-year-old Marged learns the
    hard way about the meaning of forgiveness. (I)

683 North, Sterling. So Dear to My Heart. Ill. by Brad
    Holland. Doubleday, 1947-68. A lyrical book,
    full of Biblical sayings, old saws from the Scotch-
    Irish mountain folk of Kentucky, earthy humor, and
    the natural beauty of the Indiana countryside in
    1903, about a boy, his black lamb, and his stern
    but loving Granny. (I and Up)

684 Pace, Mildred Mastin. Home Is Where the Heart Is.
    Jacket and end papers by Robert Henneberger.
    McGraw-Hill, 1954. A Whittlesey House Book. A
    novel of the Kentucky mountain people in the times
    just before the coming of the railroads there and
    a young girl who comes to the aid of a "furriner,"
    surveying for a railroad. (I and YA)

685 Potter, Marian. Copperfield Summer. Ill. by Jo

Polseno. Follett, 1967. Two children are sent to spend the summer on an uncle's farm in southern Illinois and run into unexpected mysteries (land stealing and a valuable letter) and barely escape from a cyclone. (I)

686 Reed, Meredith. Our Year Began in April. Jacket by Leonard Weisgard. Lothrop, Lee and Shepard, 1963. A story set in New Hampshire of an adolescent girl in the adolescent years of the 20th century and of her family who are forced to move all too frequently as her father is a Methodist minister. The introduction of the poet, Robert Frost, as the girl's English teacher, adds interest. (I and YA)

687 Sullivan, Peggy. The O'Donnells. Ill. by Mary Stevens. Follett, 1956. A light-hearted story about an Irish policeman's family in the early 1900s--five daughters, little money, plenty of love and jollity. (I)

688 Wellman, Manley Wade. Mountain Feud. Ives Washburn, 1969. An ancient feud breaks out between two families in the summer of 1906 in a remote part of the Smoky Mountains in North Carolina, and grows as fast and furiously as a forest fire. Communications are cut off so completely that there seems no chance for even a ceasefire long enough to solve the mystery of the cause of the feud, until--young love intervenes. (YA)

689 Whitehead, Ruth. The Mother Tree. Ill. by Charles Robinson Seabury, 1971. A touching little story about the loss of a young mother and the acceptance of the loss by a very little girl. Texas in the early 1900s. (I)

WORLD WAR I

690 Jablonski, Edward. Warriors with Wings. Ill. with photographs. Bobbs-Merrill, 1966. A dramatic story of the 38 men who served with the Lafayette Escadrille before it was transferred to the American Air Force as the Lafayette Flying Corps in World War I. (YA)

691 Knight, Clayton and K. S. We Were There with the Lafayette Escadrille. Ill. by Clayton Knight. Grosset, 1961. The true story of those early American flyers in France in World War I, with a list of the volunteers in the Escadrille. (I)

692   Leckie, Robert. The Story of World War I, adapted
      for Young Readers from the American Heritage His-
      tory of World War I. Ill. with contemporary paint-
      ings, sketches, maps, and prints. Narrative by
      S. L. A. Marshall. Random Landmark Giant, 1965.
      (I and YA)
693   Nordhoff, Charles and James Norman Hall. Falcons
      of France. Little, Brown, 1929. A novel of the
      Lafayette Flying Corps in World War I. (A)

BIOGRAPHY AND HISTORY

694   Faber, Doris. Clarence Darrow, Defender of the Peo-
      ple. Ill. by Paul Frame. Prentice-Hall, 1965.
      Biography of a famous lawyer (1857-1938), defender of
      unpopular causes, with particular attention on the
      case of a schoolteacher, John Thomas Scopes,
      whose teaching of the theory of evolution was de-
      fended by Darrow, in 1925. (I)
695   Lindop, Edmund. The Dazzling Twenties. Ill. with
      photographs. Franklin Watts, 1970. The well-
      chosen pictures and well organized subject matter
      should have a nostalgic appeal to the elders and
      lively interest for young readers. (I and Up)
696   Meyer, Edith Patterson. That Remarkable Man:
      Justice Oliver Wendell Holmes. Jacket by Robert
      G. Lowe and photographs. Little Brown, 1967. A
      biography of the Supreme Court Justice (1841-1935)
      who served until the age of 91 and was famous for
      his dissenting opinions as well as his scholarly
      works on the law. Son of a famous father, he had
      to struggle to establish his own identity and im-
      portance. (YA)
697   Werstein, Irving. Shattered Decade. Jacket by Ger-
      trude Huston. Charles Scribner's Sons, 1970. The
      beginnings of many current social, economic and
      racial problems can be found in this period from
      1919 to 1929. (YA)

THE SECOND QUARTER OF THE 20th CENTURY

BIOGRAPHIES

698 Burke, John. Winged Legend: The Story of Amelia Earhart. Jacket by Bob Abbett. G. P. Putnam's Sons, 1970. Biography of the pioneer woman flyer (1898-1937). (A)

699 deLeeuw, Adele. The Story of Amelia Earhart. Ill. by Harry Beckhoff. Grosset and Dunlap, 1955. The story of Amelia (1898-1937) as a nurse's aide in Canada, in 1918, as a social worker in Boston in 1926, as she flew the Atlantic alone in 1932, and was lost over the Pacific Ocean in 1937. (I and YA)

700 Fisk, Nicholas. Lindbergh, The Lone Flyer. Ill. by Raymond Briggs. Coward McCann, 1968. A vivid (both in pictures and text) story of Charles Lindbergh's epic flight in May 1927 from New York to Paris, 3600 miles, in 33 hours and 30 minutes. (I)

701 Fleming, Alice. The Senator from Maine: Margaret Chase Smith. Thomas Y. Crowell, 1969. A biography of the first woman to date (1972) ever to serve in both houses of Congress, the first to be elected to four full terms in the Senate, and the first to stand up to Senator Joseph McCarthy. (I and YA)

702 Henry, Marguerite. Mustang, Wild Spirit of the West. Ill. by Robert Lougheed. Rand-McNally, 1966. The story ends in the 1950s, but the main action takes place during the second quarter of the 20th century. It is the usual fine, exciting horse story one expects from this author, but more than that, the story of a great conservationist, known as "Wild Horse Annie" and how she fought to keep the wild mustangs and burros of the west from being cruelly pursued and inhumanely trapped to be ground up into "pet meat." (I and YA)

703 Howe, Jane Moore. Amelia Earhart, Kansas Girl. Ill. by Paul Laune. Bobbs-Merrill, 1950. Child-

hood of Famous Americans Series. Amelia could
never bear to be the "little lady" her grandmother
hoped for, and from the time she saw her first
airplane, she dreamed of flying one.   (E)

704 Kugelmass, J. Alvin. Ralph J. Bunche, Fighter for
Peace. Julian Messner, 1952-62. A biography of
the statesman, grandson of slaves, who became a
Nobel Peace Prize winner in 1950 and who has been
a leading figure in the United Nations. Born in
1904. (YA)

705 Lawson, Don. Frances Perkins, First Lady of the
Cabinet. Ill. with photographs. Abelard Schuman,
1966. A biography of Franklin Roosevelt's
Secretary of Labor (1882-1965) and of her part in
setting up public works programs and social security
and other important innovations of the New Deal; a
dedicated public servant in the period of the Great
Depression and during the Democratic administrations from 1932 to 1952.   (YA)

706 Mann, Peggy. Amelia Earhart, First Lady of Flight.
Ill. by Kiyo Komoda. Coward McCann, 1970. The
legend still persists that Amelia (1898-1937), some-
where, is still alive. In any case this biography
brings her vividly and delightfully "to life."   (I)

707 Parlin, John. Amelia Earhart. Ill. by Anthony
D'Adamo. Garrard, 1962. A Discovery Book. A
short biography of the intrepid woman flyer (1898-
1937). (E)

708 Radford, Ruby L. Dwight D. Eisenhower. Ill. by
Paul Frame. G. P. Putnam's Sons, 1970. A See
and Read Beginning to Read Biography.   (E)

THE 1930s AND THE DEPRESSION

709 d'Angeli, Marguerite. Henner's Lydia. Ill. by the
author with lithographs in four colors. Doubleday
Junior Books, 1936. A story about a little Amish
girl in Pennsylvania, near Lancaster, living in the
old ways in the new times.   (E)

710 _____. Up the Hill. Ill. by the author. Doubleday, 1942. A story of a Polish immigrant family in
the mining country of Pennsylvania, with a pro-
nunciation list of foreign words and their meanings
and how the Polish letters sound in English. A good
bit of Polish history and a little about the children
of other immigrants, from Slovakia, Bohemia and
Wales. (I)

711 Hunt, Irene. No Promises in the Wind: A Novel of
      the Great Depression. Jacket by Allen Carr.
      Follett, 1970. A sensitive, realistic novel about a
      15-year-old and his brother, five years younger,
      leaving their home in Chicago because of the des-
      peration of their unemployed father who takes out
      his fear, frustration, and sense of failure on his
      wife and sons; of their fight for survival, their
      meetings with all kinds of people, and the older
      boy's final growth in understanding of his father.
      (I and YA)

712 Lindop, Edmund. The Turbulent Thirties. Ill. with
      photographs. Franklin Watts, 1970. (I and Up)

713 Means, Florence Crannell. Great Day in the Morning.
      Houghton Mifflin, 1946. A novel about an indomitable
      young black woman from the Sea Islands off Caro-
      lina, not only a civil rights story, but also one of
      all young people striving to find their true goals in
      life, with an interesting introduction of George Wash-
      ington Carver in the Tuskegee section of the novel.
      (YA)

714 Richard, Adrienne. Pistol. Jacket by Lorence Bjork-
      lund. Little Brown, 1965. A realistic novel of the
      Great Depression in the ranch country of Montana; of
      a boy who grew up fast, from 14 to 18, during those
      drought-ridden, desperately hard years between 1930
      and 1934. No punches are pulled, but there is com-
      passion for the "rainbow-chasing" father, the brave
      worn-out mother and the sons, experiencing even
      more than usual growing pains. (YA and Up)

WORLD WAR II

715 Appel, Banjamin. We Were There at the Battle for
      Bataan. Historical consultant, Maj. Gen. Courtney
      Whitney, U.S.A. ret. Ill. by Irv Docktor. Grosset
      and Dunlap, 1957. Beginning with the attack on
      Pearl Harbor on December 7, 1941, this story takes
      a brother and sister and their father into the Philip-
      pine hills where they all become guerrilla fighters,
      along with Filipino soldiers. (I)

716 Archer, Jules. Battlefield President, Dwight D. Eisen-
      hower. Jacket by Stephen Haas. Julian Messner,
      1967. This biography is listed here instead of else-
      where because of the emphasis on Eisenhower's
      military leadership in World War II. (YA and Up)

717 Bliven, Bruce. From Pearl Harbor to Okinawa, The
     War in the Pacific, 1941-45. Ill. with 12 pages of
     photographs and maps by Fritz and Stephen Kredel.
     Random Landmark, 1960. A book describing every
     major action in the Pacific, from Bataan to
     Hiroshima. (I and YA)
718 Bonham, Frank. Burma Rifles: A Story of Merrill's
     Marauders. Jacket by Arthur Shilstone. Thomas
     Y. Crowell, 1960. A story specifically written (as
     the dedication states) to commemorate the heroism of
     the 14 Nisei volunteers with the 5307th Composite
     Union, popularly known as Merrill's Marauders--
     men whose very presence behind the enemy lines in
     Burma involved courage beyond the call of duty.
     (YA)
719 _____. War Beneath the Sea. Jacket by W. T.
     Mars. Thomas Y. Crowell, 1962. A grimly
     realistic novel of the part played by the sub-
     mariners in the Pacific, but also one of courage
     and Yankee humor. There is an explanation of
     naval terms and phrases and an "Author's Note"
     at the end. (YA and Up)
720 Clagett, John. Surprise Attack. Jacket by Don
     Lambo. Julian Messner, 1968. A thrilling story
     of the Battle of Leyte Gulf, as experienced by five
     young men (fictional) just out of boot training.
     (YA)
721 _____. Torpedo Run on Bottomed Bay. Ill. by
     Dennis Fritz. Cowles Book Co., 1969. On board
     a PT boat, a 17-year-old Larry Cushing and a
     Japanese-American of the same age become close
     friends. When at Guadalcanal the Nisei performs
     in a suspicious way and is accused of treason,
     Larry tries hard to believe in his innocence. A
     realistic story of the Battle for Guadalcanal by one
     who was himself a PT commander during that bat-
     tle. (I and YA)
722 Hine, Al. D-Day: The Invasion of Europe. Consult-
     tant, S. L. A. Marshall. Ill. with maps, drawings,
     paintings and photographs. American Heritage,
     1962. A detailed story of the preparations and ac-
     tion of the American and British invasion. (YA)
723 Meader, Stephen. The Sea Snake. Ill. by Edward
     Shenton. Harcourt, Brace and World, 1943. A
     story of 1942; the setting, a camouflaged German
     submarine base on an island off the Bahamas; the
     hero, a 16-year-old son of a North Carolina

fisherman; the villain, a Nazi agent. (YA)

724 _____ . Shadows in the Pines. Ill. by Edward
Shenton. Harcourt, Brace and World, 1942. A
15-year-old boy of the New Jersey Pine Barrens
back of the Fort Dix reservation helps the U.S.
army round up a gang of Nazi fifth columnists en-
dangering the fort. (YA)

725 Oneal, Zibby. War Work. Ill. by George Porter.
Viking, 1971. An entertaining period piece of the
homefront during World War II--the rationing, sal-
vaging, practice blackouts, etc., and above all the
ardent desire of all to support "our boys in Europe," a desire which leads three children, in a
small midwestern town, into some scary spy detecting yielding unexpected results. (I and YA)

726 Uchida, Yoshiko. Journey to Topaz. Ill. by Donald
Carrick. Scribners, 1971. After Pearl Harbor,
the Japanese-Americans were evacuated from their
California homes to a bleak, dusty, cold concentration camp in Utah. With fictional names, this story
is true to the disgraceful facts, yet 11-year-old Yuki
learned from her aristocratic parents to accept the
injustice with dignity, realizing that some day the
United States would come to regret their treatment
of loyal Japanese-Americans. (I and YA)

727 Whipple, Chandler. Code Word Ferdinand: Adventures
of the Coast Watchers. Jacket by Albert Orbaan.
G. P. Putnam's Sons, 1971. Stories of many unsung
heroes of the war in the Pacific, who braved death
in lonely outposts in island jungles, to report by
radio the movements of the Japanese. (YA and Up)

728 White, Robb. Surrender. Jacket by Robert Shore.
Doubleday, 1966. The harrowing experiences of
two young Americans in the Philippines, whose
father has been killed at Pearl Harbor and who
evade the Japanese with courage and skill. (YA)

PART II: SUBJECTS

ALASKA AND HAWAII

ALASKA: LEGENDS, ESKIMO LORE

729 Houston, James. Akavak, An Eskimo Journey. Ill.
by the author. Harcourt, Brace and World, 1968.
An old man seeking his brother over the icy
mountains, in bitter Alaskan cold, with the help of
his young grandson. (I)

730 _____. The White Archer: An Eskimo Legend.
Ill. by the author. Harcourt, Brace and World,
1967. About a young Eskimo's search for revenge
and his final conquest of hatred. (I)

731 Shannon, Terry. Kidlik's Kayak. Ill. by Charles
Payzant. Albert Whitman and Co., 1959. Story of
an Alaskan Indian boy, with a list of Eskimo words
and diagrams of an igloo. (E)

ALASKA, 18th CENTURY

732 Bell, Margaret E. Touched With Fire: Alaska's
George William Steller. Jacket by Walter Buhr,
maps by Bob Ritter. Morrow Junior Books, 1960.
The dramatic story of the German-born scientist-
physician-theologian who accompanied Bering on his
last expedition, and first sighted Alaska in 1741.
(I and YA)

733 Granberg, W. J. Voyage into Darkness: To Alaska
with Bering. Ill. by Gil Walker. E. P. Dutton,
1960. The story of Bering's long expedition which
finally resulted in the discovery of Alaska in 1741
but also in the death of Bering and several others,
as narrated by 17-year-old Laurentz Waxel. The
Russian claim to Alaska was dearly paid for by suffering and death, caused largely by Russian governmental corruption, wrangling and incompetence, and
also Bering's belief in a land which he called

Gamaland. (I and YA)
734 Harris, Christie. Raven's Cry. Ill. by Bill Reid.
     Atheneum, 1966. A novel set in British Columbia
     and Alaska, about the Haida Indians who were lords
     of the waters west of Canada until 1775 (when this
     story begins). It also carries the history of the
     tribe and its art up to the present. (YA)

ALASKA: 19th CENTURY

735 Appel, Benjamin. We Were There in the Klondike
     Gold Rush. Ill. by Irv Docktor. Grosset and Dun-
     lap, 1956. A rough, tough, fictional account of
     what it was like to be a young Alaskan gold seeker
     in the winter of 1897/98, suffering from scurvy and
     snowblindness, and the dishonesty of fellow-travelers.
     But discovered also is the kindness and self-sacri-
     fice exhibited by some of the apparently toughest
     characters. (I)
736 Bell, Margaret E. Daughter of Wolf House. Jacket
     by Louis Darling. William Morrow, 1957. Novel
     about a half-Indian, half-white girl whose progress-
     ive Indian grandfather brings her up in the "new
     fashion" thus incurring the enmity of the Shaman of
     the Killer Whale House and his family who still
     hold with the cruel superstitious customs pertaining
     to adolescent girls in 1888. (YA)
737 _____. Love is Forever. Jacket by Louis Dar-
     ling. William Morrow, 1954. A novel about an
     18-year-old bride, Florence Monroe, starting house-
     keeping in an isolated region where her young hus-
     band has a salmon saltery. It follows "The Totem
     Casts Its Shadow" [738]. (YA)
738 _____. The Totem Casts Its Shadow. Frontispiece
     by Louis Darling. William Morrow, 1948. A
     sequel to "Watch for a Tall White Sail" [739], the
     story running parallel to that of "Daughter of Wolf
     House" [736], and dealing with the lives of the
     pioneer Monroe family in 1888. (YA)
739 _____. Watch for a Tall White Sail. Frontispiece
     by Louis Darling. William Morrow, 1948. A novel
     about a young girl's loneliness and courage in the
     wilderness of Prince of Wales Island in 1887; about
     her hard work in keeping house for her father and
     brothers, and about her first love. (YA)
740 Bosco, Antoinette. Charles John Seghers, Pioneer in

Alaska. Ill. by Matthew Kalmenoff. P. J. Kenedy
and Sons, 1960. The story of a Belgian priest,
only 24 years old when he came to Vancouver Island
in 1863 to bring the faith to settlers and natives of
a territory which included Alaska. A map shows the
Alaskan missions he founded at a cost of dreadful
hardships and dangers. (YA)

741 Clarke, Tom E. No Furs for the Czar. Lothrop, Lee
and Shepard, 1962. A novel set in Russian Alaska
in 1804, among the Tlinkets and Kenartze tribes, its
main theme a young Russian nobleman's growing re-
alization of the evils of serfdom. (YA)

742 Herron, Edward A. First Scientist of Alaska: William
Healey Dall. Jacket by Rus Anderson. Julian
Messner, 1958. Always first and foremost a scientist, Dall also acted as physician as he led a Western
Union expedition organized to survey the Alaskan
coast for a telegraph line to be built there and con-
nect with Siberia, with a cable under the Bering
Strait. The story of Dall's adventures and achievements reads like a well constructed novel. (YA)

742a _____. Conqueror of Mount McKinley: Hudson
Stuck. Jacket by Barry Martin. Julian Messner,
1964. A story of an unquenchable spirit. Stuck,
English-born in 1863, landed in Texas, sick with
tuberculosis, when he was 22, became a cowboy
first, and then an Episcopal priest and dean of St.
Matthew's Cathedral in Dallas. At the age of 40 he
became a missionary in the coldest and most remote
parts of Alaska, and finally scaled Mt. McKinley.
What a man! What a story! (YA)

743 Janes, Edward C. When Men Panned Gold in the
Klondike. Ill. by William Hutchinson and with photographs. Garrard Pub. Co., 1968. A good telling of
discovery of gold in the Yukon by George Cormack,
the gold rush that followed, the rise and decline of
Dawson, and finally the discoveries at Nome. (I)

744 Pedersen, Elsa. Dangerous Flight. Ill. by Anthony
D'Adamo. Abingdon Press, 1960. An exciting
story about Russian America in 1867 just before the
United States purchased Alaska. An English-Russian
boy and his Russian uncle are pursued by a vin-
dictive Russian trader and are aided by Indians who
endanger their own lives by sheltering the fugitives.
Suspense to the end. (I and YA)

745 Pohlman, Lillian. Wolfskin. W. W. Norton, 1968.
A 12-year-old boy, Johnny Clemens, is taken by his

reckless father to Alaska after gold, but a short
experience of the hazards of the Gold Rush and the
death of his father on the trail turns him back and
makes him determined to get home to San Francisco.
A girl, a dog, and a wolfskin influence his decision.
(I)

ALASKA: 20th CENTURY

746   Finney, Gertrude E.   To Survive We Must Be Clever.
      Ill. by Carl Kidwell.   David McKay, 1966.   A novel
      of an Aleutian island in 1900 and the dangerous lives
      of the Aleuts, particularly a 16-year-old chap
      aspiring to be a "Top Whaler." (I and YA)
747   Pinkerton, Kathrene.   Hidden Harbor.   Harcourt, Brace,
      and World, 1951.   Story of the pioneering Baird
      family in 1910 on the islands and shore lines south of
      Juneau, a story to arouse envy in the hearts of teen-
      age readers with a love of the sea and its challenges.
      Map.   (YA)
748   Redding, Robert H.   North to the Wilderness: The
      Story of an Alaska Boy.   Doubleday, 1970.   True
      adventures, in what was still pioneer country, of a
      ten-year-old boy (known as a "gangster" and a "lout")
      in interior Alaska in the late 1920s and '30s and who
      would now be called a "juvenile delinquent." (I and
      YA)
749   Taylor, Theodore.   The Children's War.   Jacket by
      Charles Mikolaycak.   Doubleday, 1971.   Purely fic-
      tional but highly credible is this story told in the
      first person by the son of a naval chief on an island
      just a short way from the Arctic Circle at the be-
      ginning of World War II when the Japanese actually
      did invade a couple of Aleutian islands.   (I and YA)

HAWAII: MYTH AND LEGEND

750   Colum, Padraic.   Legends of Hawaii.   Ill. by Don
      Farrer.   Yale paperbound, 1960.   Colum went to
      the Islands in 1923 under the auspices of a Com-
      mission on Myth and Folklore.   He learned some-
      thing of the language and used several sources for
      these stories, some from people who still had the
      tradition of Hawaiian romance.   He also learned
      much from a distinguished group of Polynesian
      scholars in Honolulu and he retold all that he heard

in his exceptionally gifted manner. (All ages)

751 Lipkind, Will. Boy of the Islands. Ill. by Nicolas.
    Harcourt, Brace and World, 1954. A story of the
    leadership training of a Hawaiian boy long before
    the coming of the white man. (E and I)

752 Michener, James. Hawaii. Random, 1959. A long,
    epic narrative history of the islands, with fictional
    characters: the story of Hawaii from the most re-
    mote ages conceivable to the time when it became
    the 50th state. (A)

753 Sperry, Armstrong. Call it Courage. Macmillan,
    1940, Collier paperbound, 1971. A Polynesian
    legend of a ten-year-old boy who sets out alone to
    conquer his fear of the sea. (I)

754 Thompson, Vivian L. Hawaiian Myths of Earth, Sea
    and Sky. Ill. by Leonard Weisgard. Holiday
    House, 1966. (I)

755 Titcomb, Margaret. The Voyage of the Flying Bird.
    Ill. by Joseph Feher. Dodd Mead, 1963. An
    imaginative story of the discovery of Hawaii by
    Polynesians from Tahiti, based, however, on sound
    research. (I and YA)

HAWAII: 19th Century

756 Engle, Eloise. Princess of Paradise. John Day,
    1962. The story of Lilioukalaini's girlhood in the
    mid 19th century, a period of great change in
    Hawaiian culture and tragic, rapid decline of the
    race caused by diseases, brought by foreigners, to
    which the natives were not immune. The "Au-
    thor's Note" gives some further history and there
    is a "Guide to Hawaiian Names and Words." (YA)

757 Stone, Adrienne. Hawaii's Queen, Lilioukalaini. Ill.
    by Raymond Lufkin. Julian Messner, 1947. A
    biography (1838-1917) of the last queen of the Ha-
    wiian Islands (reigned 1891-93) which also contains
    a good measure of history of 19th-century Hawaii
    and should greatly enhance the pleasure of a trip
    to the Islands. (YA)

758 Webb, Nancy and Jean Francis. Kaiulani, Crown
    Princess of Hawaii. Viking, 1962. A sad story
    of the short life of the lovely young princess who
    led her people to peaceful acceptance of their
    country's annexation by the United States and thus
    a more favorable status for Hawaii than might have

been the case if there had been violence when independence was lost. A long interesting "Note about
Hawaiian words" and a chart of the royal succession
in Hawaii introduce this biography of the Princess.
(1875-99). (YA and Up)

HAWAII: 20th CENTURY

759 Gugliotta, Bobette. Nolle Smith; Cowboy, Engineer,
     Statesman. Ill. with photographs. Jacket by
     Richard Cuffari. Dodd Mead, 1971. Hawaii is
     Smith's "realest" home though he was born in Wy-
     oming in 1888 of Scotch-Irish (on his father's side)
     and Negro-Indian (on his mother's) descent and has
     served the United States in many places, particular-
     ly the Virgin Islands, Ecuador and Brazil. Too
     full a life to begin to describe in a brief note. (YA
     and Up)
760 Heyerdahl, Thor. Kon-Tiki, for Young People. Color
     illustrations painted by William Neebe; also illus-
     trated with photographs, old engravings, prints,
     charts and diagrams. A Special Rand McNally Color
     Edition for Young People, the original having been
     published in 1960. What a Book! What a story!
     and true at that. In support of his theory that the
     Indians of Peru had voyaged 4300 miles across the
     Pacific to Polynesia on a raft, Heyerdahl and five
     companions sailed for 101 days on a similar craft--
     an incredible voyage. (I and YA)

THE ARCTIC

761 Angell, Pauline K. To The Top of the World; The
   Story of Peary and Henson. Ill. with maps and
   photographs. Rand McNally, 1964 (Bantam edition,
   1966). Biographies of the two (Henson, 1867-1955,
   and Peary, 1856-1920) and a history of Arctic explorations, covering the years from 1856, when
   Peary was born, to 1955, when Henson died. (I
   and YA)

762 Berry, Erick (Best). Robert E. Peary. Ill. by
   Frederick T. Chapman. Garrard, 1963. A Discovery Book. A biography of a man whose motto
   was: "I will find a way or make one" and who,
   with Matthew Henson, after numerous unsuccessful
   attempts and narrow escapes from death, discovered
   the North Pole in 1909. (E)

763 Graves, Charles. Matthew A. Henson. Ill. by Ronald
   Dorfman. G. P. Putnam's Sons, A See and Read,
   Beginning to Read Biography. The story of the
   valiant Negro explorer who, with Robert Peary, was
   the first to reach the North Pole in April of 1909.
   (E)

764 Hall, Anna Gertrude. Nansen. Ill. by Boris Artzy-
   basheff. Viking, 1940. A beautiful book in every
   way. Illustrations, maps, and especially the
   story of the great Norwegian Arctic explorer, scientist, statesman and humanitarian (1861-1930)
   whose ship, the Fram, may be seen today in Oslo.
   (I and YA)

765 Henson, Matthew A. A Black Explorer at the North
   Pole: An Autobiography. Ill. with photographs;
   jacket by Lena Fong Lueg. Walker, 1969. A book
   showing the modesty, courage and humor of its
   author, the co-discoverer, with Peary, of the North
   Pole in 1909. It also gives us vivid descriptions
   of Arctic scenery, the behavior of sled dogs, the
   cold, hunger and fatigue suffered by the members

of the expedition and his own saving sense of humor
in the darkest hours.   (A)
766 Lord, Walter.   Peary to the North Pole.   Ill. with 27
photographs.   Harper and Row, A Breakthrough
Book, 1963.   Greatly enhanced by the photographs,
this is the heroic story of a man (1856-1920) who
wouldn't give up in his attempts to reach the Pole
and was finally successful in 1909, after 22 years
of effort and six attempts.   (I)
767 Miller, Floyd.   Ahdoolo.   Jacket by Charles McVicker.
E. P. Dutton, 1963.   A biography of Matthew A.
Henson (1867-1955), the Black hero of the Polar expedition, co-discoverer with Peary of the North Pole
in 1909.   (YA and Up)
768 Peary, Marie.   The Discoverer of the North Pole;
The Story of Robert E. Peary.   Ill. by Walter
Buehr.   William Morrow, 1959.   A biography of
the North Pole discoverer in 1909, written by his
daughter who was born in Greenland in 1893 at 77°
44' north latitude, in one of her father's unsuccessful attempts to reach the Pole.   A story of hazardous
adventure and indomitable courage, not only of Peary
but also, certainly, of Mrs. Peary.   (YA)
769 Syme, Ronald.   On Foot to the Arctic: The Story of
Samuel Hearne.   Ill. by William Stobbs.   Morrow
Junior Books, 1959.   Biography of a Canadian Arctic explorer, not well known in the U.S. but de-
serving more notice for his perseverance and endurance in attempting to find a land route to the
Pacific.   Against continual obstacles, including extreme cold and hunger, he walked, between December 1770 and July 1771, 2000 miles.   (I)

THE ANTARCTIC

770 Bixby, William.   The Race to the South Pole.   Jacket
by Bruno Junker.   Longmans Green, 1961.   Stories
of the following expeditions: the Discovery Expedition
(1901-04), Scott's first unsuccessful attempt; the
Nimrod Expedition (1907-09), led by Ernest Schackle-
ton, also unsuccessful; the Fram Expedition (1910-
12), led by Roald Amundsen; and the Terra Nova Expedition, Scott's disastrous last try.   (YA and Up)
771 Byrd, Richard E.   Alone.   Ill. by Richard E. Hanson.
G. P. Putnam's Sons, 1938.   The first-hand story
of Admiral Byrd's self-imposed isolation, in which

he came close to death, for several months of the
Arctic winter, 123 miles south of Little America, in
1934. (A)

772 DeLeeuw, Cateau. Roald Amundsen, A World Explorer.
Ill. by George I. Parrish. Garrard, 1965. The exciting story of Amundsen's explorations and discovery
of the South Pole in 1911. (E and I)

773 Gladych, Michael. Admiral Byrd of Antarctica. Jacket
by Don Lambo. Julian Messner, 1960. A biography
of the intrepid resolute explorer who flew over the
North Pole in 1936, the South Pole in 1929, and who
made three expeditions to Antarctica (1928-30, 1933-
35, and 1939). Flights to the moon may sound more
daring, but it must be remembered that astronauts
have the benefit of greatly advanced technology and
financial and governmental support. (YA)

774 Ronne, Finn and Liss, Howard. The Ronne Expedition
to Antarctica. Ill. with photographs and jacket by
Virginia Soulé. Julian Messner, 1971. Finn Ronne
was a member of Admiral Byrd's expedition to Little
America in 1933-35, and again in 1939 he went to
Antarctica with a United States crew, but it
is about his own long-dreamed-of expedition in 1947
that this book is written. Incidentally, two wives
went along--the first women to spend the winter in
Antarctica. (YA)

775 Sperry, Armstrong. South of Cape Horn: A Saga of
Nat Palmer's Early Antarctic Exploration. Ill. by
the author. John C. Winston, 1958. The story of
a young American sea captain (1799-1877) who first
sighted what came to be called "Palmer Peninsula"
in the Antarctic, while on a whaling expedition. A
bang-up sea story with a sea-going glossary. (I
and YA)

THE ARTS

ARCHITECTURE

776 Jacobs, Herbert. Frank Lloyd Wright, America's
     Greatest Architect. Ill. with photographs. Har-
     court, Brace and World, 1965. This biography
     (1869-1959), written by a journalist who knew
     F.L.W. as a client, friend and reporter for 25
     years, is an intimate one, with a great deal of de-
     tail about his engineering skills as well as his ar-
     tistic genius. The title may be open to question,
     but there can be no question about Wright's influence
     on American architecture. (YA)
777 Kaufman, Mervyn. Father of Skyscrapers: A Biogra-
     phy of Louis Sullivan. Ill. with photographs. Little
     Brown, 1969. Illustrations and text in this book
     complement each other so well that this story of the
     unhappy architectural genius (1856-1924) is compelling
     reading from start to finish, leaving a vivid and last-
     ing impression of Sullivan's originality and creativity.
     (YA and Up)
778 Rosen, Sidney. Wizard of the Dome: R. Buckminster
     Fuller, Designer for the Future. Ill. with photo-
     graphs through the courtesy of Mr. Fuller [1895-]
     and diagrams by Edmund DeWan. Little Brown,
     1969. (YA)

PAINTING AND SCULPTURE

779 Agle, Nan Hayden and Frances Atchison Bacon. The
     Ingenious John Barnard. Ill. by Joseph Papin.
     Seabury Press, 1966. The story of an inventive
     young artist of the mid-19th century who for his
     vast panoramic painting of the Mississippi River,
     unrolled in 1846 for a two-hour showing--the first
     "moving picture"--was praised by Charles Dickens,
     Queen Victoria and the United States Congress.
     Barnard also wrote plays and poems and produced
     many other paintings and dioramas all of which,

unfortunately, have disappeared. The book also contains interesting material about a mid-19th-century
art colony in New Harmony, Indiana. (I and YA)

780 Armstrong, William H. Barefoot in the Grass; The
Story of Grandma Moses. Ill. with reproductions of
her paintings. Doubleday, 1970. The long-life
(1860-1961) story of the artist which will appeal to
young children for its account of Anna Mary as a
child, making dull oak leaves "pretty" with home-
made coloring; and to the aged, for the way she
"made tracks" for 30 years after her threescore
years and ten; and to all those in between who ap-
preciate beauty that money can't buy. (All ages)

781 Ayers, James Sterling. John James Audubon. Ill. by
George I. Parrish. Garrard, A Discovery Book.
The story of the artist whose book "The Birds of
America" gave him lasting fame. (E)

782 Coatsworth, Elizabeth. Boston Bells. Ill. by Manning
deV. Lee. Macmillan, 1952. The story in fictional
form of the exciting experience of John Singleton
Copley when, in 1747 at the age of nine, he was almost impressed into His Majesty's Navy at the time
of the Knowles riots and how his paintings on the
walls of his bedroom affected his escape from the
press gang in a fortuitous and fortunate way. (E
and I)

783 Colver, Anne. Yankee Doodle Painter. Ill. by Lee
Ames. Alfred A. Knopf, 1955. A story, out of
family archives, about Archibald M. Willard, the
painter of "The Spirit of '76" and his nephew,
Will Colver, who became one of the first Scripps-
Howard editors, the action taking place in the
1860s and '70s and culminating in the hanging of
the picture at the Philadelphia Centennial Exposition
of 1876. (I)

784 Friermood, Elizabeth Hamilton. Focus the Bright Land.
Doubleday, 1967. A novel about a young lady
photographer of Ohio and Indiana in 1881, a member
of a family of photographers, who realized the po-
tential of photography at a time when it had not yet
developed into an art. (YA)

785 Graves, Charles P. Grandma Moses, Favorite Painter.
Ill. by Victor Mays. Garrard, 1969. A biography
(1860-1961) which should inspire children to start
painting very young and continue forever. (E)

786 Kerr, Laura. Wonder of His World: Charles Wilson
Peale. Funk and Wagnalls, 1968. A biography

(1741-1827) of a great painter and also inventor and
scientist.   (YA)

787   Kuhn, Lois Harris.   The World of Jo Davidson.   Ill.
by Leonard Everett Fisher.   Farrar, Straus and
Cudahy, 1958.   This world famous sculptor was born
of Russian-Jewish parents on New York's Lower East
Side, in 1883.   The almost incredible amount of work
he accomplished in his 69 years brought him into
contact with most of the world's greats of the period
as he "busted" them, making a veritable "plastic
history."   (YA)

788   McKown, Robin.   Painter of the Wild West: Frederic
Remington.   Jacket by Lorence F. Bjorklund.   Julian
Messner, 1959.   Biography of a prolific artist and
adventurous character who, in his 48 years (1861-
1909) completed over 2700 drawings and paintings
which appeared in over 40 periodicals and 42 books,
eight of which he had written.   Horse lovers, take
particular note.   (YA)

789   Miller, Helen Markley.   Lens on the West: The Story
of William Henry Jackson.   Ill. with his drawings
and photographs.   Doubleday, 1966.   No one inter-
ested in the development of the West and our great
national parks there should miss this lively story
and the remarkable illustrations.   Jackson's century
(1843-1942) covered the history of photography as
well as of the U.S., including five wars--the war
with Mexico, the Civil War, the Spanish-American,
and the two World Wars, for the second had started
when he died at 99.   (YA and Up)

790   Moore, Clyde B.   Frederic Remington, Young Artist.
Ill. by Robert Doremus.   Bobbs-Merrill, 1971,
Childhood of Famous Americans Series.   This biography of the artist (1861-1909), famed for his pictures of horses, Indians, cowboys and the wild west,
is "dedicated to boys and girls who express themselves through sketches, color and verse."   (E)

791   Nugent, Frances Roberts.   George Bellows, American
Painter.   Ill. with reproductions of some of Bellows'
most famous paintings.   Rand McNally, 1963.   A
portrait of the artist, more than a biography (1882-
1925), and a study of his techniques and procedures,
plus highlights of his life and analysis of his works,
with a list of museums and galleries in the United
States that show his works.   (I and YA)

792   Peare, Catherine Owens.   Painter of Patriots: Charles
Wilson Peale.   Ill. by Joan Berg.   Holt, Rinehart

and Winston, 1964. Biography of patriot, inventor, craftsman, scientist and painter (1741-1827). (YA)

793 Price, Willadene. Bartholdi and the Statue of Liberty. Ill. with photographs. Rand McNally, 1959. A biography of the French sculptor and the story of his big statue. (I and YA)

794 Ripley, Elizabeth. Copley. Ill. with reproductions of his paintings. Lippincott, 1967. A combined biography and art book, each page of text faced with an appropriate reproduction of a painting. John Singleton Copley (1738-1815) was born in Boston but went to England in 1774 where he spent the remainder of his life. (YA)

795 Rockwell, Anne. Paintbrush and Peacepipe; The Story of George Catlin. Ill. with adaptations in sinopia pencil of portraits and sketches made by Catlin. Atheneum, 1971. A biography of the artist (1796-1872) who traveled up and down the Missouri River making friends among, and painting, the Indians still living free. He also collected artifacts and took his exhibition to England when the U.S. government would not buy it. Later he traveled over the wilds of South America as an archaeologist-anthropologist. (I)

796 Smaridge, Norah. Audubon, The Man Who Painted Birds. Ill. by Charles Robinson. World, 1970. A large portion of this biography of John James Audubon (1785-1851) is about his childhood and youth in France where he went from Haiti, where he was born, at the age of eight. He was sent to America as a young man, married and finally died there, but his quest for birds to paint took him far afield--even to Labrador. (I)

797 Wilson, Ellen. American Painter in France: A Life of Mary Cassatt. Ill. with many reproductions of her paintings--Farrar, Straus and Giroux, 1971. The story of an unusually "liberated" woman for her times (1844-1926), who at 16 startled her parents by begging permission to go to Paris to study painting. At 22 she was granted her wish, and remained in France for the rest of her life, gaining lasting fame as one of the Impressionists. (YA)

798 Yates, Elizabeth. Patterns on the Wall. Jacket by Fritz Kredel. Ill. by Warren Chappell. E. P. Dutton, 1943. A novel about an itinerant painter (or stencilist) who, because of his extraordinary talents and interests, seems suspicious to the stolid New

Hampshire farmers in the early 1800s. (YA)

MUSIC

799 Montgomery, Elizabeth Rider. William C. Handy,
       Father of the Blues.   Ill. by David Hodges and with
       photographs. Garrard, 1968. A biography (1873-
       1958) of the little Negro boy from Florence, Ala-
       bama, who, to quote Deems Taylor, "has contributed
       something to the world's music that is absolutely
       new and absolutely American."   (I)
800 Peare, Catherine O. Stephen Foster: His Life. Ill.
       by Margaret Ayer. Holt, Rinehart and Winston,
       1952. The short sad life (1826-1864) of the com-
       poser and author of many old favorites, such as
       "Old Black Joe" and "Jeannie with the Light Brown
       Hair." (I)
801 Wheeler, Opal. Stephen Foster and His Little Dog
       Tray. Ill. by Mary Greenwalt. E. P. Dutton,
       1941. Stephen Foster (1826-64) never seemed
       aware of the evils of slavery, but fortunately music
       does not need to be concerned with social issues.
       Thirteen songs, words and music, are included. (I)

THE STAGE

802 Butler, Mildred Allen. Actress in Spite of Herself:
       The Life of Anna Cora Mowat. Jacket and ill. by
       Mimi Korach. Funk and Wagnalls, 1966. Biogra-
       phy of a beautiful and most remarkable young
       woman (1819-1870) who was able to make a stage
       career respectable in the early 19th century. She
       also wrote novels and plays and became a foreign
       correspondent in her middle years and was very in-
       fluential in saving Mt. Vernon for posterity. Amer-
       ican by parentage, she was born in France and died
       in England. (YA)
803 Fox, Mary Virginia. Ethel Barrymore: A Portrait.
       Reilly and Lee, 1970. A biography in short form
       of the great American actress (1879-1959) and her
       family--"the Royal Family" of Drews and Barry-
       mores. (YA)
804 Latham, Jean Lee. On Stage: Mr. Jefferson. Ill. by
       Edward Shenton. Harper and Bros., 1958. The
       story of the theatrical career of Joseph Jefferson

III (1829-1905) also introducing Abraham Lincoln,
and Edwin and John Wilkes Booth. (YA)

805 Malone, Mary. Actor in Exile: The Life of Ira Aldridge. Ill. by Eros Keith. Crowell-Collier, 1969.
Often called "the greatest Othello of them all, "
Aldridge, born a free Negro in New York in 1807,
felt compelled to go to England at the age of 17 to
study for the stage. There, and on the continent,
he became a famous actor of white as well as Black
roles and died there in 1867, never having obtained
recognition in the country of his birth. (YA and Up)

806 Shaw, Dale. Titans of the American Stage: Edwin
Forrest, the Booths, the O'Neills. Ill. with photographs. Jacket by Michael Loundas. Westminster
Press, 1971. A chronicle of the development of
the American theater in biographies. (YA and Up)

ENTERTAINERS

807 Borland, Kathryn Kilby. Harry Houdini, Boy Magician.
Ill. by Fred Irvin. Bobbs-Merrill, 1969, Childhood
of Famous Americans Series. Houdini (1873-1926)
in his childhood began acrobatics and lock picking;
both skills, along with his phenomenal muscular
control, made him a world famous magician. (E
and I)

808 Cone, Molly. The Ringling Brothers. Ill. by James
and Ruth McCrea. Thomas Y. Crowell, 1957.
There were seven brothers, but only five were
partners in the circus which opened in Baraboo,
Wisconsin in 1884. The illustrators attended the
Ringling School of Art in Sarasota, Florida, so the
illustrations are a circus in themselves. (E and I)

809 Eaton, Jeanette. Trumpeter's Tale: The Story of
Young Louis Armstrong. Ill. by Elton C. Fox.
William Morrow, 1955. A success story that
beats Horatio Alger and a must for devotees of New
Orleans jazz. (I and YA)

810 Friermood, Elizabeth Hamilton. Circus Sequins.
Jacket by Charles McCurry. Doubleday, 1968. A
romance of the circus world and a girl's difficult
choice between its glamor or life as a farmer's
wife. (YA)

811 Garst, Shannon. Will Rogers, Immortal Cowboy.
Ill. by Charles Gabriel. Julian Messner, 1950.
After many drop-outs and failures, Will finally

discovered his own unique gift for making people
laugh, with him and at themselves (even presidents)
(1879-1935). (I and YA)

811a   Hunt, Mabel Leigh. Have You Seen Tom Thumb?
Ill. by Fritz Eichenberg. J. B. Lippincott, 1942.
The true story of an exceptionally small and smart
midget (1838-83) whose real name was Charles
Stratton. It reads, however, like a fairy story in
which the tiny knight finally finds his princess.
Along with Tom Thumb's story runs that of his
promoter, Phineas T. Barnum. (I and YA)

812   Kendall, Lace (Stoutenberg). Houdini, Master of
Escape. Jacket by Clifford Schule. Macrae Smith,
1960. The story of the almost superhuman magician
(1873-1926) who could never be successfully hand-
cuffed, tied, strait-jacketed, or restrained in any
way. His wife deserves a biography too and their
marriage was one of the memorable love affairs in
stage history. His real name was Weise, but the
name he adopted is so familiar it has even been
made into a verb meaning to escape--"houdinize."
(YA)

813   Wormser, Richard. Kidnapped Circus. Ill. by Don
Bolognese. William Morrow, 1968. A picaresque
novel about a 12-year-old boy who joins a circus
and is kidnapped with it by a mad owner of a
hacienda. (I)

POETS, NOVELISTS, AND OTHERS

814   Barth, Edna. I'm Nobody! Who Are You? The Story of
Emily Dickinson. Ill. by Richard Cuffari. Seabury
Press, 1971. A well-drawn profile of the recluse
of Amhurst, Mass., and major American poet (1831-
85) with a section of Selected Poems. (YA)

815   Borland, Kathryn Kilby and Helen Ross Speicher.
Phillis Wheatley, Young Colonial Poet. Ill. by William K. Plummer. Bobbs-Merrill, 1968. Childhood of Famous Americans Series. The remarkable
story of an African girl who, at about seven was
bought by a kind Mrs. Wheatly of Boston who taught
her to talk English (she could hardly talk at all at
first). At age 12 she began writing poetry which
made her so famous that she was invited to England.
She barely missed being presented to King George
III and did later (ca. 1754-84) meet George Washing-

ton. (E and I)

816   Branham, Janet. Bret Harte, Young Storyteller. Ill.
by Robert Doremus. Bobbs-Merrill, 1969, Childhood of Famous Americans Series. Bret Harte
was born in Albany in 1836 and died in England in
1902, but he established himself as a writer in
California with his realistic tales of the West. (I)

817   Burnett, Constance Buel. Happily Ever After: A
Portrait of Frances Hodgson Burnett. Jacket by
Carl Smith. Vanguard Press, n.d. The story of
a born story teller and hard worker (1849-1924),
born in England but brought quite early in life to
Tennessee. Her best-known book was "Little
Lord Fauntleroy" but she was also a prolific author
of adult novels, plays and short stories. At the
end of the book is her good advice to 8th graders
who want to become writers. (YA)

818   Calder-Marshall, Arthur. Lone Wolf: The Story of
Jack London. Ill. by Biro-. Jacket by Robert
Jones. Duell-Sloan and Pearce. As dramatic,
extraordinary and tragic as any of his stories and
novels, this biography of London (1876-1916) shows
the many mistakes he made, the most serious
caused by his lack of self-understanding. An appendix on "Books by and about Jack London."
(YA and Up)

819   Coolidge, Olivia. Edith Wharton, 1862-1937. Jacket
by Hildegarde Rath. Charles Scribner's Sons,
1964. With the possible exception of "Ethan Frome,"
it is doubtful whether many young adults of the lat-
ter half of the 20th century will have much interest
in her books or her life, but she holds and important place in American literature even though
she lived much of her life in London and Paris.
(YA and Up)

820   Cooper, Lettice. The Young Edgar Allan Poe. Ill.
by William Randall, Roy, 1964. A fictionalized
story of the youth of Poe, his lack of security and
need for love, and his dedication to poetry from
babyhood to the age of 18 when he ran away from
his adopted parents. (1809-49). (I)

821   Daugherty, Charles Michael. Samuel Clemens. Ill.
by Kent Wurth. Crowell, 1970. A short biography of the early life of Mark Twain (and why
wasn't that name used in the title?). (E)

822   Dunham, Montrew. Anne Bradstreet, Young Puritan
Poet. Ill. by Paul and Patty Karch. Bobbs-

Merrill Co., 1969.   Childhood of Famous American Series.   The story of the English childhood of
Anne Dudley Bradstreet who came to America in
1630 and became America's first woman poet; with
a chronology, lists of things to remember, look up,
and do, bibliography and vocabulary of interesting
words.   (E and I)

823   Eaton, Jeanette.   America's Own Mark Twain.   Ill. by
Leonard Everett Fisher.   William Morrow, 1958.
An excellent biography (1835-1910).   (YA)

824   Fisher, Aileen and Rabe, Olive.   We Alcotts.   Ill. by
Ellen Raskin.   Atheneum, 1968.   The story of
Louisa M. Alcott's family as seen through the eyes
of Marmee, mother of "Little Women," based on
journals, letters, and other writings of the Alcotts.
(YA)

825   Franchere, Ruth.   Carl Sandburg, Voice of the People.
Ill. by Victor Mays-Garrard, 1970.   A short biography (1878-1967) of the great American poet and
writer of Swedish extraction, who was largely self-
educated.   He was born and brought up in Gales-
burg, Ill., a poor boy in worldly wealth but rich in
his happy, courageous nature, his tremendous
energy, his singing imagination and absolute origin-
ality.   (I and YA)

826   .   Jack London: the Pursuit of a Dream.
Jacket by Milton Glaser.   Thomas Y. Crowell, 1962.
This describes the tough adventurous life (1876-
1916) of a man with a burning desire to educate
himself and become a successful writer.   (YA)

827   .   Stephen Crane: The Story of an American
Writer.   Jacket by Romano-Ross.   Thomas Y.
Crowell, 1961.   The sad story of the short life
(1871-1900) of the author of "The Red Badge of
Courage," a driven, tortured young man, unable to
find peace of mind in failure or success, even when
his talent was recognized and appreciated by such
other writers as Hamlin Garland, W. D. Howells,
Joseph Conrad and many others.   (YA)

828   .   Willa.   Ill. by Leonard Weisgard.   Thomas
Y. Crowell, 1958.   The story of Willa Cather's
"growing up" to the age of 16, from 1873 to 1889.
She died in 1947.   (YA)

829   Fuller, Miriam Morris, Phillis Wheatley, America's
First Black Poetess.   Ill. by Victor Mays.   Garrard, 1971.   What a dramatic short life she led!
(1754?-84).   She was brought from Africa as a

little child in chains to be sold at auction in Boston, was educated by her kindly buyer and sent to England to be royally feted there, was received by George Washington, and died poor and alone. (I)

830 Geismar, Maxwell. Ring Lardner and the Portrait of Folly. Jacket by Giulio Maestro. Thomas Y. Crowell, 1972. Biography of a satirist (1885-1933) continuously interlaced with quotations from Lardner's writings which beg to be read aloud--so funny, and at the same time so true to the life of the '20s. (YA and Up)

831 Gould, Jean. That Dunbar Boy. Ill. by Charles Walker. Dodd Mead, 1958. The story of an unusually happy and successful poet who made use of his Negro origins to preserve plantation dialect in light verse. (I and YA)

832 Gurko, Miriam. Restless Spirit: The Life of Edna St. Vincent Millay. Thomas Y. Crowell, 1962. A biography (1892-1950) with lines of Millay's poetry interspersed in the story just as her poetry was part of the fabric of her life. (A)

833 Harlow, Alvin F. Joel Chandler Harris (Uncle Remus): Plantation Story Teller. Ill. by W. C. Nims. Julian Messner. Harris' own name is seldom remembered now, 64 years after his death (he was born in 1848 and died in 1908), but "Uncle Remus" will probably never be forgotten and he deserves our deep gratitude for his conservation of Negro folk tales, some of which may well have come originally from Africa. (YA)

834 Higgins, Helen Boyd. Noah Webster, Boy of Words. Ill. by Gray Morrow. Bobbs-Merrill, 1951. Childhood of Famous Americans Series. (E)

835 Jackson, Phyllis Wynn. Victorian Cinderella: The Story of Harriet Beecher Stowe. Portraits by Elliott Means. Holiday House, 1947. A fictionalized biography of the writer (1811-96) whose "Uncle Tom's Cabin" suddenly raised her from poverty and obscurity to wealth and world renown. (YA)

836 Kane, Harnett T. Young Mark Twain and the Mississippi. Ill. by Lorence Bjorklund. Random House, 1966. What a boy that young Sam Clemens was! Over 100 years later he would have been put in a detention home. The stories of his escapades told here are based on his own recollections, and the thrilling responsibilities he assumed as a "pirate's cub," and then a pilot, are founded on his story of

his early life on the big river.   This book covers
his life from 1835 to the beginning of the Civil War.
He died in 1910.   (I)

837 Longworth, Polly. Emily Dickinson: Her Letter to
the World. Thomas Y. Crowell, 1965. The autobiography of one of America's greatest poets, remarkably advanced for her time in technique and
form, but too much a recluse to allow publication
in her lifetime. (YA)

838 Manley, Seon. Nathaniel Hawthorne, Captain of the
Imagination. Ill. with prints and photographs.
Vanguard, 1968. A biography of one of the great
19th-century writers (1804-1864), friend of Thoreau,
Emerson, the Alcotts, et al., with a chronology of
his life. (YA and Up)

839 Mason, Miriam. Yours with Love, Kate. Ill. by
Barbara Cooney. Riverside Press. Houghton
Mifflin, 1952. It may come as a surprise to
many who only remember her from "Rebecca of
Sunnybrook Farm" that Kate Douglas Wiggin [later
Riggs] (1856-1923) was also one of the earliest
kindergarten teachers and was particularly noted for
her Silver Street kindergarten in the slums of San
Francisco. Her writing career later grew out of
her interest in children. An exceptionally happy
personality, her motto was, "expect everything good
and some of it is bound to happen." (I and YA)

840 Meigs, Cornelia. Invincible Louisa. Ill. with photographs and portraits. Little Brown, 1933. An inspiring biography of Louisa May Alcott (1832-88),
showing how she drew her stories from her own
life, and also the hardships she bravely endured.
(YA)

841 Meltzer, Milton. Langston Hughes: A Biography.
Jacket by Tracy Sugarman. Thomas Y. Crowell,
1968. Biography of the Negro poet (1902-67) written with deep insight into the racial problems of
the '60s, their roots and development. (YA)

842 Merriam, Eve. The Voice of Liberty: The Story of
Emma Lazarus. Ill. by Charles W. Walker.
Farrar, Straus and Cudahy, Jewish Publication
Society. Known to most of us only for her verses
on the Statue of Liberty, Emma Lazarus (1849-
1887) was an author of other poetry, respected by
poets, and an outstanding proponent of Jewish pride
in Jewish heritage and the establishment of a home-
land in Palestine. (YA)

843 Myers, Elisabeth P. Langston Hughes, Poet of His
     People. Ill. by Russell Hoover. Garrard, 1970.
     A fine short biography (1902-1967) of the Black poet
     born in Kansas, whose life took him to Mexico,
     Africa, Europe and Harlem (where he felt most at
     home), with several quotations from his poetry.
     (YA and Up)

844 North, Sterling. Thoreau of Walden Pond. Ill. by
     Harve Stein. Houghton Mifflin, 1959. A pleasantly
     readable biography of the poet (1817-1862) as a
     naturalist, with little about his theory of civil dis-
     obedience. (I)

845 O'Connor, Richard. Sinclair Lewis. Foreword by
     Mark Schorer. McGraw-Hill, 1971. No matter
     how hard he may have tried, the author has not
     been able to make Lewis (1885-1951) seem a like-
     able personality, but he does pay tribute to the
     originality of "Main Street," "Babbitt," and the other
     works, and evokes a certain sympathy for the man
     who was a physically unattractive "misfit." He
     also shows how conscientious Lewis was about ac-
     curate detail and his own working hours. (YA)

846 Papashvily, Helen Waite. Louisa May Alcott. Ill. by
     Bea Holmes. Houghton Mifflin, 1965. The life
     story (1832-88) of the tempestuous, gifted young
     woman who was able to bring her family up out of
     poverty by the power of her pen. (I and YA)

847 Peare, Catherine Owens. Henry Wadsworth Longfellow:
     His Life. Ill. by Margaret Ayer. Holt, Rinehart
     and Winston, 1953. The biography of the poet (1807-
     1882) whose works have come down to the present
     almost as folk saga--Hiawatha, Evangeline, and
     others. (I)

848 _____. Louisa May Alcott: Her Life. Ill. by
     Margaret Ayer. Holt, Rinehart and Winston, 1954.
     A short biography of the author of "Little Women"
     who was also a Civil War nurse and later an editor.
     (I)

849 _____. Washington Irving: His Life. Ill. by
     Margaret Ayer. Henry Holt, 1957. A charming
     biography of a delightful author, diplomat, and tra-
     veler (1783-1859) who contributed Rip Van Winkle
     and Ichabod Crane to American folklore. (I and YA)

850 Porges, Irwin. Edgar Allan Poe. Jacket by Harsh
     Finegold. Chilton Books, 1963. A biography (1809-
     1849) including summaries of many of Poe's best-
     known tales and refuting much of the accepted

opinions about his use of drugs and alcohol. (YA
and Up)

851 Proudfit, Isabel. Noah Webster, Father of the Dictionary. Ill. by I. B. Hazelton. Julian Messner,
1942. Biography of a man (1758-1843) who in spite
of constant financial pressures lived a happy life because of his love of words and his work with them,
beginning with a speller, grammar and readers. At
age 49 he began his 20-year-project--a truly American Dictionary. (I)

852 Rink, Paul. Remaking Modern Fiction: Ernest Hemingway. Ill. by Robert Boehmer. Encyclopaedia
Britannica, 1962. The story of Hemingway (1899-
1961) as a man, as a writer, and as a legend, and
the basis of the legends about him. (YA and Up)

853 Robinson, Martha. The Young Louisa M. Alcott. Ill.
by William Randell. Roy, 1963. The story of
Louisa's life from 1840, when she was eight, to
1853 when she was 21 and her writing career was
launched with the publication of "Flower Fables"
(actually written when she was 16); a story of courage, determination, and the love of family which
pervades her first real success, "Little Women." Of
particular interest to older readers is the account of
the Alcott's life at "Fruitlands," the experiment in
communal living which caused "Marmee" great un-
happiness. (I and YA)

854 Rollins, Charlemae. Black Troubadour: Langston
Hughes. Ill. with photographs. Rand McNally,
1970. A biography of the kind Black poet (1902-67)
by a librarian and writer who met him during the
Depression and became his warm friend to the end
of his life. Contains lists of Langston Hughes' published works, and of his awards and honors. (YA)

855 No Entry.

856 Seton, Anya. Washington Irving. Ill. by Harve Stein.
Houghton, 1960. A biography of the writer who made
Diedrich Knickerbocker, Ichabod Crane, and Rip Van
Winkle figures of American folklore. (YA)

857 Sterling, Philip. Sea and Earth: The Life of Rachel
Carson. Ill. with photographs taken by the author.
Thomas Y. Crowell, 1970. A modest little woman,
naturalist and poet (1907-64), who started the big
war against insecticides. (YA and Up)

858 Stevenson, Augusta. Francis Scott Key, Maryland Boy.
Ill. by Gray Morrow. Bobbs-Merrill, 1960, Childhood of Famous Americans Series. A story of Key's

exciting boyhood during the early years of the Republic and his love of reading and writing verses
even then; ending with his watching the bombardment
of Fort McHenry from imprisonment on a British
warship, the inspiration for "The Star Spangled
Banner."

859 Stoutenburg, Adrien and Laura Nelson Baker. Dear,
Dear Livy: The Story of Mark Twain's Wife.
Scribner's Sons, 1963. Olivia Louise Langdon
(1845-1904) was 22 when she married Mark Twain
and this story of a loving marriage that lasted 37
years shows a side of his character which is not
often revealed. (YA)

860 _____. Listen America. Scribner's, 1968. A
fine biography of the poet Walt Whitman (1819-92)
who was neglected and even maligned during his
lifetime but who is now considered among the best.
(YA and Up)

861 White, Hilda. Truth Is My Country: Portraits of
Eight New England Authors. Ill. with portraits.
Doubleday, 1971. Profiles of Hawthorne, Emerson,
Thoreau, Stone, Dickinson, Robinson, Milley,
Frost. (YA and Up)

862 Winders, Gertrude Hecker. James Fenimore Cooper,
Leatherstocking Boy. Ill. by Clotilde Embree Funk.
Bobbs-Merrill, 1951. Childhood of Famous Ameri-
cans Series. The adventures of Cooper as a boy
which provided much of the material for his popular
"Leatherstocking Tales." (E and I)

863 Wise, Winifred. Harriet Beecher Stowe, Woman with
a Cause. Jacket by Frank Aloise. G. P. Putnam's Sons, 1965. Told in engrossing story form
this biography of "the little woman who started a
great big war" (1811-1896) should be an inspiration
to all women who think that marriage and mother-
hood deter them from writing careers or involve-
ment in a great cause. Until the success of "Uncle
Tom's Cabin" in 1852, Harriet was very poor and
often discontented with her lot but even after the
book brought fame and fortune she "never became
puffed up." (YA)

864 Wood, James Playsted. A Hound, A Bay Horse and
a Turtle Dove: The Life of Thoreau for the Young
Reader. Ill. by Douglas Gorsline. A Pantheon
Portrait, 1963. Don't let the words "young reader"
deter older ones from this biography of the author
of "Walden" (1817-1862). His "Essay on Civil Dis-

obedience" will appeal to today's dissenters regardless of age, and the chapter on Thoreau's own writing methods and rules is useful for writers of any
age. (YA and Up)

865   .   Spunkwater, Spunkwater: A Life of Mark
Twain. Ill. with photographs. A Pantheon Portrait, 1968. An entertaining biography (1835-1910)
of the original Tom Sawyer, river pilot, miner,
newspaper man, and author. (YA)

866   .   Sunnyside: A Life of Washington Irving.
Ill. by Antony Saris. Pantheon, 1967. If one
thinks of Irving (1783-1859) mainly in relation to
Spain and his "Tales from the Alhambra" or his
folk tales, it is revealing to read here about his
adventures in our own wild west in the early 19th
century and his friendship with John Jacob Astor.
Irving was a man who never really settled down
though he did occasionally alight in his home,
"Sunnyside." (YA)

867   .   Trust Thyself: A Life of Ralph Waldo
Emerson for the Young Reader. Ill. by Douglas
Gorsline. A Pantheon Portrait, 1964. Any writer
or would-be writer of any age can take inspiration
and good sound advice from the staunch but gentle
individualist, R.W.E. (1803-82). (YA and Up)

JOURNALISTS

868 Allen, Edward. Informing a Nation; Horace Greeley.
Ill. by Robert Boehmer. Britannica Books, 1962.
The story of a poor boy who became a powerful
newspaper editor (The New York Tribune) in the
second half of the 19th century, and who ran for
President against U.S. Grant under the Liberal Republican banner (1811-72). (I and YA)

869 Archer, Jules. Fighting Journalist, Horace Greeley.
Jacket by Harry Bjorklund. Julian Messner, 1966.
An absorbing biography of the man who, starting as
a poverty-stricken youngster, rose to prominence
as a newspaper editor with a powerful influence on
the political events of his time, including the nomi-
nation and election of Abraham Lincoln. (YA)

870 Berry, Erick (Best). The Wavering Flame. Ill. by
the author. Charles Scribner's Sons, 1953. A
novel about the beginnings of the free press and a
young printer's difficulties in deciding where his

loyalty lay. (YA)

871 Dunnahoo, Terry. Nellie Bly: A Portrait. Jacket by
     Lois and Jim Axeman. Reilly and Lee, Regnery,
     1970. Her real name was Elizabeth Cochrane (1865-
     1922) but in the 1880s, young ladies were not often
     accepted in newspaper offices. Adopting the name
     of Nellie Bly and willingly accepting dangerous as-
     signments, she secured a job under the editorship
     of the New York World's Joseph Pulitzer. (1865-
     1922) (I and YA)

872 Faber, Doris. Horace Greeley, the People's Editor.
     Ill. by Paul Frame. Prentice-Hall, 1964. Biogra-
     phy (1811-73) of the great newspaper editor, often
     remembered for words he didn't say: "Go West,
     young man." He did say simply "go west," for he
     believed firmly in America's "manifest destiny."
     (I)

873 _____. Printer's Devil to Publisher: Adolph S.
     Ochs of the New York Times. Jacket by Everett
     Raymond Kinstler. Julian Messner, 1963. Bi-
     ography of a man with tremendous determination
     and courage, who never gave up his ideals of
     what a great newspaper should be. Born in Ten-
     nessee in 1858, he was always loyal to that state,
     especially to the city of Chattanooga where he owned
     his first newspaper and where, after receiving over-
     whelming honors, he died in 1935. (YA and Up)

874 Galt, Tom. Peter Zenger, Fighter for Freedom. Ill.
     by Ralph Ray Jr. Thomas Y. Crowell, 1951. In
     fictional form this is the story of a very early
     fighter for freedom of the press (1697-1746), with
     interesting details of his court trial. (I and YA)

875 Sagarin, Mary. John Brown Russwurm; The Story of
     Freedom's Journal, Freedom's Journey. Introduc-
     tion by Ernest Kaiser. Jacket by Thomas Upshur.
     Lothrop Lee and Shepard. Son of a black slave
     woman and white Jamaican planter, and educated at
     Bowdoin College in Maine, he was founder (with
     Samuel Cornish) of the first newspaper, owned,
     operated, published and edited by Black people. He
     became an advocate of colonization and emigrated
     to Africa where he became a Liberian leader. Be-
     cause of this he was always a controversial figure
     and rejected by many Blacks as well as Whites.
     (YA)

876 Wellman, Manley Wade. Frontier Reporter. Jacket
     by William Ferguson. Ives Washburn, 1969. A

good lively novel about rival newspapers in rival
towns in southwestern Kansas, and the adventures
and dangers experienced in 1889 by a young reporter
from the east. (I and YA)

877 Williamson, Joanne B. "And Forever Free." Alfred
A. Knopf, 1966. A novel about a German immigrant
whose father died in Germany because of his ex-
pressions of protest and who is saddened to find
ethnic groups in New York fighting against each
other, uniting only against the Negro. As a news-
paperman he is an endangered observer of the Battle of Gettysburg and afterward discovers what part
he can play in the preservation of freedom. (YA)

FOLKLORE AND GENERAL

878 Carlson, Natalie Savage. Sashes Red and Blue. Ill.
by Rita Fava. Harper and Bros., 1956. Tall
stories about a big family named LeBlanc (a name
like Smith in the U.S.). (E)

879 Meyer, Edith Patterson. The Friendly Frontier: The
Story of the Canadian-American Border. Ill. by
W. T. Mars. Little Brown, 1947. This well-put-
together and eminently readable book blends American and Canadian stories and biographies into a
continuous narrative about their common border
from 1497 to the present. (YA)

THE 17th CENTURY

880 Baker, Laura Nelson. O Children of the Wind and
Pines. Ill. by Inez Storer. J. B. Lippincott,
1967. A story of the first American Christmas
carol, written about 1641 by a Jesuit priest for the
Huron Indians, the words and music of the song at
the end of the small book. (All ages)

881 Berry, Erick (Best). Valiant Captive. Chilton, 1962.
A story based on fact, of a girl captured by the
Indians in 1676, from what later became Framing-
ham, Mass., during King Philip's War, and taken
as a prisoner to Quebec where she was ransomed
by the French. (YA)

882 Bull, Ethel C. Madeleine Takes Command. Ill. by
Bruce Adams. McGraw-Hill, 1946. The story behind the statue of Madeleine de la Vercheres which
stands above the St. Lawrence River near Montreal--
how at the age of 14 and with only two younger brothers (10 and 12) and a garrison of seven people,
she guarded her father's "seignory" against the Mohawks for a whole week. (YA)

883 Cather, Willa. Shadows on the Rock. Knopf, 1931.
A novel about an apothecary and his young mother-

less daughter in Quebec at the end of the 17th century, in the last years of the Comte de Frontenac.
It is also about the emergence of Canada as a country apart from its French parentage. (A)

884 Coatsworth, Elizabeth. Sword of the Wilderness. A
boy of the Maine fishing village of Pernaquoit is
captured by Abenaki Indians in 1689 and taken to
their village near Quebec. There he finds compara-
tive comfort but is never completely free of fear
for his own fate and that of another captive whom he
much admires for his courage. An interesting
"Author's Note" describes French-Indian-English relations on the border at the end of the 17th century.
(I and YA)

885 Heiderstadt, Dorothy. Marie Tanglehair. Ill. by
Ursula Koering. David McKay, 1965. How a young
Huron Indian girl has great difficulty in adapting to
Ursuline convent life in Quebec and finally runs
away to find her own village, and what it is that takes
her back to the convent. (I and YA)

886 Malkus, Alida. Outpost of Peril. Jacket and title
page by Neil O'Keefe. John Day, 1961. The story
of Canada's Joan of Arc, Madeleine de la Vercheres, who in 1692 defended her parents' fortress
against the Indians, with only a force of seven, for
a whole week until help arrived. The author's
note at the end tells of Madeleine's later exploits.
(YA)

887 Syme, Ronald. Frontenac of New France. Ill. by
William Stobbs. Morrow Junior Books, 1969. Story
of late 17th-century Canada under the governorship
of Louis Frontenac (1620-98) who was sent to Quebec by Louis XIV in 1672 to try to weld small settlements of French into a united colony able to de-
fend itself against hostile Indians and neighboring
British forces. (YA)

THE 18th CENTURY

888 Alderman, Clifford Lindsay. The Way of Eagles.
Doubleday, 1965. A novel about the American as-
sault on Quebec, led first by General Montgomery,
and later by Benedict Arnold, and the fictional adventures of a young colonial who tries to save the
day for the Americans. (YA)

889 Bowers, Gwendolyn. Journey for Jemima. Jacket by

Patricia Secord. Henry Z. Walck, 1960. A clever-
ly plotted romance, set in Maine and Quebec and
points in between, about a young lady stolen by Indians because of their belief in the magic of her red
hair and about a young painter who also admires her
red hair and goes on a long journey in search of
her. (I and YA)

890   Butler, Beverly. The Fur Lodge. Ill. by Herb Mott.
Dodd Mead, 1959. A strong novel about a 14-year-
old voyageur, pitted against starvation, loneliness,
wolves and ghosts on the treeless plains of Canada.
(I and YA)

891   Downie, Mary Alice and John. Honor Bound. Ill. by
by Joan Huffman. Henry Z. Walck, 1971. A loyalist family, the Averys, are forced to leave their
Philadelphia home after the American Revolution and
to travel stealthily to Cataraqui (now Kingston)
Canada without, however, their 17-year-old daughter,
Honor, who had been away on a visit and whose
whereabouts are uncertain. How they survive their
first rugged winter in the Canadian wilderness and
how the younger children attempt to find Honor, are
all told with humor and gusto. (I)

892   Dwight, Allan. Guns at Quebec. Macmillan, 1962.
A novel about the French and English conflict in
1759 and 1760--the battles between Montcalm and
Wolfe, other battles, and skirmishes with the Indians, with a mystery about a Massachusetts boy
captured by the Indians and sold to a merchant in
Quebec. (YA)

893   Hays, Wilma Pitchford. Drummer Boy for Montcalm.
Ill. by Alan Mayler. Macmillan, 1959. A novel
about the siege of Quebec and the battle on the
Plains of Abraham in which Wolfe and Montcalm
led the opposing armies, with a chronology of the
events of the summer of 1759 and a map of the
area. (I and YA)

894   Henty, G. A. With Wolfe in Canada. Ill. by Gordon
Browne. Chicago: Thompson and Thomas, n.d.
(Author's dates are 1893-1902). Grandparents of
today's young readers may remember with pleasure
some of Henty's historical novels, and this particular one is given simply as an example of 19th-cen-
tury historical fiction for the young. Good reading.
(YA)

895   Longfellow, Henry Wadsworth. Evangeline: A Tale of
Acadie, 1847. The British Expulsion of the

Acadians from Nova Scotia, edited by Mina Lewiton
and with an introduction by her. Ill. by Howard
Simon. Duell, Sloan and Pearce, 1966. The book
also contains a brief biography of Longfellow. (A)

896 Meader, Stephen W. River of the Wolves. Ill. by
Edward Shenton. Harcourt, Brace and World,
1948. A boy and girl, captured in Maine by the
Abenaki Indians, are taken to Canada where their
show of courage makes them accepted by their captors and where the boy, especially, becomes well
versed in Indian lore. However, in spite of good
treatment after a harrowing trek through the wilderness, they constantly plan and hope for escape. (I
and YA)

897 Roberts, Kenneth. Arundel. Doubleday, 1930. A novel
about Benedict Arnold's expedition against Quebec,
the first of a series, followed by "Rabble in Arms."
[see 237]. Arundel was the original name of Kenne-
bunk, Maine. (A)

898 Speare, Elizabeth George. Calico Captive. Ill. by
W. T. Mars. Houghton Mifflin, 1957. A love
story of 1754, in which a young girl, captured by
the Indians in Charlestown, New Hampshire, is
taken with her family to Montreal. She and her sister are sold into servitude to a French family.
The journey with the Indians is based on the sister's
diary. (YA)

899 Syme, Ronald. Alexander Mackenzie, Canadian Explorer. Ill. by William Stobbs. William Morrow,
1964. A biography of the Scotsman (1763-1820) who,
in 1788, took over the management of Fort Chipewi-
jan for the Northwest Fur Co. and finally discovered
the overland route to the Pacific which several others
had sought in vain, thus establishing a new westward
route for fur traders, first, and, later, settlers. (I)

900 _____. Vancouver, Explorer of the Pacific Coast.
Ill. by William Stobbs. William Morrow, 1970.
Biography of the man (1757-98) for whom the city
of Vancouver is named. He first went to sea, with
Captain Cook, at the age of 15, and his career end-
ed in 1795 after a voyage lasting four and a half
years in search of the legendary Northwest Passage.
His charts were used for 100 years after his death.
(I)

901 Tomkinson, Grace. Welcome Wilderness. Ives Washburn, 1946. A novel about the loyalists who, after
having been harrassed and burned out of the colonies

by the Sons of Liberty, fled to Nova Scotia. The
principal character is a young woman who goes as a
bride into the icy, foggy wilderness. (A)

902 Vance, Marguerite. Esther Wheelwright, Indian Captive. Ill. by Lorence F. Bjorklund. E. P. Dutton,
1964. A biographical story of a woman who was
stolen by Indians when she was only six years old
but rescued by a Catholic priest with the help of
the Governor of Quebec. She became an Ursuline
nun and finally, in 1760, the first English Ursuline
Mother Superior. (I)

THE 19th CENTURY

903 de la Roche, Mazo. The Building of Jalna. Little
Brown, 1944. For those who enjoy family sagas,
the Whiteoaks Chronicle will be richly rewarding,
there being 16 books about the Whiteoaks family
besides a play, "The Whiteoaks." In point of time
this is the first story of the family, the migration
to Canada in the mid 19th century, and the foundation of the homestead of Jalna. (A)

904 Eckert, Allan W. Incident at Hawk's Hill. Jacket by
John Schoenherr. Little, Brown, 1971. A deeply
moving story, based on an actual incident, of a
six-year-old boy--a boy not like other boys--and
his survival in the wilds of Manitoba under the care
and protection of a female badger. The most poignant aspect of the story is the differing attitudes of
the boys' parents toward his strange ability to com-
municate with animals and inability to do so with
humans. (YA and Up)

905 Harris, Christie. West With the White Chiefs. Woodcuts by Walter Ferro. Atheneum, 1965. A true
story, based on the journals of two Englishmen,
Viscount Milton and Dr. Cheadle, about their adventures as they traveled with an Assineboine
Indian family through western Canada and over the
Rockies to the Cariboo gold diggings. (I and YA)

906 Harrison, Thad. Westward to Adventure. Ill. by
Lawrence Hoffman. Criterion Books, 1960. An
exciting novel, based on the adventures of an actual
character whose descendents still live in Minnesota
(where he spent his later life). As a young Swedish
orphan he sailed to America but was accidentally
stranded ashore when the ship put into Hudson's Bay

for fresh food.   A long hard trek brought him to
an Ojibway couple who adopted him and taught him
their Indian ways.   (YA)
907   Howard, Elizabeth.   North Winds Blow Free.   William
Morrow, 1949.   A novel about the love affairs of a
young girl who, with her family, was moved by the
father to Canada in order to start a settlement for
escaped Negroes after the Fugitive Slave law was
adopted in the States.   (YA)
908   Vineberg, Ethel.   Grandmother Came from Dvoritz;
A Jewish Story.   Ill. by Rita Briansky.   Tundra
Books of Montreal, 1969.   This story goes back to
the author's grandmother's life in the Jewish "Pale"
of Russian Poland, during the second half of the
19th century and carries through her Mother's immi-
gration to the U.S. and final settlement in New
Brunswick.   (I and YA)

THE 20th CENTURY

909   Kumin, Maxine.   When Great Grandmother Was Young.
Ill. by Don Almquist.   G. P. Putnam's Sons, 1971.
A bright colorful period piece about the life of a
little girl on a small island off the coast of Nova
Scotia at the turn of the 20th century, with pictures
telling the story as clearly as the text.   (E)
910   Levine, I. E.   The Discoverer of Insulin; Dr. Frederick G. Banting.   Jacket by Frank Kramer.   Julian
Messner, 1959.   The biography of this great bene-
factor of mankind (1891-1941) includes material
about other eminent Canadian doctors and medical
progress in that country.   (YA and Up)
911   Noble, Iris.   Megan.   Julian Messner, 1965.   A love
story set in Alberta, Canada in the beginning of the
20th century when that part of the country was being
homesteaded by immigrants from many countries.
The 16-year-old heroine is a "hired girl, " an orphan
from Wales, and underlying her story is the theme
of the amalgamation of "foreigners" into "Canadians. "
(YA)
912   Pumphrey, George H.   Grenfell of Labrador.   Ill. with
photographs.   Dodd Mead, 1959.   The story of the
adventures and narrow escapes of Sir Wilfred Grenfell (1865-1940) in his medical mission to Labrador.
The book ends with his own words: "We are not
here to be safe.   We must have faith and take

risks... I would not have lost the opportunity of
going to Labrador for anything. " (I and YA)
913 Wees, Frances Shelley. <u>Mystery in Newfoundland.</u>
     Ill. by Douglas Bisset. Abelard-Schuman, 1965.
     This contemporary treasure hunt reveals a surpris-
     ing amount of information about Newfoundland history.
     Did you know, for instance, that the city of St.
     Johns on that island is the oldest city in North
     America? An excellent mystery plot to boot. (I
     and YA)

EDUCATION

914 Blackburn, Joyce. Martha Berry: Little Woman with
a Big Dream. Jacket by Robert Parker. J. B.
Lippincott, 1968. A biography (1866-1942) of the
remarkable woman who founded the Berry Schools,
in Georgia, in 1902, for underprivileged mountain
children. (YA)

915 Carruth, Ella Kaiser. She Wanted to Read: The Story
of Mary McLeod Bethune. Ill. by Herbert McClure.
Abingdon, 1966. A biography (1875-1955) of the
Negro educator, founder of Daytona Normal and Industrial Institute for Negro Girls in 1904 (now
Bethune-Cookman College) and its president for 38
years, but who started life as a cotton picker. (I)

916 Fleming, Alice. Alice Freeman Palmer, Pioneer
College President. Ill. by Donn Albright. Prentice-
Hall, 1970. So much accomplished in so short a
life (1855-1902): president of Wellesley College at
26, dean of women at the New University of Chicago
in 1892, promoter of many preparatory schools for
girls, and founder of the American Association of
University Women, besides holding many other important positions and being the devoted wife of George
Herbert Palmer, a famous Harvard professor. (YA)

917 Franchere, Ruth. Hannah Herself. Thomas Y. Crowell, 1964. A novel about a 16-year-old girl from
Connecticut, facing the challenge of the educational
needs in a frontier community in Illinois in the
1830s. (YA)

918 Graham, Shirley. Booker T. Washington. Jacket and
frontispiece by Donald W. Lambo. Julian Messner,
1955. A biographical novel about the famous Negro,
Booker Taliaferro Washington (1858-1915), born in
slavery, who became the friend of Presidents and
royalty, largely because of his development of Tuskegee Institute, the man who wrote these words: "No
race can prosper til it learns that there is as much
dignity in tilling a field as in writing a poem." (YA)

919 Howard, Elizabeth. The Courage of Bethea. Jacket
     by Ezra Jack Keats. William Morrow, 1959. A
     story of boarding school days in Oxford, Ohio, in
     1860, based on a real seminary, now Western
     College for Women. Not much plot, but a good
     picture of the education of young ladies in that time
     and place. (I)

920 _____. A Girl of the North Country. Jacket by
     Attilia Sinagra. William Morrow, 1957. A novel
     of a young lady school teacher in northern Michigan,
     on the coast of Lake Michigan across from Mackinac
     Island, in 1855. There is a mystery too: a strange
     light causes frequent shipwrecks and casts suspicion
     on the man she loves. (YA)

921 Patterson, Lillie G. Booker T. Washington, Leader
     of His People. Ill. by Anthony D'Adamo. Garrard,
     1962. A fine short biography (1858-1915), easy and
     interesting to read. (E)

922 Peare, Catherine Owens. Mary McLeod Bethune.
     Vanguard, 1951. A full-length, inspiring biography
     of a great woman (1875-1955), born of slave parents,
     whose accomplishments are too many to be included
     in these brief notes. Starting life as a cotton pick-
     er, she founded and became the head of a great
     Negro college and served the cause of Negro ad-
     vancement in many fields, held a government posi-
     tion in the administration of Franklin Roosevelt,
     and was a consultant at the United Nations San Fran-
     cisco Conference in 1945, among other notable
     achievements. (YA)

923 Wellman, Manley Wade. The Master of Scare Hollow.
     Jacket by William Ferguson. Ives Washburn, 1964.
     A novel, with a slight detective story line, about
     a young schoolmaster meeting the challenge of a
     one-room school in the North Carolina mountains
     in 1882--the feuding and the fighting and all. (I)

SOCIAL SERVICE

924 Bigland, Eileen. Helen Keller. Ill. by Lili Cassel
     Wronker. S. G. Phillips, 1967. A biography of
     a truly miraculous woman (1880-1968) and her de-
     velopment, from the age of 19 months when she
     lost her sight and hearing, through her growth into
     womanhood and world fame. Her service and in-
     spiration to others seemed to fit her into the

category of "social service" as well as any. (YA)

925 Block, Irvin. Neighbor to the World: The Story of
Lillian Wald. Ill. with photographs. Thomas Y.
Crowell, 1969. A biography (1867-1938) of a
trained nurse and social settlement pioneer, a
fighter against war, child labor, sweat shops, and
ill treatment of immigrants, and friend of presidents
and prime ministers, she was always concerned with
her "neighbors" as individuals. This daughter of
Jewish parents was, like Jane Addams, "all religions."
(I and YA)

926 Brown, Marion Marsh. The Silent Storm. Ill. by
Fritz Kredel. Abingdon, 1963. A biographical novel
about Helen Keller's "Teacher," a fiery, but in-
finitely patient Irish girl of 20 when she started
work with Helen and with bad eyes herself. The
story ends with Helen's graduation from Radcliffe in
1904 and Annie Sullivan's marriage to John Macy.
(YA)

927 Dunnahoo, Terry. Annie Sullivan: A Portrait. Jacket
by Lois and Jim Axeman. Reilly and Lee, n.d.
A story of the woman (1866-1936) chiefly remembered
for her miracle working with Helen Keller but who
should also be recognized for the overcoming of her
own handicaps--an incredibly cruel and deprived childhood, partial blindness, and an Irish temper. (I and
YA)

928 Gilbert, Miriam. Jane Addams, World Neighbor. Ill.
by Corinne Boyd Dillon. Abingdon, 1960. The
story of the founder (1860-1935) of Hull House, the
first social settlement house in Chicago, who was
active in many civic enterprises and winner of the
Nobel Peace Prize in 1931. (I)

929 Graff, Stewart and Polly Anne. Helen Keller. Ill.
by Paul Frame. Garrard, 1965. A Discovery
Book. A short story of Helen's life and the important part in it played by her "Teacher," Annie
Sullivan. (E)

930 Hickok, Lorena A. The Story of Helen Keller. Ill.
by Jo Polseno. Grosset and Dunlap, 1971. The
story of the miracle wrought by two great women,
Helen and her teacher; just how Annie Sullivan
taught her and how Helen, blind, deaf, and dumb,
learned the lessons. The "manual alphabet" is
given at the end. (I)

931 Judson, Clara Ingram. City Neighbor: The Story of
Jane Addams. Ill. by Ralph Ray. Charles Scribner's Sons, 1951. A biography (1860-1935) by one

who knew Jane Addams personally, and the story of
Hull House, one of America's first settlements,
with a partial list of internationally famous people
who have been residents of Hull House, and a list of
honors and awards given to Miss Addams.   (I)

932 Lavine, Sigmund A. Evangeline Booth, Daughter of
Salvation. Jacket by Thomas Upshur. Ill. with
photographs. Dodd Mead, 1970. A biography (1865-
1950) of the remarkable daughter of the founder, in
England, of the Salvation Army, who became Commander in America until the death of her brother (the
second S.A. general) when she became General Booth
herself at the age of 69.   (YA)

933 Marshall, Catherine. Christy. McGraw-Hill, 1967.
A novel about the struggle of a 19-year-old girl
missionary to understand and help the Scotch-Irish
mountain people in Tennessee, in 1912. Full of
mountain lore and speech.   (A)

934 Meigs, Cornelia. Jane Addams, Pioneer for Social
Justice. Ill. with photographs. Jacket by Sarah El
Bindari. Little Brown, 1970. A full-length biography of the great woman (1860-1935), a character
study, and a record of an era.   (YA and Up)

935 Pace, Mildred Mastin. Juliette Low. Ill. by Jane
Castle. Charles Scribner's Sons, 1947. A biography
(1860-1927) of the founder of the Girl Scouts, in
Savannah, Georgia, in 1912.   (I)

936 Peterson, Helen Stone. Jane Addams, Pioneer of Hull
House. Ill. by Hobe Hays. Garrard, 1965. A
Discovery Book. A good lively biography, (1860-
1935).   (E)

937 Radford, Ruby. Juliette Low, Girl Scout Founder. Ill.
by Vic Dowd. Garrard, 1965. A biography,
especially for Brownies.   (E)

938 Tibble, J. W. and Anne. Helen Keller. Ill. by Harper
Johnson. G. P. Putnam's, 1958. The always thrilling story of how, in conjunction with her remarkable
teacher, Annie Sullivan, a deaf, dumb, and blind
baby became a world-famous woman and an inspiration
to the sighted as well as the blind and deaf.   (I and
YA)

939 Wagoner, Jean Brown. Jane Addams, Little Lame Girl.
Ill. by Gray Morrow. Bobbs-Merrill, 1944-62.
Childhood of Famous Americans Series. The story
of the young Jane Addams who grew up to be the
founder of Hull House in Chicago, and a Nobel Peace
Prize winner.   (E and I)

940 Ziegler, Elsie Reif. Light a Little Lamp. Jacket by
     Neil O'Keefe. John Day, 1961. A novel in "the
     Daughters of Valor" series about Mary McDowell
     and the Great Chicago Fire in 1871, with a brief
     factual biography at the end. (I)

FOLKLORE

941 Aliki [pseud. for Aliki Brandenberg]. The Story of
    Johnny Appleseed. Ill. by the author. Prentice-
    Hall, 1963. The legend of a real man, John
    Chapman, 1774-1845. (Picture Book)

942 Ayers, Rebecca Caudill and James. Contrary Jenkins.
    Ill. by Glen Rounds. Holt, Rinehart and Winston,
    1969. A tall tale, based on a real character, about
    a mountain man who "lived by the rule of contrary"
    and who may still be living thus, for all we know.
    (E)

943 Bowman, Dr. James Cloyd. Pecos Bill, The Greatest
    Cowboy. Ill. by Laura Bannon. Albert Whitman,
    1937. Stories of the legendary hero of the cattle
    country. (I and YA)

944 Carmer, Carl. The Hurricane's Children. Ill. by
    Elizabeth Black Carmer. David McKay, 1937 and
    1965. Rather than fairy stories, "giant stories"
    seem to be the favorites of Americans, and here
    is a collection of mighty yarns about larger-than-
    life characters: Mike Fink, Davy Crockett, Tony
    Beaver, and more and more. Each section is in-
    troduced by a "speech" as colorful as the stories
    that follow. (E and I)

945 _____, (with Elizabeth Carmer). Pecos Bill and the
    Long Lasso. Ill. by Mimi Korach. Garrard, 1968.
    Tall tales of the fabulous Texas cowboy. (E)

946 Classic Press. Paul Bunyan. Ill. by William Demp-
    ster, cover by Don Irwin. Children's Press, 1968.
    This Paul Bunyan-sized book with its Bunyan
    "geography" and its afterword, "The Lure of Folk-
    lore," its marginal notes and illustrations, is every-
    thing one could ask for on the subject. (I)

947 Coatsworth, Elizabeth. Daniel Webster's Horses. Ill.
    by Cary. Garrard, 1971. A folk-ghost story about a
    boy who loved animals and worked on Daniel Web-
    sters farm because Daniel too loved animals and
    had his favorite horses buried standing upright,
    newly shod and harnessed. (E and I)

948 Courlander, Harold. Terrapin's Pot of Sense. Ill.

by Elton Fox. Henry Holt, 1957. A collection of
Negro folk tales told in the manner of a Negro
storyteller. (I)

949 deLeeuw, Adele. John Henry, Steel-Drivin' Man. Ill.
by Gordon Laite. Garrard, 1966. Tales of the
great tunnel and railroad builder who could do anything he put his mind to. (E)

950 _____. Paul Bunyan and His Blue Ox. Ill. by Ted
Schroeder. Garrard, 1968. The fantastic story of
the legendary lumberman and his gigantic ox. (E)

951 _____. Paul Bunyan Finds a Wife. Ill. by Ted
Schroeder. Garrard, 1969. And a fabulous wife
she was who made stacks of pancakes as high as a
pine tree. (E)

952 Felton, Harold W. John Henry and His Hammer.
Ill. by Alden A. Watson. Alfred A. Knopf, 1950.
Based on a ballad about the power of man in com-
petition with steam. (E and I)

953 _____. Legends of Paul Bunyan. Ill. by Richard
Bennett. Alfred A. Knopf, 1961. With a foreword
by James Stevens in which he makes a guess that
the Irish and French lumberjacks of the Great Lakes
area started the Paul Bunyan cycle and it just grew
and grew as people of all sorts and places added
figments of their imaginations and humor. A great
collection. (I)

954 _____. New Tall Tales of Pecos Bill. Ill. by
William Moyers. Prentice-Hall, 1958. A new col-
lection of stories about the mighty hero of the Old
West and his friends of the Hell's Gate Gulch
Ranch. (I)

955 _____. True Tall Tales of Stormalong, Sailor of
the Seas. Ill. by Joan Sandin. Prentice-Hall,
1968. The format of this book will appeal to very
young readers and those not yet ready to read to
themselves. (E and I)

956 Harris, Joel Chandler. The Favorite Uncle Remus,
selected and arranged and edited by George Van
Santvoord and Archibald C. Coolidge. Ill. with
the original illustrations of A. B. Frost. Houghton
Mifflin, 1948. A collection of stories from various
Uncle Remus books as written by Joel Chandler
Harris in the dialect of the cotton plantations of
middle Georgia. (I)

957 Hunt, Irene. Trail of Apple Blossoms. Ill. by Don
Bolognese. Follett, 1968.
A delicate poetic version of the Johnny Appleseed

legend. (I)

958 Hunt, Mabel Leigh. Better Known as Johnny Appleseed. Ill. by James Daugherty. J. B. Lippincott,
1950. A book of stories and legends told by and
about John Chapman, a sort of American St. Francis, in the poetic language of backwoods Ohio and
Indiana. (All ages)

959 Irving, Washington. The Bold Dragoon and Other
Ghostly Tales. Selected and edited by Anne Carroll
Moore. Ill. by James Daugherty. Alfred A. Knopf,
1930 and 1966. The book includes, besides the
title story, "The Devil and Tom Walker," "Wolfert
Webber or Golden Dreams," "Guests From Gibbet
Island," and "Dolph Heyliger." (I and Up.)

960 _____. The Legend of Sleepy Hollow and Rip Van
Winkle (1819). Ill. by Leonard Everett Fisher.
Large Type edition; a Keith Jennison Book.
Franklin Watts, 1967. A double entry, complete
and unabridged. (I)

961 Justus, May. It Happened in No-End Hollow. Ill. by
Mimi Korach. Garrard, 1968. Three jolly folk
stories of the mountain people retold--good to listen
to for those who can't read them to themselves.
(E)

961a Lester, Julius. The Knee-High Man and Other Tales.
Ill. by Ralph Pinto. Dial, 1972. Some of these
animal stories, originally told by slaves, have a
deeper meaning--the relations between slaves and
their owners. (E and I)

962 LeSueur, Meridel. Little Brother of the Wilderness:
The Story of Johnny Appleseed. Ill. by Betty Alden.
Alfred A. Knopf, 1947. John Chapman was a real
person (1774-1845) who became a legend. (E)

963 Malcolmson, Anne. Yankee Doodle's Cousins. Ill. by
Robert McCloskey. Houghton Mifflin, 1941. This
fine volume of American folklore is usefully arranged by regions: East, South, Mississippi Valley,
and West. (I)

964 _____, and McCormick, Dell J. Mister Stormalong.
Ill. by Joshua Tolford. Houghton Mifflin, 1952.
Stormy is the creation of the great days of American
seafaring in all waters and periods, and Anne Malcolmson points out some parallels in the Bible and
the Odyssey of Homer. (I)

965 Raskin, Joseph and Edith. Tales Our Settlers Told.
Ill. by William Sauts Bock. Lothrop Lee and
Shepard, 1971. A baker's dozen of tales and legends

from Colonial days in New England, taken from
old documents, diaries and old collections. (I)

966 Rees, Eunis. The Song of Paul Bunyan and Tony
Beaver. Ill. by Robert Osborn. Pantheon, 1964.
A collection of the best Paul Bunyan stories in un-
rhymed verse, along with some of his southern
counterparts who had a camp in West Virginia. (I)

967 Richter, Conrad. Over the Blue Mountain. Ill. by
Herbert Danska. Alfred A. Knopf, 1967. A
combination of old Pennsylvania Dutch reality and
legend in the humorous vernacular. (I)

968 Shapiro, Irwin. Tall Tales of America. Ill. by Al
Schmidt. Simon and Schuster, 1958. A collection
of stories about Pecos Bill, Anthony and the Moss-
bunker, Old Stormalong, Johnny Appleseed, Davy
Crockett, Sun Patch, Paul Bunyan, John Henry,
and Joe Magarac the Steel Man. (I)

969 Steele, William O. Daniel Boone's Echo. Ill. by
Nicolas. Harcourt, Brace and World, 1957. A
Davy Crockett-Paul Bunyan type of story to make a
body laugh out loud, and, at the same time, learn
the lesson that Aaron learned that "a body can't be
scared of something til he knows what it is." (E)

970 Turkle, Brinton. The Fiddler of High Lonesome. Ill.
by the author. Viking, 1968. A mountain folk story
picture book. (All Ages)

971 Wadsworth, Wallace. Paul Bunyan and His Great
Blue Ox. Ill. by Enrico Arno. Doubleday, 1926 and
1964. Many of the legends. (I)

INDIANS--THE NATIVE AMERICANS

Legends, Myths, Folklore and Pre-history

972 Bell, Corydon. John Battling-Gourd of Big Cove:
A Collection of Cherokee Legends. Ill. by the author. Macmillan, 1955. Stories as told to contemporary children in the North Carolina mountains
by an old man who remembers them from his boyhood. (I)

973 Buff, Mary and Conrad. Hah-Nee. Ill. by Conrad
Buff. Houghton Mifflin, 1956. A beautifully illustrated book about the cliff-dwelling Indians during
the Great Drought of 1276 and after. (I)

974 _____. Kemi. Ill. by the authors. Ward Ritchie
Press, 1966. A story of a boy of the Indian stone
age, hundreds of years before Columbus discovered
America. (I)

975 Christensen, Gardell Dano. Buffalo Kill. Ill. by the
author. Thomas Nelson, 1959. Vividly imaginative
drawings make this recreation of prehistorical
Indians as exciting as tales of later days--about a
12-year-old's initiation into manhood. (E and I)

976 Coatsworth, Elizabeth. Indian Encounters. Ill. by
Frederick T. Chapman. Macmillan, 1960. An
anthology of stories and poems about the American
Indian. (I and YA)

977 de Angelo, Jaime. Indian Tales. Ill. by the author.
Foreword by Carl Carmer. A. A. Wyn, 1953.
Mr. de Angelo, an anthropologist, lived for 40
years among the Pit River Indians of California and
has woven the tales and legends he learned from
them into a long, poetic narrative about animal-
humans, a story full of magic and humor and descriptions of the western landscape as it was before cor-
rupted by the white man. (All Ages)

977a Houston, James. Ghost Paddle, A Northwest Coast
Indian Tale. Ill. by the author. Harcourt, Brace
Jovanovich, 1972. A story inspired by the legendary
Indian carvers on the Northwest Coast of Canada.
(I)

978 May, Julian. Before the Indians Came. Ill. by
     Symeon Shimin. Holiday House, 1969. A book
     about how archaeologists work and what has been
     discovered so far about the dim distant past and
     the people from whom the Indians descended.

979 Penny, Grace Jackson. Tales of the Cheyennes. Ill.
     by Walter Richard West. Houghton Mifflin, 1953.
     These legends were kept alive, long before the
     coming of the white man, by honored story-tellers
     who, in the evenings, with solemn ceremony, tied
     one story onto another until, as the camp fire
     burned low, he would say, "this cuts it off." Here
     is the Cheyenne story of creation and also some
     tales told simply for entertainment. (I)

980 Rushmore, Helen, with Wolf Robe Hunt. The Dancing
     Horses of Acoma and Other Acoma Indian Stories.
     Ill. by Wolf Robe Hunt. World, 1963. In the famed
     "Sky City" of the Acoma Indians in New Mexico,
     these stories are still told and here recorded for
     the first time by Helen Rushmore as they were told
     to her by the artist Wolf Robe Hunt, a chief who
     was born on the Acoma Reservation. (I)

981 Scheer, George F. Cherokee Animal Tales. Ill. by
     Robert Frankenberg. Holiday House, 1968. The
     introduction, by the editor, Mr. Scheer, gives a
     history of the Cherokee tribes, with the tragic
     story of the Trail of Tears. The tales themselves
     show the basis of many Uncle Remus stories. (I)

THE 16th and 17th CENTURIES

982 Agle, Nan Hayden. Makon and the Dauphin. Ill. by
     Robert Frankenberg. Charles Scribner's Sons,
     1961. Based on a true incident of the early 16th
     century, this is the story "as it might have been"
     of a little Indian boy, captured by an Italian sailing
     a French ship, and taken to France where he be-
     came companion to the King's son. (I)

983 Alderman, Clifford Lindsey. The Vengeance of Abel
     Wright. Jacket by Richard Powers. Doubleday,
     1964. A novel of King Philip's War (1675-76) in
     which two boys, 14 and 15, are captured and re-
     captured by Indians. Abel Wright blames King
     Philip for the massacre in which his father was
     killed, but his desire for vengeance weakens after
     he comes to know Philip's wife and young son. (I
     and YA)

984 Anderson, A. M. Squanto and the Pilgrims. Ill. by
     John Osebold. Harper and Row, 1949 and 1962.
     The adventurous life of the Pilgrims' good friend,
     with a pronunciation list. (E)
985 Averill, Esther. King Philip and the Indian Chief.
     Ill. by Vera Belsky. Harper and Bros., 1950.
     The story of Massasoit's son who invited many
     Indian tribes to unite against the white man in "King
     Philip's War" (in 1675) a war probably brought on
     by the injustice of the Plymouth settlers who came
     later than the early friends of Massasoit. The il-
     lustrations are especially helpful for an understand-
     ing of the area in which the war took place. There
     is also a glossary of Indian names. (I and YA)
986 Balch, Glenn. Horse of Two Colors. Ill. by Lorence
     Bjorklund. Thomas Y. Crowell, 1969. In a sus-
     penseful, informative, and action-packed novel,
     Mr. Balch has developed a theory of how the
     Appaloosa breed of horses might have had its
     origin with the Nez Percé Indians of the southwest
     at the end of the 17th century. The story begins
     with the vision of an Indian boy, escaping from en-
     slavement by the Spanish, with a silvery-white stal-
     lion and a red mare. (I and YA)
987 Bulla, Clyde Robert. Pocahontas and the Strangers.
     Ill. by Peter Burchard. Thomas Y. Crowell,
     1971. This story of the Indian princess is derived
     from new facts brought to light by the author's re-
     search, and told with new insight into Pocahontas'
     inner conflicts caused by her devotion to Captain
     John Smith and her marriage to John Rolfe. (I)
988 _____ Squanto, Friend of the White Men. Ill. by
     Peter Burchard. Thomas Y. Crowell, 1954. An
     amazing story of an Indian Patuxet boy who was
     taken to England in the early 1600s, then, on his
     return to America, captured by a sea captain who
     tried to sell him into slavery. For what happened
     next, read and see. (E)
989 d'Aulaire, Ingri and Edgar Parin. Pocahontas. Ill. by
     the authors. Doubleday, 1946. A picture book bi-
     ography. (E)
990 Faber, Doris. The Life of Pocahontas. Ill. by Elinor
     Jaeger. Prentice-Hall, 1963. A good short biogra-
     phy of the Indian princess (1595-1627) who saved
     the life of Captain John Smith, married John Rolfe
     and died on her way home from England. (E and I)
991 Faulkner, Nancy. Tomahawk Shadow. Doubleday,

1959. A story of an escaped apprentice from Plymouth, his refuge in the Providence colony, and how King Philip's War affected his life. Roger Williams enters the story. (YA)

992   Hall-Quest, Olga. Flames Over New England: The Story of King Philip's War--1675-76). Ill. by Christine Price. E. P. Dutton, 1967. A vivid, readable story of the final defeat of Philip and the Wampanoag tribe with a map of New England at that period. (YA)

993   _____. Powhatan and Captain John Smith. Ill. by Douglas Gorsline. Farrar, Straus and Cudahy, 1957. Stories about the Chief (ca. 1550-1618), his daughter Pocahontas (ca. 1595-1617), later Lady Rebecca Rolfe, Captain Smith, and the settlement of Jamestown. (I and YA)

994   Longfellow, Henry Wadsworth. The Story of Hiawatha, adapted by Allen Chaffee. Ill. by Armstrong Sperry. Random House, 1951. With an introduction and editing by Mina Lewiton. A good edition for very young readers. (E)

995   Malkus, Alida Sims. There Really Was a Hiawatha. Ill. by Jon Nielson. Grosset and Dunlap, 1963. A recreation of the man behind the myth, an Iroquois of the Onondago nation who united five Indian nations (later six) into a "League for Peace." The Iroquois League of the Five Nations, in the Finger Lakes Region of New York State. (YA)

996   Martin, Patricia Miles. Pocahontas. Ill. by Portia Takakjian. G. P. Putnam's Sons, 1964. A Beginning to Read Biography. (E)

996a   Molloy, Anne. Five Kidnapped Indians. Ill. by Robin Jacques. Hastings House, 1968. A fictionalized account of the 1605 kidnapping of five Indians (including Squanto) by a Captain George Waymouth of England. (YA)

997   Richter, Conrad. The Light in the Forest. Ill. by Warren Chappell. Alfred A. Knopf, 1953 and 1966. A strong, tragic novel of a white boy, stolen and adopted at the age of four, by a Tuscarora Indian who was forced to relinquish him to his white parents when he was about 15, along with other white prisoners. The central theme of the story is freedom, showing the Indians to have possessed more than the whites. (YA)

998   Stephens, Peter John. Towappu, Puritan Renegade. Ill. by William Moyers. Atheneum, 1966. A

story of the moral and physical courage of a boy who
tried to prevent King Philip's War, and the subsequent
disaster, told from the Indian viewpoint. (YA)
999 Stiles, Martha Bennett. One Among the Indians. Jacket
by Donald Bolognese. Dial Press, 1962. A cross
between fiction and biography, this is a novel, based
on extensive research, about actual characters--Tom
Savage, the principal one, Powhatan, Pocahontas,
Captain John Smith and others lesser known. Tom
Savage, arriving at Jamestown in 1608, as a cabin
boy on the John and Francis, is exchanged to Powhatan as a hostage, for Powhatan's son, Nantauquas
thereby becoming "one among the Indians." (YA)
1000 Ziner, Feenie. Dark Pilgrim: The Story of Squanto.
Jacket by George L. Connelly. Chilton Books,
1965. A biography (15?-1622), for older readers,
of the friend of the Pilgrims who had been twice
captured by the English (and once sold into slavery),
valuable because of its notes and bibliography. It is also exceptionally interesting in showing
the early settlements of New England from the
Indian as well as the English viewpoint. (YA)

THE 18th CENTURY

1001 Allen, Leroy. Shawnee Lance. Delacorte, 1970. Captured by a Shawnee chief who adopts him as a son,
Daniel, aged 14, is made to run the gauntlet and
otherwise prove his strength in fights with a young
brave who is out to get his scalp. He has other bitter enemies among the Shawnees before he helps
them in their warfare against the Miamis, yet, when
his chance comes to escape, he has to make a difficult decision. (I and YA)
1002 Allen, Merritt. Parmelee. Red Heritage. Ill. by Ralph
Ray. David McKay, 1946. A 17-year-old joins
General Herkimer in the battle of Oriskany, is captured and imprisoned by Joseph Brant, Chief of the
Mohawks, and finally makes his escape as a tough,
self-reliant young man. (YA)
1003 Alter, Robert Edmond. Time of the Tomahawks. Ill.
by Dirk Gringhuis. G. P. Putnam's Sons, 1964.
A novel, constructed on the facts of Pontiac's rebellion, 1862-66, in which, by trickery, he conquered
many English forts. However, he failed to defeat
the besieged Fort Pitt, at the confluence of the

Allegheny and Monongahela Rivers, when an English
captive and his adopted Abenaki father come to the
rescue of the besieged. (YA)

1004 Arnold, Elliott. White Falcon. Ill. by Frederick T.
Chapman. Alfred A. Knopf, 1955. John Tanner
was stolen from his Kentucky home as a small boy,
in the late 1770s. Later, with his foster Indian
mother, he was taken on the long journey to her native
Chippewa tribal home on what is now the Minnesota-
Canadian border. With the Chippewas he fought
against the Sioux, and still later became involved in
the struggle between the Northwest Company and the
Hudson Bay Company for the fur trade. More Indian
than White in training and disposition, he was influential in the settlement of the Scotch in the Red River
Valley. (YA)

1005 Brick, John. Captives of the Senecas. Duell, Sloan
and Pearce, 1964. Two young Continental Army
soldiers go AWOL to hunt deer and are captured
by the Senecas. (I)

1006 Carper, Jean and Grace Leslie Dickerson. Little
Turtle. Ill. by Grace Leslie Dickerson. Albert
Whitman, 1959. The true story of an Indian chief
who twice outsmarted the white man, but who, as
head of a large Indian confederation, was finally
defeated by "Mad" Anthony Wayne. (I)

1007 Colver, Anne. Bread-and-Butter Indian. Ill. by
Garth Williams. Holt, Rinehart and Winston,
1964. A story of a little Pennsylvania frontier
girl kidnapped by Indians, based on Barbara Graff's
own account of adventures and rescue. (I)

1008 Cooper, James Fennimore. The Last of the Mohicans:
A Narrative of 1757. With an introduction by May
Lambertson Becker. Ill. by James Daugherty.
World Rainbow Classics, 1957. The second of the
Leather-Stocking Tales, about the French and
Indian War and the efforts of two young ladies to
join their father, the British Commander at Fort
William Henry near Lake Champlain--efforts
blocked by the Huron Indians. Attacks, captures,
flights and rescues! (A)

1009 DeLeeuw, Cateau. One Week of Danger. Ill. by
Kurt Werth. Thomas Nelson, 1959. A thriller of
a story about two boys captured by Shawnees, in
Ohio, from whom they escape only to fall into the
grasp of two white renegades. (I)

1010 Doughty, Wayne Dyre. Crimson Moccasins. Jacket

by Merle Shore. Harper and Row, 1966. The sad
story of a young man who cannot decide whether he
is Indian or white and finally leaves the Miami nation to go to Jennison Station in Kentucky Territory. In an expedition with George Rogers Clark
against forts held by the British, he finds himself
opposing his former Miami father, and seeks within his own heart to bridge the river between Indians and whites. (YA)

1011 Edmonds, Walter D. In the Hands of the Senecas.
Jacket by Alan Tompkins. Little Brown, 1937.
The separate stories of several white people captured by the Indians after their town had been
burned, during the Revolutionary period, showing
the cruel side of some New York State Indians.
(A)

1012 Goodnough, David. The Cherry Valley Massacre,
November 11, 1778. Ill. with photographs and
contemporary prints. Franklin Watts, 1968. A
Focus Book. Because of the attention attracted by
this Iroquois massacre of 32 whites, mostly
women and children, there grew up in New York
State and elsewhere, ever increasing enmity toward the Indians. This relatively small, though
terrible event, kindled fierce racial conflict.
Among important characters involved in this episode of the Revolution were the Mohawk chief,
Joseph Brant, commander of a force of old
Tories and Iroquois, and Sir William Johnson,
who negotiated the Treaty of Fort Stanwix, opening
up the Northeast for settlement. (YA)

1013 Hays, Wilma Pitchford. Pontiac, Lion in the Forest.
Ill. by Lorence Bjorklund. Houghton Mifflin, 1965.
The story of the great Ottawa chief (1721-69) who
united many Indian tribes of the Middlewest in
support of the French and who planned a conspiracy against the English after their conquest of Fort
Detroit and then managed a year-long siege of
that fort. "Historical Note" included. (I)

1014 Jakes, John. Mohawk: The Life of Joseph Brant.
Ill. by Roger Hane. Crowell-Collier, 1969. A
biography of an educated Christian Indian (1742-1807)
who twice went to England, first to try to persuade
King George to let the Five Tribes fight with the
British against the Colonists, and later to obtain
land for his people. He also tried to teach the
Indians mercy toward captives. A story too of

the Revolutionary warfare in the Mohawk Valley
and of the Cherry Valley massacre. Mostly it is
the story of the conflict within Brant himself between his Indian heritage and his loyalty to Sir
William Johnson who had brought him up as a son.
(YA)

1015 Lenski, Lois. Indian Captive: The Story of Mary
      Jemison. Ill. by the author. J. B. Lippincott,
      1941. The story of a little girl captured by the
      Senecas who, after several attempts to escape,
      decided to stay with the Indians and did until her
      death in 1833, when she was 90 years old, "the
      White Woman of the Genesee." It is based on her
      memories as told, when she was 80, to James
      Everett Seaver, M.D. A detailed picture in text
      and illustrations of Seneca Indian life between 1758
      and 1760. (I)

1016 Richmond, Robert P. The Day the Indians Came. Ill.
      by Anita Bernarde. Van Nostrand, 1966. A story
      based on fact about a boy, Eben, who with his
      father defended their homestead against a large
      force of Indians. (I and YA)

1017 Steele, William O. Flaming Arrows. Ill. by Paul
      Galdone. Harcourt, Brace and World, 1957. A
      story of split-second action in defense of a small
      fort in Tennessee by nine men, a dozen boys with
      guns, and some women and children, against 50 or
      more Chickamauga Indians, with the underlying
      theme of the pioneers' (and our) need to face prob-
      lems together and trust each other. (I)

1018 _____. Tomahawks and Trouble. Ill. by Paul
      Galdone. Harcourt, Brace and Co., 1955. A
      story of the almost superhuman courage and endur-
      ance of three children captured by Shawnee Indians
      on the Wilderness Trail, told with this author's
      customary humor and zest. (I and YA)

1019 _____. Wayah of the Real People. Ill. by Isa
      Barnett. Holt, Rinehart and Winston, 1964. An
      unusual story of a Chota Cherokee boy sent to
      learn the ways of the white man at William and
      Mary College in Williamsburg, Virginia, in 1752.
      His difficulties in adjusting to the white man's
      world, make understandable, to a large degree,
      why Indians have chosen to remain in their own.
      (YA)

1020 Tomerlin, John. Prisoner of the Iroquois. Jacket by
      Douglas Gorsline, frontispiece map by Lili Cassell
      Wronker. E. P. Dutton, 1965. At the beginning

of the War for Independence, the Indians of the
Five Nations were mostly on the side of the
British, but the 15-year-old hero of this exciting
story has an Oneida friend who, with his tribe, is
friendly to the Colonists. However, it is an
Onandagua leader who captures him and an Onandagua boy who aids his escape. (I)

1021 Underhill, Ruth. Beaverbird. Ill. by Robert Garland.
Coward McCann, 1959. A Kalapuya Indian, of a
great hunting tribe in the forests of Oregon, is
captured by Indian pirates and traded to a west
coast tribe with a completely different culture from
that in which he had been raised. These "water
people" lived on the ocean front and did little hunting, living on fish, berries, roots, ferns, etc.
Kept there as a slave, he is befriended by the
chief's daughter and promises her he will not try
to escape until after the fall potlatch. (I and YA)

THE 19th CENTURY--General

1022 Brown, Dee. Bury My Heart at Wounded Knee; An
Indian History of the American West. Ill. with
photographs. Jacket by Winston Potter. Holt,
Rinehart and Winston, 1971. A skillfully constructed narrative history of the West, between
1860 and 1890, from the Indian point of view as
nearly as such viewpoint could be obtained. Each
chapter is introduced by a chronology of the
events of the specific year and statements of an
Indian chief of the period. (A)

1023 Meyer, John W. Famous Indian Chiefs. Ill. by
James D. Vlasaty. M. A. Donahue, 1957. The
chiefs whose brief biographies are included in
this handsome book are: Red Jacket (Seneca),
Black Hawk (Sauk and Fox), Tecumseh (Shawnee),
Yaholo-Micco (Creek), Osceola (Seminole), Red
Cloud (Sioux), Dull Knife (Cheyenne), Sitting Bull
(Sioux), Geronimo (Apache), Chief Joseph (Nez
Percé), and Quanah Parker (Comanche). (I)

THE 19th CENTURY--First Half

1024 Arnold, Elliott. Broken Arrow. Ill. by Frank
Nicholas. Duell, Sloane and Pearce, 1947. A

young reader's edition of "Blood Brother" by the
same author, about the last of the great Indian
wars. Main characters are Cochise, the Apache
chief, and Tom Jeffors, the American scout.
Among others, Geronimo. (YA)

1025 Baker, Betty. And One Was a Wooden Indian.
Jacket by Emmanuel Shongut. Macmillan, 1970.
A story about the confusion caused when two young
Apaches are brought into sudden contact with
"White-eyes" (U.S. soldiers), Mexicans and Indians
of other tribes, Papagos and Yumas. 1850s. (YA)

1026 _____. Killer-of-Death. Ill. by John Kaufmann.
Harper and Row, 1963. A novel about the Apache
wars and the enmity between Mexicanos and a tribe
of Apaches, some of whom still live in the White
Mountains of Arizona. (YA)

1027 Beals, Frank L. Chief Black Hawk. Ill. by Jack
Merryweather. Harper and Row, 1943-60-61. The
adventures of the great Sauk chief (1767-1838), culminating in his surrender after the Black Hawk War
of 1830. (I)

1028 Blassingame, Wyatt. Osceola, Seminole War Chief.
Ill. by Al Fiorentino. Garrard, 1967. The story
of Osceola's leadership of the Seminole wars in
the 1830s, which finally ended without complete
surrender by the Indians. (E)

1029 _____. Sacajawea, Indian Guide. Ill. by Edward
Shenton. Garrard, 1965. The story of the Shoshone
Indian girl, stolen from her tribe when about 12
years old, sold to a French trapper, and taken
as a guide by Lewis and Clark on their expedition
of 1803-6. (I)

1030 Burt, Olive. The Cave of Shouting Silence. Ill. by
a map of Zion National Park and a photograph.
John Day, 1960. A novel set in what is now the
park, about a young Mormon in 1855 searching
for proof that his grandfather had found a salt
cave there. His friendship with a young Paiute
Indian boy and his growing understanding of Indian
traditions and rights provide a moral problem for
Caleb Wilson which adds to the suspense of the
story. An "Author's Note" gives the authentic
historical background. (I and YA)

1031 Capron, Louis. White Moccasins. Ill. by Douglas
Gorsline. Henry Holt, 1955. An orphan boy in
search of an uncle in Florida becomes a friend
of the Seminole Indians there, shortly before the

Seminole War in 1835. (I and YA)
1032 Ceder, Georgianna Dorcas. Little Thunder. Ill. by
      Robert L. Jefferson. Abingdon, 1966. Story of
      a Shawnee boy of Tippecanoe, Indiana, whose chief
      is the great Tecumseh; of how the British, during
      the war of 1812, entice the Indians to fight against
      the Americans and how the latter trick the Indians
      with treaties. Sauganash is also important in the
      story. (I)
1033 Clark, Electa. Cherokee Chief: The Life of John
      Ross. Ill. by John Wagner. Macmillan, 1970.
      A biography of a great man (1790-1866) who was
      seven-eighths white but a Cherokee by choice, a
      leader and believer in non-violence. It is also
      the tragic story of the Trail of Tears (1838) when
      the Cherokees were cheated out of their eastern
      homeland and forced to take the long trek to
      Oklahoma. Presidents Jackson and Van Buren
      came out very badly in this story, but Polk and
      Lincoln are shown as compassionate and just. The
      book includes a history of the Cherokee nation and
      stories of other famous Cherokees, including Se-
      quoya, inventor of their alphabet. (I and YA)
1034 Dunsing, Dee. War Chant. Ill. by E. Harper John-
      son. Longmans Green, 1954. A stirring novel
      of the second Seminole War in 1836 in which a
      young woodsman becomes a scout for the U.S.
      army against Osceola and his braves, is captured
      by the Indians first and by a white slave catcher
      later, and finally brings help to an army outpost.
      (YA)
1035 Eckert, Allan W. Blue Jacket, War Chief of the
      Shawnees. Jacket and map by Lorence Bjorklund.
      Little Brown 1969. A biographical novel about a
      man whose real name was Marmaduke Von Swear-
      ingen but who changed it when he allowed himself
      to become adopted by the Shawnees, in order to
      save the life of his little brother (and also because
      he had always had great interest in and sympathy
      for the Indians). During the period of the story,
      1771 to 1810, he fought with the Shawnees against
      the encroachments of the Whites. (I and YA)
1036 Farnsworth, Frances Joyce. Winged Moccasins; The
      Story of Sacajawea. Ill. by Lorence F. Bjorklund.
      Julian Messner, 1954. A biographical novel about
      the Shoshone Indian girl (1788?-1884), married to
      a French trapper, who acted as interpreter and
      guide for the Lewis and Clark expedition of 1802-6

over the Rockies. The story is based on the
painstaking research of Dr. Grace Raymond Hebard
and Dr. Charles Alexander Eastman, a Sioux Indian; their explorations were made separately but
produced like results (I and YA)

1037 Fox, Mary Virginia. Ambush at Fort Dearborn. Ill.
by Lorence F. Bjorklund. St. Martin's, 1962.
An unusual story of the Fort Dearborn Massacre in
1812, beginning with the threat of Indian trouble
and ending after the attack. The main character
is a boy captured by the Senecas and learning their
ways to his advantage. (I and YA)

1038 Franklin, George Cory. Indian Uprising. Ill. by
William Hofmann. Houghton Mifflin, 1962. A
short, easy-to-read book about the settlement of
the San Louis Valley in Colorado in the 1840s, and
the first white boy to enter it. (E and I)

1039 Frazier, Neta Lohnes. Sacajawea, The Girl Nobody
Knows. Ill. with a map. David McKay, 1967. A
thoroughly researched book which raises more
questions than it answers and piques the reader's
curiosity and imagination. It is written almost in
the form of a mystery or detective story. (YA
and Up)

1040 Fuller, Iola. The Loon Feather. Harcourt, Brace
and World, 1940. Fiction winner in the Avery
and Julie Hopwood Awards contest for 1939. It
is a long novel, vividly recreating the little world
of Mackinac Island in the 1820s and early '30s,
with its fort, its Ojibways, voyageurs, and the
mixed marriages of Indians and French before the
Indians were pushed off into Wisconsin. (A)

1041 _____. The Shining Trail. Ill. by Dale Nichols.
Duell, Sloane and Pearce, 1943-51. A long novel
about events leading up to Blackhawk's War and
the war itself, pointing up the poor faith and judg-
ment of the Whites and the nobility of Black Hawk
and some of his followers and at the same time
showing Chief Keokuk and his followers as being
less than "noble" Indians. (A)

1042 Giles, Janice Holt. Johnny Osage. Houghton Mifflin,
1960. A novel of the Cherokee-Osage wars in
the early 19th century, especially in 1821 at Three
Forks, Arkansas, and of Johnny Fowler whose
sympathy for the Osage Indians was so deep that
he came to think like them and adopt their ideas
and ideals. Johnny is a fictional character but

there are many historical ones among the soldiers,
traders and missionaries in the novel. (A)

1043 Hunt, Mabel Leigh. Michel's Island. Ill. by Kate
Seredy. Frederick A. Stokes, 1940. A story of
Michilimakinac (Mackinac Island) and the love of
one boy, half French and half Indian, for the
place and its legends and landscape and way of
life in the period of the late 18th and early 19th
centuries. (I and YA)

1044 Jones, Weyman. Edge of Two Worlds. Ill. by
J. C. Koesis. Dial, 1968. A sensitive story of
a white boy, the only survivor of a Comanche
raid, and the old Cherokee Sequoyah, who is seeking in Texas for the origins of his people. Both
in danger--the boy from Comanches and the old
man from white buffalo-killers--they help each
other, even though in the beginning each fears the
other. Sequoyah's Cherokee alphabet is given in
the "Author's Notes," and also the facts upon which
the story is based. (I and YA)

1045 _____. The Talking Leaf. Ill. by Harper Johnson. Dial, 1965. A story about Sequoyah's influence upon a little Cherokee boy who yearns to
know what a "talking leaf," given him by his
father, has to say. (I)

1046 Lampman, Evelyn Sibley. Half-Breed. Ill. by Ann
Frifalconi. Doubleday, 1967. The problem of a
boy whose father is white and whose mother is a
Crow Indian, as he tries to fit into the environ-
ment of early Portland, Oregon, shortly after the
Whitman massacre by the Indians. (I)

1047 Lauritzen, Jonreed. The Legend of Billy Bluesage.
Ill. by Edward Chavez. Little Brown, 1961.
A beautiful book about a young Spanish boy's faith
in the powers of a certain mysterious character,
against the hostile Ute Indians. (YA)

1048 Lawson, Marian. Proud Warrior, The Story of Black
Hawk. Ill. by W. T. Mars. Hawthorne Books,
1968. A fine biography of the great Sauk Chief
(1767-1838), who was forced to surrender to
white men in 1832, and a sad story of broken
treaties and intertribal warfare and treachery.
(YA)

1049 McGraw, Eloise Jarvis. Moccasin Trail. Coward
McCann, 1952. A novel about a young man who
grew up from the age of ten with the Crow Indians.
Suddenly finding his brothers and sisters on their

way to Oregon, in 1844, he joins them and tries
to adjust to the ways of his own people. (YA)

1050 McNeer, May. War Chief of the Seminoles. Ill. by
Lynd Ward. Random House Landmark, 1954.
The story of Osceola (1804-38) and the Seminole
Wars (1835-42), bringing Seminole history up to
date. (I)

1051 Marriott, Alice. The Black Stone Knife. Ill. by
Harvey Weiss. Thomas Y. Crowell, 1957. A
story about a small group of Kiowa Indians who
trekked from Oklahoma to the southern tip of
Mexico in 1825 and about a 12-year-old who ran
away to join them but was captured by the Apaches.
(I)

1052 _____. Sequoyah, Leader of the Cherokees. Ill.
by Bob Riger. Random Landmark, 1956. A
splendid history of the Cherokees begins the book.
Sequoyah, "the Lame One," claimed to have been
born in 1776, of an Indian woman and white father
and seems to have died in 1844. His invention of
the Cherokee alphabet was a unique achievement.
(I)

1053 Montgomery, Jean. The Wrath of Coyote. Woodcuts
by Anne Siberell. William Morrow, 1968. A novel
based on the life of the legendary Chief Marin
(1840 and before) and the conflicts between the various California Indians inhabiting the area of present-
day San Francisco. (YA)

1054 Parish, Peggy. Granny and the Indians. Ill. by
Brinton Turkle. Macmillan, 1969. How a tough
little granny puts one over on the Indians--and not
just one. (E)

1055 Penney, Grace Jackson. Moki. Ill. by Gil Miret.
Houghton Mifflin, 1960. Avon Books, 1970. A
little Cheyenne maiden wishes she were a boy and
had her "name called" for a brave deed, but is
constantly frustrated when she tries to copy the
young braves and finally has to find her own kind
of courage. (I)

1056 Radford, Ruby L. Sequoyah. Ill. by Unada. G. P.
Putnam's Sons, 1969. A See and Read Beginning
to Read Book. A short biography of the Cherokee
scholar (1770-1843) who invented the Cherokee
alphabet, whose statue is in the Capitol Building in
Washington, D.C., and for whom the Sequoyah National Forest was named. (E)

1057 Seymour, Flora Warren. Bird Girl Sacajawea. Ill.

by Edward C. Caswell. Bobbs-Merrill, 1945.
Childhood of Famous Americans Series. A story
of the childhood of the Indian girl who became in-
terpreter and guide for Lewis and Clark on the
1803-6 expedition. (E)

1058   Smith, Fredrika Shumway. Wilderness Adventure.
Ill. by Jack Merryweather. Rand McNally, 1958.
A white boy and his Potawatomie blood-brother go
to the rescue of the white boy's sister who has been
stolen by Fox Indians from her home near Fort
Dearborn just before the Indian massacre there.
(I)

1059   Snow, Dorothea J. Sequoyah, Young Cherokee Guide.
Ill. by Frank Giacoia. Bobbs-Merrill, 1960.
Childhood of Famous Americans Series. The youth
of the Cherokee (1770-1843) who invented the
Cherokee alphabet, a list of important dates,
questions about the story and suggestions of interesting things to look up and to do, and definitions
of interesting words. (E)

1060   Underhill, Ruth M. Antelope Singer. Ill. by Ursula
Koering. Coward McCann, 1961. Written by an
anthropologist who has spent years on reservations
and served in the U.S. Indian Service, this is a
story about a family separated from their wagon
train in the 1840s who spend a winter with the
friendly Paiutes and of the friendship that grows
up between 10-year-old Tad and a sad little Indian boy with a withered arm and of all that the
white folks learned from the Indians. (I)

1061   Wilson, Holly. Double Heritage. Jacket by John Gist.
Westminster Press, 1971. A love story, set in
the period of Black Hawk's War, 1832 and 1833,
in Detroit. A half-Chippewa girl is in love with
a young man of aristocratic French descent and
he with her, but her loyalty is divided between
him and her Indian grandmother and half-brother.
(YA)

1062   Worcester, Donald. Lone Hunter's First Buffalo
Hunt. Ill. by Harper Johnson. Henry Z. Walck,
1958. A sequel to "Lone Hunter's Gray Pony"
[1963] in which an Indian boy has a dream about
where a buffalo herd can be found, but no one
will believe him even though his Oglala tribe is
close to starvation. Finally he runs the risk of
being beaten by running off to find the herd. (I)

1063   _____. Lone Hunter's Gray Pony. Ill. by

Harper Johnson. Oxford University Press, 1956.
Combined with interesting information about the
Oglala tribes of the Sioux family, in the Dakota
Territory in the early 19th century, and their
enemies, the Assiniboins and the Kiowas, is an
exciting story of an Indian boy whose pony has
been stolen and who goes to retrieve it at great
risk to his scalp. (I)

THE 19th CENTURY--Second Half

1064 Altschuler, Joseph A. The Great Sioux Trail: A
      Story of Mountain and Plain. D. Appleton, 1918.
      The first of a series of romances about the open-
      ing of the West just after the Civil War and about
      the life and customs of the Sioux Indians. If you
      can overlook the old-fashioned, stilted style, you
      may want to read more books by this prolific
      writer. (YA)
1065 Anderson, Lavere. Sitting Bull, Great Sioux Chief.
      Ill. by Cary. Garrard, 1970. The story of one
      of the strongest, wisest and best-remembered
      Indian chiefs, known mainly for his victory over
      Custer in the Battle of Little Big Horn. (E and I)
1065a Benchley, Nathaniel. Only Earth and Sky Last For-
      ever. Jacket by Jay J. Smith. Harper and Row,
      1972. A touching novel of a southern Cheyenne
      lad who had been adopted by the Oglala Sioux when
      he was 12 years old, after his father and mother
      had both been killed by the whites. His love for
      a girl with a tyrannical grandmother makes him
      yearn to perform some outstanding deeds of cour-
      age and win horses in order to gain the grand-
      mother's consent to their marriage. But nothing
      ever works out as he hopes, though he is involved
      in the fighting climaxed by the Battle of Little
      Big Horn. A powerful novel of the events leading
      up to that battle, and of the deeds and character
      of Crazy Horse. (YA and Up)
1066 Bontemps, Alex. Black Comanche Boy. Ill. by
      Johnny Mercer. Hill and Wang, 1970. Story about
      a Negro boy at the end of the Civil War and the
      lessons in courage he learned from the Comanche
      Indians. (I)
1067 Cochise, Ciyo "Niño" (as told to A. Kenney Griffith).
      The First Hundred Years of Niño Cochise: The

Untold Story of an Apache Chief. Ill. with photographs. Abelard-Schuman, 1971. Mr. Griffith
has done a remarkable feat in plumbing Niño
Cochise's powers of total recall, so that we can
read about what it was like to be the grandson
(1874-) of the famous Apache Chief, Cochise,
and about life in a mountain hideaway where a
group of Apaches lived, the "Nameless Ones." A
long, rich autobiography and story of treachery
among the Mexicans, Americans and Apaches and
of Niño Cochise's attempts to adapt himself to
white men's ways. (A)

1068 Cooke, David. Apache Warrior. Ill. with photographs. W. W. Norton, 1963. A story of the
Apaches and their chief, Magnus Colorado, the
greatest leader in their hopeless war against Mexicans and the American army. Other more widely
known Apaches are part of the story, as Cochise,
Geronimo, Victorio and Nana. A sad story of
betrayal by the whites, ruthless cruelty by the
Indians, and the death of the Apache way of life.
(I and YA)

1069 Davis, Russell and Ashabramer Brent. Chief Joseph,
War Chief of the Nez Percé. Ill. by Jo Polseno.
McGraw-Hill, 1962. The sad story of the attempts
of Chief Joseph (ca. 1840-1904) to control the mili-
tants of his tribe in the face of broken treaties on
the side of the U.S. government, and of the long,
harrowing trek of the Nez Percés in their attempt
to join Sitting Bull in Canada. (I and YA)

1070 _____. The Choctaw Code. Jacket and endpaper
design by W. N. Wilson. Whittlesey House, 1961.
A novel about the code of ethics of the Choctaw
tribe in Oklahoma, and how a young white man
came to understand it. (YA)

1071 Fall, Thomas (Donald Clifford Snow). Edge of Manhood. Ill. by Henry C. Pitz. Dial, 1964. A
short poignant story of a Shawnee boy living on
land given to both the Pottowatomies and the
Shawnees and therefore a cause of trouble between
the tribes, and of the boy's rescue by a Pottowa-
tomie youth, and of his determination to prove his
own manhood. (I)

1072 Fast, Howard. The Last Frontier. Crown, 1941 and
1968, Signet paperbound, 1971. A novel of the
desperate struggle of some 300 Cheyenne Indians
to return from the dry, hot, blighted Oklahoma

reservation to the home in the north which was
their's by treaty with the U.S. government. (A)

1073 Forman, James. People of the Dream. Jacket by
Karl Stuklen. Farrar, Straus and Giroux, 1972.
A novel of the tragic last years of Chief Joseph
of the Nez Percé, with endpapers maps of their
trail toward freedom in Canada, and ending with
Joseph's famous plea for freedom. (YA and Up)

1074 Garst, Shannon. Crazy Horse, Great Warrior of
the Sioux. Ill. by William Moyers. Houghton
Mifflin, 1950. An exciting book, followed by a
chronology of the warrior's life (1849?-1877) and
a bibliography showing the extensive research to
make the story authentic, particularly the careful
planning of the Indians which led to Custer's last
stand. (I and YA)

1075 _____. Red Eagle. Ill. by Hubert Buel. Hastings
House, 1959. The story of a handicapped boy of
the Sioux who, first of all had to learn to laugh
at himself and then to overcome his handicap and
prove his mettle in an unusually daring way. (I)

1076 Goble, Paul and Dorothy. Red Hawk's Account of
Custer's Last Battle. Ill. by the authors and
printed in Hong Kong. Pantheon, 1969. A colorful,
dramatic account of the Battle of Little Big Horn,
1876, narrated by a fictional 15-year-old Sioux,
but based on published accounts of Sioux and Cheyenne participants in the battle and with a running
military analysis of the action. (YA)

1077 _____. Brave Eagle's Own Account of the
Fetterman Fight. Ill. by Paul Goble.
Pantheon, 1972. The illustrations and text of this
handsome book are so beautifully integrated that
one sees the action as one reads about it; the
terrain over which the fighting took place is clearly drawn. (I and YA)

1078 Grote, William. J. P. and the Apaches. Ill. by
Charles Waterhouse. Meredith, 1967. Fiction,
with good detail of the Sonora desert and the
Chiricahua Indians, led by Cochise, with mounting
suspense. The hero is a 12-year-old Spanish-Irish
boy who has made a good friend of an Apache lad.
A burro also plays an important role. (I and YA)

1079 Keith, Harold. Komantcia. Jacket by Peter Burchard.
Thomas Y. Crowell, 1965. A strong, realistic and
sanguinary novel about a young Spanish aristocrat
captured by a tribe of Comanche Indians in south-

western Oklahoma, after their massacre of his
mother and guardian uncle, and about the cruelty
of his captors and his constant dream of escape,
and then, very gradually, his absorption into the
tribe partly because of his love for a young Indian
girl. (YA)

1080 Kjelgaard, Jim. Wolf Brother. Jacket by Charles
      Banks Wilson. Holiday House, 1957. A story of
      a young Apache who, after spending six years in a
      white man's school, goes back to his reservation,
      hoping to teach and lead his tribe out of their hope-
      lessness. He is forced by circumstances to join a
      band of Apache outlaws, is captured and finally
      freed by the efforts of a young white lawyer. A book
      showing that neither Apaches nor whites were all
      bad or all good. (I and YA)

1081 Lampman, Evelyn Sibley. The Year of Small Shadow.
      Jacket by Robert Parker. Harcourt, Brace Jovano-
      vich, 1971. A pleasant little story of an 11-year-
      old Rogue River boy spending a winter with the
      "whites" while his father is in jail for "borrowing
      a horse." The strained relations between whites and
      Indians in the Northwest of the 1880s is depicted
      with humor and compassion. (I)

1082 Maloy, Lois. Swift Thunder of the Prairie. Ill. by
      the author. Charles Scribner's Sons, 1942. An
      exciting story of how a little Indian boy saves a
      train from being wrecked by young Indian braves,
      enraged by the encroachments of the railroads. (E)

1083 Marriott, Alice. Indian Annie, Kiowa Captive. Ill. by
      Allan Thomas. David McKay, 1965. Stolen by the
      Kiowas in Oklahoma, at the age of ten, Annie learns
      all their ways and teaches them much about the ways
      of the whites. Finally she has to decide between
      marrying an Indian or going back to her own people.
      (I)

1084 Meader, Stephen W. Everglades Adventure. Ill. by
      Charles Beck. Harcourt Brace, 1957. Less plot
      than in most of Meader's books, but lots of Ever-
      glades lore, the flora and fauna and the Caloosa
      Indians. (I)

1085 Meigs, Cornelia. The Willow Whistle. Ill. by E.
      Boyd Smith. Macmillan, 1931. This story of
      Pioneer children on the western prairies and their
      Indian friends and foes is of particular interest in
      showing the hostility between some tribes--in this
      story, the Sioux and the Arickeree. (I)

1086   Miller, Helen Markley. Thunder Rólling; The Story of
       Chief Joseph. Ill. by Albert Orbaan. G. P.
       Putnam's Sons, 1959. A tragic but inspiring biogra-
       phy of the noble Nez Percé chief (1840-1904) whose
       only plea to the white man was that promises be
       kept and that he and his people be "free and equal"
       and able to live on the land of their fathers. (I
       and YA)

1087   O'Connor, Richard. Sitting Bull, War Chief of the
       Sioux. Ill. by Eric von Schmidt. McGraw-Hill,
       1968. The story of the man famous for his defeat
       of Custer at Little Big Horn in 1876, a poet, a
       man of mercy, and a strategist in war. (I and YA)

1088   O'Dell, Scott. Sing Down the Moon. Houghton Mifflin,
       1970. A beautiful, sad story of the Navajos being
       driven out of their home canyon in 1864, and, after
       a long painful trek (known as the Long Walk) made
       to settle at Fort Sumner until 1868 when they were
       "freed" to live as best they could in the four-corner
       wilderness where the states of Utah, Arizona,
       Colorado and New Mexico join. The heroine is an
       Indian maiden named Bright Morning who, in spite
       of all hardships, never gave up hope. There is a
       disillusioning mention of Kit Carson in connection
       with the harsh treatment accorded the Navajos.
       (I and YA)

1089   Randall, Janet. Buffalo Box. Ill. by Ursula Koering.
       David McKay, 1969. A young Nez Percé maiden
       goes through harrowing experiences when her peo-
       ple are driven from their homes in central Idaho
       (homes given them by treaty in 1855) to the small-
       er Lapwai reservation. Under Chief Joseph, 700
       of them tried to escape to Canada, among them
       the girl Willow, carrying with her a dangerous
       secret. (I)

1090   Rush, William Marshall. Red Fox of the Kinapoo.
       Ill. by Charles Banks Wilson. Longmans Green,
       1949. A novel of the wars between the Nez Percés
       and the United States army, the principal character
       being Red Fox, a lad who has been to school under
       a white teacher and acts as an interpreter for
       Chief Joseph. (YA)

1091   Schultz, James Willard. The Quest of the Fish Dog
       Skin. Ill. by Lorence Bjorklund. Houghton Mifflin,
       1960. This is the second book of a trilogy [see
       1093]. The two young men, Tom and his Blackfoot
       "almost brother," make their way, beset by hostile

tribes, to the Pacific in search of a sealskin to take back as a cure for a sick old chief. (I and YA)

1092 _____. The Trail of the Spanish Horse. Ill. by Lorence Bjorklund. Houghton Mifflin, 1960. The third of a series about Tom Fox and his "almost brother" in which they determine to get Tom's Uncle's Spanish horse back from the Blue Paint raiders. All three books [see 1093] are recommended to readers of any age who wish to learn more about the various Northwest Indian tribes. (I and YA)

1093 _____. With the Indians in the Rockies. Ill. by Lorence Bjorklund. Houghton Mifflin, 1960. This is the first of a trilogy about Tom Fox and his Indian "almost brother." The author, who joined the Blackfoot tribe when young and married into it, has written up the adventures of an actual young trader who told him about them. The result is a novel of the tribal varieties and ways of the Plains and Northwest Indians as well as hairbreadth escapes and suspense, as Tom Fox and his "almost brother" are left to survive the winter in the Rockies without any equipment whatsoever, their possessions having been stolen by Kootenays. (I and YA)

1094 Spies, Victor C. Sun Dance. Ill. by Lorence F. Bjorklund. Follett, 1954. A story of Indian life in the southwest when the traders began coming through. The plot concerns a boy, an old mountain lion, and an all-black skunk whose skin has a very special value for the boy. (I)

1095 Wyatt, Edgar. Cochise, Apache Warrior and Statesman. Ill. by Allan Houser, direct descendent of Geronimo. McGraw-Hill, 1953. The story of the Apache (ca. 1815-74) who tried to be a peacemaker, but, not trusted by the Whites, turned into an enemy. (I)

1096 _____. Geronimo, the Last Apache War Chief. Ill. by Allan Houser, direct Descendent of Geronimo. McGraw-Hill, 1952. The story of the fierce Apache wars and the unforgiving leader (1829-1909). (I)

THE 20th CENTURY

1097 Barnouw, Victor. Dream of the Blue Heron. Ill.
      by Lynd Ward de la Corte, 1966. A novel about
      a young Chippewa (Wisconsin) Indian, taken from
      the reservation and put into an Indian school and
      his adaptation to the White world. The period
      about 1905. (YA)

1098 Beatty, Patricia. The Sea Pair. Ill. by Frank
      Altschuler. William Morrow, 1970. A unique
      novel, set in 1940, in Washington State, tracing
      the parallels in the lives of a mother sea otter
      and her pup and those of a young Quilente boy
      and his new teacher, a "white squaw." Essentially
      it is a story of conservation of both animal and
      human life. (I and YA)

1099 Clark, Ann Nolan. Medicine Man's Daughter. Ill.
      Donald Bolegnese. Bell Books, Farrar Straus,
      1963. A regional novel of the Navajos in New
      Mexico in which a young girl, training to be a
      medicine woman in the ways of her tribe, is sent
      to school and exposed to Christianity and still does
      not forsake all of her native culture.

1100 Coates, Belle. The Sign of the Open Hand. Ill. by
      Albert Micale. Charles Scribner's Sons, 1962. A
      good story about a little Valley Indian girl in the
      early 20th century in Montana, and her aged grand-
      father who loves to tell stories about the past, but
      is smarter about the present than the younger peo-
      ple realize. (E and I)

1101 Norton, André [i.e., Alice M.]. Fur Magic. Ill. by
      John Kaufmann. World, 1968. A contemporary
      and legendary novel about a boy whose father is
      in Viet Nam and who goes to stay with an adopted
      Indian father in Idaho. There, through some
      mysterious magic, he is turned into a mythical
      animal of the age before the coming of man. The
      story is based on Nez Percé folklore. (I and YA)

1102 Robinson, Barbara. Across From Indian Shore. Ill.
      by Evaline Ness. Lothrop Lee and Shepard, 1962.
      With a 20th-century setting in Massachusetts, this
      story involves a Wamponoag princess, the great
      (times six) granddaughter of Massasoit. (I)

1103 Rushmore, Helen. The Magnificent House of Man
      Alone. Ill. by Frank Vaughn. Garrard, 1968.
      A sort of contemporary folk tale of an old Osage
      Indian in Oklahoma who finds that oil money can

build a fine house but cannot make a home. (I)

1104 Westreich, Budd. Please Stand Clear of the Apache Arrows. Ill. by Ray Abel. David McKay, 1969. A first rate mystery story concerning some treasure hidden in deep, bat-ridden caves with dark tunnels and bottomless pits and the search for it by a city boy and the pretty daughter of an archaeologist with whom he is spending his Christmas vacation. The girl has almost been killed by an Apache arrow, and the plot thickens as the two try to solve the riddle, all told with light humor but reminiscent of the search of the Conquistadores for the Seven Cities of Cibola. (YA)

1105 White, Ray. Sunset for Red Elk. Ill. by Victor Mays. Dodd Mead, 1968. A story of pioneer life near Missoula, Montana in 1904, and of the blood brotherhood of Indian and white boys. (I)

1106 Williams, Jay. The Hawkstone. Jacket by Robert Quackenbush. Henry Z. Walck, 1971. A present and past story about the finding of an Indian hawkstone which gives a strange power to the finder. (I and YA)

INDUSTRY AND TECHNOLOGY

INVENTORS

1107 Asimov, Isaac. The Kite that Won the Revolution.
Ill. by Victor Mays. Houghton Mifflin, 1963. A
biography of Ben Franklin (1706-1790), through
which is woven a history of electricity from
mythological theories to its uses in the present,
and the story of how Franklin's discovery and inventions affected the Revolution. (I)

1108 Bare, Bargaret. John Deere, Blacksmith Boy. Ill.
by Robert Doremus. Bobbs-Merrill, 1964. Childhood of Famous Americans Series. The man who
gave the world the steel plow was born in Vermont
in 1804 and died in Moline, Illinois, in 1886. His
boyhood and young manhood were spent in New England, but his great invention was born in Grand De-
tour, Illinois. A chronology, interesting things to
do, other books recommended, and a vocabulary
are at the end. (E)

1109 Burlingame, Roger. Out of Silence into Sound: The
Life of Alexander Graham Bell. Ill. with photographs. Macmillan, 1964. Biography (1847-1922)
of a man, born in Scotland and brought to Canada
as a youth, who became a United States citizen
in 1874. He was not only the inventor of the telephone, but also worked all his life to bring sound
to the deaf and speech to the mute. (YA)

1110 Glines, Carroll V. The Wright Brothers, Pioneers
of Power Flight. Ill. with photographs. Franklin
Watts, 1968. The two Ohio boys, Wilbur (1867-
1912) and Orville (1871-1948) were regular "Mr.
Fixits," even as children, and with their mother's
encouragement became inventors while still young.
Their first power flight at Kitty Hawk, December
1903, ushered in the air age, but their hardest
fight was to protect their patent. (YA)

1111 Gurko, Miriam. The Lives and Times of Peter
Cooper. Ill. by Jerome Snyder. Diagrams by
Ava Morgan. Thomas Y. Crowell, 1959. A

biography (1791-1883) of a manufacturer, reformer,
philanthropist and inventor of many important
products and processes now taken for granted and
a pioneer in the promotion of free education. It is
also a lively story of the growth of New York City.
(YA)

1112 Hays, Wilma Pitchford. Eli Whitney and the Machine
Age. Ill. by Alfred Peterson. Franklin Watts,
1959. Though Whitney (1765-1825) is most often
remembered for his invention of the cotton "gin"
(short for engine) in 1793, his first use of "inter-
changeable parts" introduced the machine age and
mass production which influenced many other inventors and led to many other important inventions. (I)

1113 Latham, Jean Lee. Samuel F. B. Morse, Artist--
Inventor. Ill. by Jo Polseno. Garrard, 1961.
A Discovery Book. The story of the invention of
the telegraph in 1844. (E and I)

1114 Lawson, Robert. Ben and Me. Ill. by the author.
Little Brown, 1939. "A New and Astonishing Life
of Benjamin Franklin As Written by His Good
Mouse, Amos." This delightful nonsensical story
of Franklin, the inventor, contains more historical
fact than one might expect to find. (I)

1115 Levine, I. E. Inventive Wizard, George Westinghouse.
Jacket by Barry Martin. Julian Messner, 1962.
A biography (1846-1914) written in story form,
about a man who at 23 was president of his own
company producing air brakes for railroads, who
later devised a way to furnish Pittsburgh with
natural gas and a way of harnessing the power of
Niagara Falls, who invented shock absorbers for
autos and made many other contributions to the
industrial age, not least of which was the introduction of benefits for his employees. Other giants of
invention and industry are brought into the story and
an account of Westinghouse's struggle with his com-
petitors. (YA)

1116 Markey, Dorothy. The Little Giant of Schenectady:
A Story of Charles Steinmetz. Ill. by E. Harper
Johnson. Aladdin Books, 1956. A biography
(1865-1923) of the little humpbacked electrical engineer with a mind like a modern computer one of
whose many miraculous achievements was the building of a generator for producing artificial lightning.
(I)

1117 Miller, Floyd. The Electrical Genius of Liberty Hall:

Charles Proteus Steinmetz, with a foreword by
Clyde Wagoner. Ill. with photographs. McGraw-
Hill, 1962. Biography (1865-1923) of the electrical
engineer, forced out of Bismarck's Germany because he belonged to a student socialist club, who,
among his many other great contributions to his
adopted country, developed a practical calculation
method for alternating current. (YA and Up)

1117a Monjo, F. N. Slater's Mill. Ill. by Laszlo Kubinyi.
Simon and Schuster, 1972. A true story of a remarkable young Englishman named Samuel Slater,
who came to Rhode Island in 1789 and built from
memory (as he had seen them in England) every
single part of the carding and spinning machine of
America's first wholly automated spinning mill.
(I)

1118 Montgomery, Elizabeth Rider. Alexander Graham
Bell. Ill. by Gray Morrow. Garrard, 1963. A
Discovery Book. A short biography (1847-1922)
of the dedicated teacher of the deaf, and inventor
of, among many other things, the telephone. (E
and I)

1119 Pratt, Fletcher. Famous Inventors and Their Inven-
tions. Ill. by Rus Anderson. Random House,
1955. Short biographies of Robert Fulton, the
Wright brothers, Eli Whitney, Cyrus McCormick,
Benjamin Franklin, Samuel F. B. Morse, Alex-
ander Graham Bell, Christopher Shoes, Ottmar
Morgenthaler, Elias Howe, Thomas A. Edison,
Samuel Colt, John Ericsson, John Holland, Clarence
Birdseye, Lee DeForest, Enrico Fermi, and
Robert Oppenheimer. (I)

1120 Reynolds, Quentin. The Wright Brothers, Pioneers
of American Aviation. Ill. by Jacob Landau.
Random Landmark, 1950. A dual biography of
Wilbur (1867-1912) and Orville (1871-1948), who
even as small boys started "fixing things," later
manufactured bicycles, and after practicing with
their own gliders were able to add a motor and be
the very first pioneers of modern aviation. Special
credit for their skills and their imaginations is
given in this book to their mother. (I)

1121 Shapp, Martha and Charles. Let's Find Out about
Thomas Alva Edison. Ill. by Marvin Friedman.
Franklin Watts, 1966. An easy to read biography
(1847-1931).

1122 Shippen, Katherine. Mr. Bell Invents the Telephone.
      Random Landmark, 1952. Not a biography but the
      story of the trials and perseverence of Alexander
      Graham Bell, from the time he first arrived in
      Boston as a young man to teach in a school for
      the deaf, until the day when telephone calls could
      be made across the continent. (I)

1123 Stevenson, Augusta. Wilbur and Orville Wright: Boys
      with Wings. Ill. by Paul Laune. Bobbs-Merrill,
      1951. This story of the inventors of the first man-
      carrying airplane, gives us a picture of their
      typical middle-western background in the 1880s and
      their constant experimenting which led to their
      great achievement. (E)

1124 Thomas, Henry. George Westinghouse. Ill. by
      Charles Beck. G. P. Putnam's Sons, 1960.
      Biography of the inventor (1846-1914) who started
      inventing (and successfully) at the age of 12 and
      never stopped until he died at the age of 68. Air
      brakes for trains and shock absorbers for cars are
      only two of his memorable inventions, but he is
      also remembered for his good labor relations and
      business ethics, both causing him trouble with his
      competitors. (I and YA)

ENGINEERS

1125 Latham, Jean Lee. George W. Goethals, Panama
      Canal Engineer. Ill. by Hamilton Green. Garrard,
      1965. A Discovery Book. Biography (1858-1928)
      of the West Pointer, a member of the Army En-
      gineers for 40 years, chief engineer of the Panama
      Canal from 1907 to 1914, and later, governor of
      the Canal Zone. (E)

1126   . Young Man in a Hurry: The Story of Cyrus
      W. Field. Ill. by Victor Mays. Harper, 1958.
      The thrilling story of the laying of the Atlantic
      cable, and the financier (1819-92) who refused,
      against almost insuperable obstacles, to give up
      the project. (YA)

1127 Veglahn, Nancy. The Spider of Brooklyn Heights. Ill.
      with photographs. Charles Scribner's Sons, 1967.
      Biography of John Augustus Roebling (1806-69),
      German-American engineer, builder of suspension
      bridges, who died in an accident during the con-
      struction of the Brooklyn bridge. The story con-

tinues with the work of his son, Washington Au-
gustus Roebling. (YA)
1128 Widdemer, Mabel Cleland. DeWitt Clinton, Boy
Builder. Ill. by Robert Doremus. Bobbs-Merrill,
1961. Childhood of Famous Americans Series.
The childhood of the man (1769-1828) who promoted
the building of the Erie Canal was exceptionally full
of danger and adventure. The Canal was finally
opened in 1825. (E)

LABOR

1129 Gould, Jean. Sidney Hillman, Great American.
Houghton Mifflin, 1952. Biography (1887-1946)
of the Lithuanian-born labor leader, especially in
the garment trades, who came to Chicago in 1907;
the organizer of the C.I.O. Political Action Com-
mittee in 1943. (YA and Up)
1129a Myers, Elisabeth P. Madame Secretary, Frances
Perkins. Jacket by Don Lambo. Julian Messner,
1972. This book might have been listed in a num-
ber of categories, but in her position as Secretary
of Labor under F.D.R., Miss Perkins (1880-1965)
seems best listed here. The first woman Cabinet
member, she attained that position by hard work
and scrupulous attention to facts and statistics,
while at the same time she showed deep compassion for children, minorities, immigrants, and the
unemployed. Written dramatically and excitingly,
Frances Perkins' story covers the political history
of the first half of the 20th century. (YA and Up)
1130 Nadin, Corinne J. The Haymarket Affair, Chicago,
1886. Ill. with photographs. Franklin Watts,
1968. A short, well organized account of the riot
of May 4, 1886, and the trial that followed, the
results of the trial, and the courage of Governor
Altgeld. (YA)
1131 Noble, Iris. Labor's Advocate, Eugene V. Debs.
Julian Messner, 1966. An engrossing biography
(1855-1926) of an idealistic labor leader and socialist (a presidential candidate while in prison),
a nonviolent revolutionist in his way. It is also
the story of the growth of unionism, the Haymarket
Riot, and the Pullman strike of 1894. (YA)
1132 Shulman, Alix. To the Barricades: The Anarchist
Life of Emma Goldman. Jacket by Bob Levering;

photographs. Thomas Y. Crowell, 1971. Biography (1869-1940) of a woman whose childhood had
been so brutally oppressed that it is small wonder
she turned into an ardent anarchist, against all
governments. She was almost as enthusiastically
feminist as anarchist, and this biography was
written by a feminist. (YA and Up)

1133 Selvin, David F. Champions of Labor. Ill. with
photographs. Abelard-Schuman, 1967. Stories of
the following labor leaders, with a running account
of the labor movement in the U.S. from 1806 to
the present: William H. Sylva, Terence V. Pow-
derly, Samuel Gompers, Eugene V. Debs, Bill
Haywood, William Green, John L. Lewis, Sidney
Hillman, David Dubinsky, Philip Murray, Walter
Reuther, George Meany, and Philip Randolph. With
three appendixes: 1) glossary of terms frequently
used in trade unions and in industrial relations in
general, 2) biographical data on each leader, and
3) some notes on further reading. (YA and Up)

1134 _____. Sam Gompers, Labor's Pioneer. Ill. with
photographs. Abelard-Schuman, 1964. The story
of Gomper's life (1850-1963) is also the story of
the early labor movement, the formation of the
A.F.L. in 1866, the mobilization of industry and
manpower in World War I, and creation of the
International Labor Organization after that war.
(YA)

1135 _____. The Thundering Voice of John L. Lewis.
Ill. with photographs. Lothrop Lee and Shepard,
1969. The story of the career of John L. Lewis
and the history of the United Mine Workers--the
two inseparably connected. (YA)

1136 Werstein, Irving. Labor's Defiant Lady: The Story
of Mother Jones. Thomas Y. Crowell, 1969.
Biography of the woman (1830-1930), born Mary
Harris, in Ireland, who came to America when
she was ten. She lived all over the United States,
going wherever she could to help the cause of
labor and to fight for an eight-hour day and safer
working conditions and against child labor--up to
the age of 98. (YA)

1137 _____. Strangled Voices: The Story of the Haymarket Affair. Ill. with photographs. Macmillan,
1970. The story of what happened on May 26,
1886, in Chicago--the causes and results of the
affair--is here dramatically told, with fairness

and dispassion, yet clearly showing the injustice of
the case, and the courage of Governor Altgeld,
seven years after the trial.   (YA and A)

INDUSTRY

1138 Fleming, Alice. Ida Tarbell, First of the Muckrakers.
      Ill. with photographs. Thomas Y. Crowell, 1971.
      A biography (1857-1944) of a pioneer in exposing
      corrupt practices and injustice by publishing the re-
      sults of painstaking research. Ida Tarbell was
      especially noted for her writings on John D. Rocke-
      feller's oil monopoly. (YA and Up)
1139 Judson, Clara Ingram. Andrew Carnegie. Ill. by
      Steele Savage. Follett, 1964. Biography of the
      steel manufacturer and philanthropist (1835-1919),
      the son of a Scottish weaver who moved his family
      to America when Andrew was thirteen. The story
      of how Andrew made his millions and how he spent
      them. (YA)
1140 Paradis, Adrian A. Henry Ford. Ill. by Paul Frame.
      G. P. Putnam's Sons, 1968. A See and Read Be-
      ginning to Read Biography. A very simple story of
      the man who initiated mass production of automo-
      biles (1863-1947). (E)
1141 Shippen, Katherine. Andrew Carnegie and the Age of
      Steel. Ill. by Ernie Barth. Random Landmark,
      1958. The story of the poor Scottish Weaver's
      son (1835-1919) who came to America and made a
      fortune. Carnegie Libraries were one of his great
      philanthropies. (I)
1142 Simon, Charlie May. The Andrew Carnegie Story.
      Ill. with photographs. E. P. Dutton, 1965. A
      "From Rags to Riches" story of the rise of a poor
      Scottish boy to the status of one of the richest men
      in the world, a rise accomplished by hard work,
      ingenuity, courage, and a talent for picking good
      men. Without his benefactions to libraries, this
      book might not have been written. (YA)

LATIN AMERICA AND THE WEST INDIES

CENTRAL AND SOUTH AMERICA

1143 Baker, Nina Brown. He Wouldn't Be King; The
Story of Simon Bolivar. Ill. by Camilo Egas.
Vanguard, 1941. A narrative biography of Bolivar
(1783-1830) and also a comprehensive book about
the liberation and formation of the countries of
Venezuela, Bolivia, Colombia, Ecuador and Peru,
with some additional material on Chile, Argentina
and Brazil. (YA)

1144 Brown, Rose. American Emperor Dom Pedro II of
Brazil. Ill. by C. B. Falls. Viking, 1945. An
endearing biography of Pedro II (1826-89) who
ruled from 1844 until his exile in 1888 with interesting material on slavery in Brazil as it differed
from that in the U.S. (YA)

1145 Criss, Mildred. Dom Pedro of Brazil. Ill. by
Victor J. Dowling. Dodd Mead, 1945. A biographical novel of the Portuguese Pedro II of
Brazil incorporating the history of Brazil during
his rule, 1844-89. During part of this time his
daughter Isabella, wife of Prince Louis d'Orleans,
acted as regent. A family tree at the end of the
book is helpful but rather hard to read. (YA)

1146 Schirmer, Mathilda. Latin-American Leaders. Ill.
by Dick Gringhuis. Beckley-Cardy, Chicago,
1951. Ten short biographies of Miguel Hidalgo y
Costilla, by Camilla Campbell; Francisco de
Miranda, by Olive W. Burt; José de San Martín,
by Lois Rhea; Bernardo O'Higgins, by Helen L.
Gilliun; Simón Bolívar, by Elma Martens; Antonio
José de Sucré, by Webb B. Garrison; José
Bonifácio de Andrada e Silva, by Elizabeth
Scherman; Domingo Faustino Sarmiento, by Elsie
Spicer Eels; José Martí, by Alice Mathews
Shields, Eloy Alfaro, by Mary McGowan Slappey.
(I and YA)

1147 Syme, Ronald. Bolivar the Liberator. Ill. by

William Stobbs. William Morrow, 1968. A biogra-
phy (1783-1830) introduced by a chapter on the
Spanish conquests and rule and the setting into which
Simon Bolivar was born. A good map. (I)

1148 Webb, Robert N. Simon Bolivar the Liberator. Franklin Watts, 1966. This biography of the Liberator
(1783-1830) has the special feature of a last chapter, "The Aftermath," summing up the later history of the countries liberated by Bolivar, namely:
Bolivia, Colombia, Ecuador, Peru and Venezuela.
It is a sad chapter considering Bolivar's hopes for
unity and democracy. (YA)

THE WEST INDIES

1149 Chastain, Madye Lee. Magic Island. Ill. by the author.
Harcourt, Brace and World, 1964. Any book
which winds up in the West Indies is bound to be,
partially at least, a sea story, and so this is--
set in the days of Clipper Ships. Here too one
meets friends from "Dark Treasure" and "Emmy
Keeps Her Promise." [395] (I)

1150 Diekmann, Miep. Slave Doctor. Translated from the
Dutch by Madeleine Mueller. William Morrow,
1970. Novel about a young man who signs on a
slave ship as ship doctor and about his life in the
West Indies in the 17th century. (YA)

1151 Heatter, Basil. A King in Haiti: The Story of Henri
Christophe. Ill. by Toni Evins. Farrar, Straus
and Giroux, 1972. Born a slave in 1767, as Jean
Christophe, he died in 1820 as King Henri I of
Haiti, a fearless tyrant but one who also did much
for his country. (I and YA)

1152 Howard, Elizabeth. Verity's Voyage. Jacket by
Eric Carle. William Morrow, 1964. A 17th-
century romance (1640) about a young English girl
sent to the West Indies colony of Providence, with
her cousin who is to be married to a plantation
owner. Neither girl having a dowry, their only
chance of a good marriage is on the islands where
women are scarce. Verity is soon betrothed there
but not to the one she would choose. However,
when the Spanish attack Providence, the best laid
plans go very much agley. (YA)

1153 Newcomb, Covella. Black Fire. Ill. by Avery Johnson. David McKay, 1940. The dramatic fantastic
story of the black slave, Jean Christophe, growing
up to become King Henry I of Haiti (1767-1820).
(YA)

1154 Norris, Marianne. Doña Felisa; A Biography of the
      Mayor of San Juan. Ill. with photographs. Dodd
      Mead, 1969. The story of a woman (1897-) who,
      brought up in the strict Spanish tradition, became
      deeply aware of the problems of the slums, of
      poverty and injustice. Finding politics the only
      avenue for remedying these ills, she became in-
      volved in the Popular party work and finally became
      mayor of San Juan, Puerto Rico, which office she
      held for 20 years. (I and YA)
1155 Sherlock, Philip. West Indian Folk Tales. Ill. by
      Joan Kiddell-Monroe. Henry Z. Walck, 1966.
      Some of these retold tales come from the first in-
      habitants of the West Indies, the Arawaks and the
      Caribs, living on the shore of the Caribbean before
      Columbus came, others are of African origin,
      brought by the captive slaves. The introduction
      "From Sun Spirit to Spider-Man" gives a short his-
      tory of the Arawak and Carib tribes which should
      interest older readers. (I)
1156 Sterling, Philip and Brau, Maria. The Quiet Rebels.
      Ill. by Tracy Sugarman. Zenith Books, Doubleday,
      1968. Biographies of four Puerto Rican leaders,
      José Celso Barbosa, Luis Múños Rivera, José de
      Diego, and Luis Muños Marín. A rather pedestrian
      book but good for Puerto Rican history of the last
      100 years. (YA)
1157 Syme, Ronald. Toussaint, the Black Liberator. Ill.
      by William Stobbs. William Morrow, 1971. Be-
      sides being a biography of Toussaint L'Ouverture
      (1743-1820), this is an important book for its
      story of how the republic of Haiti (the second re-
      public in the New World) came to be founded by
      an ex-slave who played not only two ends against
      the middle, but a whole tangle of ends--Spain,
      France, England--mulattos and Blacks--all of
      whom seldom cooperated. (YA)
1158 Taylor, Theodore. The Cay. Jacket by Milton Glaser.
      Doubleday, 1969. An un-put-downable book about a
      young American boy and an old West Indian Negro
      on a tiny island during World War II when the
      German U-boats were attacking Curaçao and Aruba.
      (I and Up)

MEDICINE

THE REVOLUTIONARY ERA

1159 Douty, Esther M. Patriot Doctor: The Story of Benjamin Rush. Julian Messner, 1959. Best remembered, by laymen at least, for his army medical
work during the Revolutionary War and as a signer
of the Declaration of Independence, Dr. Rush (1746-
1813) was also a pioneer in psychiatry. (YA)

THE 19th CENTURY

1160 Allen, T. D. Doctor in Buckskin. Harper, 1951.
Most of the stories and biographies of Dr. Marcus
Whitman and his wife, Narcissa, will be found
with other western expansion stories, but at least
one must be included in this category, for Marcus
was primarily a medical missionary to the Cayuse
Indians. This is a biographical novel, mainly set
in the 1820s and '40s. (A)
1161 Baker, Rachel. America's First Trained Nurse,
Linda Richards. Julian Messner, 1959. Biography of the woman (1841-1930) who, overcoming
tremendous obstacles and enduring manifold dis-
comforts and trials, became our own American
Nightingale and raised nursing to a respectable
and respected profession. (YA)
1162 _____. Angel of Mercy, The Story of Dorothea
Lynde Dix. Julian Messner, 1955. Biography
of the woman (1802-87) who brought about a
complete revolution in the care of the mentally
ill and was superintendent of nurses for the
Union forces during the Civil War. (YA)
1163 _____. Dr. Morton, Pioneer in the Use of Ether.
Ill. by Lawrence Dresser. Julian Messner,
1946. This is the story of the discovery of
ether as an anaesthetic and the frustrations and
discouragements of its discoverer, Dr. Wiliam
Thomas Green Morton (1819-68). Dr. Morton

was a Boston dentist who died leaving "$25.00, one
house, and some personal belongings" but who, at
the urging of the Drs. Mayo of Rochester, Minn.,
was finally posthumously elected to the Hall of
Fame. (YA)

1164 _____. The First Woman Doctor: The Story of
Elizabeth Blackwell. Ill. by Corinne Malvern.
Julian Messner, 1944. A biography of a woman,
born in England in 1821 and buried in Scotland in
1910, who overcame her greatest odds in the United
States as a trailblazer in the field of medicine for
women. (YA)

1165 Blassingame, Wyatt and Glendinning, Richard. The
Frontier Doctors. Franklin Watts, 1963. Stories
about the following heroic doctors: 1) "The Doctors Who Weren't" namely: Lewis and Clark who,
though not actually trained as doctors, performed
medical services on their famous journey at the
beginning of the 19th century; 2) Ephraim McDowell,
father of abdominal surgery; 3) Marcus Whitman,
medical missionary and promoter of westward expansion; 4) Henry Perrine, botanist as well as
doctor; 5) Crawford Long, pioneer in the use of
anaesthesia; 6) Bethenia Owens-Adair, an early
"female doctor"; and 7) Samuel Crumbine, pioneer
in public health. (YA)

1166 DeGering, Etta. Gallaudet, Friend of the Deaf.
Ill. by Emil Weiss. David McKay, 1964. A
biography of the man (1787-1851) who pioneered the
first permanent work for the deaf in America and
founded the first school "The American School for
the Deaf" in Hartford, Conn., in 1817. (I and YA)

1167 Higgins, Helen Boyd. Walter Reed, Boy Who Wanted
to Know. Ill. by Raymond Burnes. Bobbs-Merrill, 1958. Childhood of Famous Americans Series. The story of the boyhood of a man (1852-
1902) who in his late forties made the important
discovery about the cause of yellow fever which in
turn made it possible to exterminate the mosquitos
causing the fever when the Panama Canal was being
constructed. (E)

1168 Koob, Theodora. Surgeon's Apprentice. J. B. Lippincott, 1963. A realistic novel, though with a
romantic plot concerning the mystery of an indentured boy's background; about the son of a surgeon
in the early 1800s, and his struggle to overcome
his own weakness in the face of death and pain.
(YA)

1169 Meltzer, Milton. A Light in the Dark: The Life of
      Samuel Gridley Howe. Thomas Y. Crowell, 1964.
      The remarkable story of the life of a remarkable
      man (1801-76) who had his fingers in many pies
      but who is probably best remembered for his
      work with Laura Bridgeman, the deaf-mute child.
      (YA)

1170 Pace, Mildred Mastin. Clara Barton. Ill. by Robert
      Ball. Charles Scribner's Sons, 1941. The story
      of a determined little woman (some said "stubborn")
      (1821-1912) who nursed soldiers during the Civil
      War, became "General Correspondent for the
      Friends of Paroled Prisoners" after it, lectured,
      organized the American Red Cross in 1881, served
      in disaster areas at home and abroad, and led the
      Red Cross during the Cuban campaign of the
      Spanish-American War. (YA)

1171 Rich, Josephine. Pioneer Surgeon, Dr. Ephraim
      McDowell. Jacket by Stephen Voorhis. Julian
      Messner, 1959. A biographical novel about
      the man (1770-1830) who made medical his-
      tory by being the first surgeon to dare to cut into
      the abdominal cavity when he performed an opera-
      tion for a tumor on Christmas Day in 1809, while
      a lynch mob stood outside the door with a rope for
      him in case the patient died. (YA)

1172 Rose, Mary Catherine. Clara Barton. Ill. by E.
      Harper Johnson. Garrard, 1960. A Discovery
      Book. During her long life Clara Barton (1821-
      1912) played many parts: nurse during the Civil
      War, organizer and first president of the American
      Red Cross, and leader of it, at the age of 76, in
      the Spanish-American War. (E)

1173 Stern, Madeleine B. So Much in a Lifetime: The
      Story of Dr. Isabel Barrows. Julian Messner,
      1964. This woman's life (1845-1913) was so full
      and varied in her accomplishments that it is hard
      to summarize her achievements in a short note.
      She was the first woman eye specialist in the U.S.,
      first woman to become private secretary to the
      head of the State Department--and these are just a
      few of her "firsts." (YA)

1174 Wood, L. N. Walter Reed, Doctor in Uniform. Ill.
      by Douglas Duer. Julian Messner, 1943. This
      biography of the conqueror of yellow fever (1852-
      1902) is exciting all the way through but most
      dramatically so toward the end when his own

teammates in the work of detection offered themselves as guinea pigs, particularly two heroic young
men, Kissinger and Moran. Also not to be over-
looked is the Cuban Dr. Carlos Finlay who was
the first to believe in the mosquito theory though
he could not prove it. (YA)

THE LATE 19th and THE 20th CENTURIES

1175 Bertol, Roland. Charles Drew. Ill. by Jo Polseno.
Thomas Y. Crowell, 1970. A short, easily readable biography of the important Black doctor (1904-
50) who became the first director of the Red
Cross blood bank in 1941. (E and I)

1176 Clapsattle, Helen. The Mayo Brothers. Ill. by
Karoly and Szanto. Houghton Mifflin, 1962. These
famous surgeons, sons of a country doctor, were
born respectively in 1861 (Will) and 1865 (Charles)
and died within two months of each other in 1939.
The story of their great clinic in Rochester, Minnesota, is well known, but perhaps not so familiar
is the story of the early training the boys had
under their father, and the difference in their per-
sonalities which made them complement each other
so perfectly. (YA)

1177 Denzel, Justin F. Genius with a Scalpel: Harvey
Cushing. Jacket by Andre de Blanc. Julian
Messner, 1971. The remarkable story of the
foremost brain surgeon of his time (1869-1939)
and, after his retirement, a noted author. (YA)

1178 Dunnahoo, Terry. Emily Dunning: A Portrait.
Reilly and Lee, 1970. The story of the courageous
young woman (1876-1961) who made headlines in
the New York newspapers in 1903 as the first and
only lady ambulance surgeon in the world. Her
greatest test, however, came when her fellow interns at Bellevue Hospital tried every possible
trick to get her in trouble and force her out of the
hospital which she had worked so hard to enter.
(YA)

1179 Fleming, Alice. Doctors in Petticoats. Jacket by
Joan Berg. J. B. Lippincott, 1964. Short
biographies of ten women in medicine: Marie
Zakrzewska, Mary Pitman Jacobi, Emily Dunning
Barringer, Clara Swain, Alice Hamilton, Louise
Pearce, Sara Jordan, Karen Horney, Leona Baum-

gartner, and Corrine Meyers Guion. All of these
women had difficult obstacles to surmount--some-
times financial, sometimes parental opposition,
but mostly prejudice against their sex. (YA)

1180 Hardwick, Richard. Charles Richard Drew, Pioneer
in Blood Research. Jacket by Donald Crews.
Charles Scribner's Sons, 1967. Dr. Drew (1904-50)
was a great Negro sports figure before he took up
medicine at McGill University in Toronto, Canada.
"The best player I ever coached," Tuss McLaughry
wrote of him in a Saturday Evening Post article.
The first part of the book deals with his successes
in swimming, track, football, etc. While the
remainder shows what obstacles he had to overcome
(and did) in finally achieving recognition for his
blood research and his promotion of blood banks.
(I and YA)

1181 Harrod, Kathryn. Man of Courage, Dr. Edward L.
Troudeau. Jacket by Everett Raymond Kinstler.
Julian Messner, 1959. Biography of a man (1848-
1915) who didn't find his real goal in life until he
was 20, having been an easy-going playboy until
then. Suddenly he realized that he wanted to be
a doctor, and thus the Troudeau Sanitarium at
Saranac, New York, came to be renowned for
"consumptives" until it finally became unnecessary.
(YA and Up)

1182 Levine, I. E. The Discoverer of Insulin: Dr.
Frederick Banting. See entry 910.

1183 Lichello, Robert. Pioneer in Blood Plasma: Dr.
Charles R. Drew. Jacket by Don Lambo. Julian
Messner, 1968. A biography, written in fictional
style, of a great athlete, brilliant scientist, surgeon, teacher and researcher, who, in his too
short life (1904-1950) did much to promote the
acceptance of his fellow Blacks in the field of
medicine, and who by his pioneering in the use of
blood plasma saved countless lives in World War
II. (YA)

1184 Noble, Iris. The Doctor Who Dared: William Osler.
Jacket by Don Lambo. Julian Messner, 1959. An
inspiring story of the life of a great physician and
exceptionally loveable human being (1849-1919).
Canadian-born and raised, he became one of the
"Big Four of Johns Hopkins" and his book, "The
Principles and Practices of Medicine" not only
brought him personal fame but led to the formation

of the Rockefeller Institute of Medical Research.
In 1911 he was knighted by King George V of
England.   (YA)

1185   _____.   First Woman Ambulance Surgeon.   Reilly
and Lee, 1970.   Born Emily Dunning (see "Emily
Dunning: A Portrait" [1178]), she prepared herself for her medical career under that name, and
it was as Emily Dunning, before her marriage to
Benjamin A. Barringer, that she endured all sorts
of harassment by fellow interns at Bellevue Hospital, in their attempts to force her out.   Her
courage and stamina, in the face of sex discrimi-
nation and the actual physical dangers of ambulance
driving in New York's toughest sections, make an
inspiring story.   (YA)

1186   _____.   Physician to the Children: Dr. Bela
Schick.   Jacket by Dave Dippel.   Julian Messner,
1963.   The tender life story of the Hungarian doctor (1877-1967) who loved children so dearly that
he struggled to gain a medical education against
his father's strong opposition.   From his work and
study came the Schick test for diptheria and the
beginning of the science of pediatrics.   In 1923 he
came to America to become head pediatrician at
Mt. Sinai Hospital in New York where he also became an American citizen.   (YA)

MEXICO

GENERAL HISTORY

1187 McNeer, May and Lynd Ward. The Mexican Story.
Ill. by Lynd Ward. Farrar, Straus and Young,
1953. A good narrative history of Mexico, interspersed with vignettes of children of various
periods. Enjoyable for all ages. (I)

LEGENDS

1188 Jordan, Philip D. The Burro Benedicto and Other
Folk Tales and Legends of Mexico. Ill. by R. M.
Powers. Coward McCann, 1960. A varied collection, some old, some new, some Christian in
origin and some Aztec. (I)
1189 Niggli, Josefina. Miracle for Mexico. Ill. with
paintings by Alesandro Rangel Hidalgo. New
York Graphic Society, 1964. An historical novel
about Our Lady of Guadalupe, full of Catholic
mysticism. The prologue and End Note to the
Reader give the history of the times preceding
and following the few days of the story's action.
(YA)
1190 O'Dell, Scott. The Treasure of Topo-el-Bampo.
Ill. by Lynd Ward. Houghton Mifflin, 1972. A
story about two burros, some 200 years ago, and
how they became the saviors of the poorest village in all Mexico. (E and I)
1191 Parish, Helen Rand. Our Lady of Guadalupe. Ill.
by Jean Charlot. Viking, 1955. A beautiful
short book, retelling the story of Juan Diego and
the miracle of the roses which brought about the
building of the great Cathedral of Our Lady of
Guadalupe. (I)
1192 Tinkle, Lon. Miracle in Mexico: The Story of Juan
Diego. Ill. by Vivian Berger. Hawthorne Books,
1965. Biography of the simple peasant whose
visions of the Mother of God, in the 1530s, resulted, long after his death, in the building of the

great basilica of Our Lady of Guadalupe. (I and
YA)

THE 19th CENTURY

1193 Barnes, Nancy. Carlota, American Empress. Ill.
      by John Barber. Julian Messner, 1943. Biography
      of the Belgian princess (1840-1927) who married
      the Austrian Grand Duke Maximilian and became,
      for the years 1864 to 1866, Empress of Mexico.
      Interesting history of Mexico in the 1860s. (YA)
1194 Hazelton, Elizabeth Baldwin. Tides of Danger.
      Charles Scribner's Sons, 1967. A novel about the
      perilous adventures of pearl divers in the Sea of
      Cortez and the evils of peonage in Mexico in
      the latter 19th century. (I and YA)
1195 Lampman, Evelyn Sibley. The Tilted Sombrero.
      Ill. by May Cruz. Doubleday, 1966. An exciting
      novel about a young mestizo (part Spanish and
      part Indian) and the beginning of Mexican Inde-
      pendence in 1810. Real characters include Father
      Hidalgo, the leader of the movement, José
      Morelos, Iturbide and others. Glossary. (YA)
1196 Vance, Marguerite. Ashes of Empire. Ill. by J.
      Luis Pellicer. E. P. Dutton, 1959. A dual
      biography of Maximilian (1832-67), who was the
      brother of Austrian Emperor Franz Joseph, and
      Maximilian's wife Carlota (1840-1927), for three
      years Emperor and Empress of Mexico. A sad
      tale. (YA)
1197 Williams, J. R. Mission in Mexico. Prentice-Hall,
      1959. A novel about a "gringo" in 1867 in search
      of his father, a supporter of Emperor Maximilian
      against Juarez. A pleasant way to absorb Mexican
      history. (YA)

THE 20th CENTURY

1198 Bruckner, Karl. Vive Mexico. Ill. by Adalbert Pilch.
      Translated from the German by Stella Humphries.
      Roy, 1960. An action-packed novel about the
      Mexican revolution, 1911-13, led by Francisco
      Madero. With a list of Spanish words and expres-
      sions used in the book and their English meanings.
      (YA)

1199 Collin-Smith, Joyce. Jeremy Craven. Jacket by Lynd
      Ward. Houghton Mifflin, 1958. A novel set in the
      revolutionary years of 1911-13, with the different
      factions led respectively by Huerta, Zapata, Madero
      and Villa. A shy sensitive English boy is taken
      to Mexico by his uncle who is involved in selling
      arms to any faction who will pay the most. The
      lad, finding himself attuned to Mexico, is torn by
      loyalty to his uncle and desire for a peaceful
      studious life and career as a silversmith in Taxco.
      (YA and Up)
1200 Lewis, Thomas. Hill of Fire. Ill. by Joan Sandin.
      An I Can Read History Book. Harper and Row,
      1971. The story of the birth of a volcano in
      Mexico in 1943. (E)
1201 Rouverol, Jean. Pancho Villa. Doubleday, 1972.
      A factual biography of the revolutionist (1878-
      1923) and the complicated revolutionary activities
      in Mexico in the early 20th century, a tangle of
      characters and allegiances. (YA and Up)
1202 Syme, Ronald. Zapata, Mexican Rebel. Ill. by
      William Stobbs. William Morrow, 1971. The story
      of Zapata's revolutionary leadership from 1908,
      when he was 40, until his assassination in 1919,
      and the turbulent history of Mexico during that
      period. (I)

PRESIDENTS AND THEIR FAMILIES

COLLECTIVE BIOGRAPHIES

1203 Alvarez, Joseph. Vice Presidents of Destiny. G. P. Putnam's Sons, 1969. Profiles of the following eight Vice Presidents who became Presidents: Tyler, Fillmore, Andrew Johnson, Arthur, Theodore Roosevelt, Coolidge, Truman, and Lyndon Johnson. (YA and Up)

1204 McConnell, Jane and Burt. Our First Ladies: Martha Washington to Pat Ryan Nixon. Ill. by Isabel Dawson. Thomas Y. Crowell, revised edition, 1969. Sketches of some very important ladies and their famous husbands. An interesting approach to history. (YA)

1205 _____. Presidents of the United States. Portraits by Constance Joan Naar. Thomas Y. Crowell, 1951 and 1970. Brief biographies of 36 Presidents from Washington through Nixon [see Table of Presidents]. (I and YA)

1206 Prindiville, Kathleen. First Ladies: Stories of the Presidents' Wives with an introduction by Adrienne Foulke. Ill. with photographs and some paintings. Macmillan, 1964. From Martha Washington to Jacqueline Kennedy, with the addition of Jefferson's daughters, Martha J. Randolph and Maria J. Eppes. (I and YA)

1206a Reit, Seymour. Growing Up in the White House: The Story of the Presidents' Children. Ill. with prints and photographs. Crowell-Collier, Macmillan, 1968. These are stories of the presidents' families (not just the children) and the changes each family brought to the White House which, incidentally, was only officially named that in the administration of Theodore Roosevelt. (I and Up)

PRESIDENTS OF THE UNITED STATES
With the Dates of Their Administrations

1. George Washington, 1789-97
2. John Adams, 1797-1801
3. Thomas Jefferson, 1801-1809
4. James Madison, 1809-1817
5. James Monroe, 1817-1825
6. John Quincy Adams, 1825-1829
7. Andrew Jackson, 1829-1837
8. Martin Van Buren, 1837-1841
9. William H. Harrison, 1841
10. John Tyler, 1841-1845
11. James K. Polk, 1845-1849
12. Zachary Taylor, 1849-1850
13. Millard Fillmore, 1850-1853
14. Franklin Pierce, 1853-1857
15. James Buchanan, 1857-1861
16. Abraham Lincoln, 1861-1865
17. Andrew Johnson, 1865-1869
18. Ulysses S. Grant, 1869-1877
19. Rutherford B. Hayes, 1877-1881
20. James A. Garfield, 1881
21. Chester A. Arthur, 1881-1885
22, 24. Grover Cleveland, 1885-89 and 1893-97
23. Benjamin Harrison, 1889-1893
25. William McKinley, 1897-1901
26. Theodore Roosevelt, 1901-1909
27. William H. Taft, 1909-1913
28. Woodrow Wilson, 1913-1921
29. Warren C. Harding, 1921-1923
30. Calvin Coolidge, 1923-1929
31. Herbert Hoover, 1929-1933
32. Franklin D. Roosevelt, 1933-1945
33. Harry S Truman, 1945-1953
34. Dwight D. Eisenhower, 1953-1961
35. John F. Kennedy, 1961-1963
36. Lyndon B. Johnson, 1963-1969
37. Richard M. Nixon, 1969-

INDIVIDUAL BIOGRAPHIES [see also the Biographical Index]

GEORGE WASHINGTON

1207 D'Aulaire, Ingri and Edgar Parin. George Washing-
ton. Ill. by the authors. Doubleday, 1936.
Washington's life (1732-99) to the time he became
President, largely in pictures. (E)

1208 Desmond, Alice Curtis. George Washington's Mother.
Ill. with photographs, drawings and maps by the
author. Dodd Mead, 1961. A biographical novel
about Mary Ball Washington, a dictatorial, stubborn,
indomitable woman, and about her strained relations with her son. (A)

1209 Eaton, Jeanette. Leader by Destiny: George Washington, Man and Patriot. Ill. by Jack Manley
Rose. Harcourt, Brace, 1938. A full-length
biographical novel of the first President (1732-99).
(YA and Up)

1210 Fleming, Thomas J. First in Their Hearts: A
Biography of George Washington. Ill. with photographs and engravings. W. W. Norton, 1968. A
biography which brings the Father of his Country
to robust life as a big man in every way; a man
with great energy, impetuous will and violent temper, which he learned to control, who enjoyed fox
hunting, cards, and dancing, but who also was
strongly self-disciplined as a soldier and statesman. (YA)

1211 Fritz, Jean. George Washington's Breakfast. Ill.
by Paul Galdone. Coward-McCann, 1968. A
story of a boy who shared his name and birthday
with the first President and became quite an authority on his life, but had to do a great deal of
research to find out what the real George had for
breakfast. (E and I)

1212 Heilbrunner, Joan. Meet George Washington. Ill.
by Victor Mays. Random, Step-up Books, 1964.
A fine elementary biography with maps of George
Washington's world. (E)

1213 Judson, Clara Ingram. George Washington, Leader
of the People. Ill. by Robert Frankenberg.
Follett, 1951. A comprehensive, enjoyable readable biography (1732-99) showing the human as
well as the heroic nature of the man. (I and YA)

1214 _____. George Washington. Ill. by Bob Patterson,

Follett, 1961. A shortened, simplified version of
her book for older readers [1213], with a word
list intended for third graders. (E and I)

1215 Meadowcroft, Enid La Monte. The Story of George
Washington. Ill. by Edward A. Wilson. Grosset
and Dunlap, 1952. A biography in story form of
Washington's life to the time when he took the oath
of office as President in 1789. (E)

1216 Norman, Gertrude. A Man Named Washington. Ill.
by James Caraway. Longmans Green, A See and
Read Biography, 1960. (E)

1217 North, Sterling. George Washington, Frontier Colonel.
Ill. by Lee Ames. Random Landmark, 1957. A
biography of Washington's years from 1732 to 1775,
containing many quotations from the young Colonel's
reports and letters and even some of his "love
poems." It brings to life an intrepid, warm-
blooded and altogether human young man. (I and
YA)

1218 Steiner, Stan. George Washington: The Indian Influence. Ill. by Fermin Rocker. G. P. Putnam's
Sons, 1970. A short and easy to read biography
(1732-99) emphasizing his youthful experiences with
and against the Indians which helped him forge his
tactics during the Revolution. (E and I)

1219 Thompson, Vivian L. George Washington. Ill. by
Frank Aloise. Longmans Green, 1964. A See
and Read Biography (1732-99) with a word list,
recommended for grades two to four. (E)

1220 Vance, Marguerita. Martha, Daughter of Virginia.
Ill. by Nedda Walker. E. P. Dutton, 1947. The
story of Martha Dandridge Custis Washington,
from her 11th birthday in 1742 to 1789 when her
second husband, Washington, was elected President. (I)

1221 _____. The Beloved Friend. Ill. by Leonard
Weisgard. Colonial Williamsburg, 1963 (distrib-
uted by Holt, Rinehart and Winston.) The story of
Washington's first and hopeless love, Sally Cary
Fairfax, whose husband was Washington's close
friend. Also a story of Washington's campaigns in
the French and Indian wars. (YA)

JOHN ADAMS

1222 Kelly, Regina Z. Abigail Adams, The President's
Lady. Ill. by Robert Frankenberg. Houghton

Mifflin, 1962. The story of a "thinking, reading woman" (1744-1818), wife of the second President, and of the very beginning of the United States, with a map of Boston and its environs. (I)

1223   Peterson, Helen Stone. Abigail Adams, "Dear Partner". Ill. by Betty Fraser. Garrard, 1967. A Discovery Book. A short biography of the wife of the second president and mother of the sixth, one of the most influential first ladies in U.S. history (1744-1818). (E)

1224   Steinberg, Alfred. John Adams. G. P. Putnam's Sons, 1969. Besides being a biography of the second President, who was born in Braintree, Mass., in 1735 and died at the age of 91 on the 50th anniversary of the Declaration of Independence, this is a story of the struggle for American Independence, the problems of establishing a completely new government, and the beginning of party politics. (YA and Up)

THOMAS JEFFERSON

1225   Johnston, Johanna. Thomas Jefferson: His Many Talents. Ill. by Richard Bergen. Dodd Mead, 1961. A fine book about the third President (1743-1826), a many faceted character: statesman, archaeologist, naturalist, geographer, inventor, and outstanding architect. (YA)

1226   Komroff, Manuel. Thomas Jefferson. Julian Messner, 1961. A concise biography (1743-1826). (YA)

1227   Moscow, Henry and the Editors of American Heritage. Thomas Jefferson and His World. Ill. with paintings, prints, drawings and photographs. American Heritage, 1960. The illustrations provide a vivid background for the biographical novels by Leonard Wibberley. (YA)

1228   Wibberley, Leonard. A Dawn in the Trees: Thomas Jefferson, the Years, 1776-1789. Jacket by Enrico Arno. Farrar, Straus, 1964. The second of the four-volume biography [1228, 1229, 1231, 1232], covering the period of the American Revolution, Jefferson's mission to France, and the beginning of the French Revolution. (YA)

1229   _____. The Gales of Spring: Thomas Jefferson, the Years 1789-1801. Jacket by Enrico Arno. Farrar, Straus and Giroux, 1965. The third of the four-volume work, mainly about Jefferson as

Secretary of State and his opposition to Alexander
Hamilton. (YA)

1230   . Man of Liberty: A Life of Thomas Jefferson. Farrar, Strauss and Giroux, 1968. In one
volume, the four books listed separately in 1228,
1229, 1231 and 1232. (YA and Up)

1231   . Time of the Harvest: Thomas Jefferson,
the Years 1801-1826. Farrar, Straus and Giroux,
1966. The fourth and last book in this Jefferson
series about his two terms as President and the
building of the University of Virginia. (YA)

1232   . Young Man from Piedmont: The Youth of
Thomas Jefferson. Jacket by Enrico Arno. Farrar, Straus, 1963. The first of the four-volume
biography of Thomas Jefferson [1228, 1229, 1231,
1232], covering the years from his birth in 1743
to 1776. The author says, "This is non-fiction
fiction." (YA)

JAMES MADISON

1233 Davidson, Mary R. Dolly Madison. Ill. by Erika
Markling. Garrard, 1966, A Discovery Book. A
short biography of the wife of the fourth President,
especially remembered for saving valuable papers
and the Stuart painting of Washington when the
British burned the White House during the War of
1812 (1768-1849). (E)

1234 Mayer, Jane. Dolly Madison. Ill. by Walter Buehr.
Random, 1954. It is interesting that among books
for young people there are more about the wife
of the fourth President than about the chief executive.

1235 Melick, Arden Davis. Dolley Madison, First Lady.
Ill. by Ronald Dorfman. G. P. Putnam's Sons,
1970. A biography with exciting adventures of
possibly the most colorful first lady in the history
of the White House (1768-1849), a famous hostess
whose second husband was the fourth President.
Her name is spelled both ways--Dolly and Dolley.
(I)

1236 Monsell, Helen Albee. Dolly Madison, Quaker Girl.
Ill. by Gray Morrow. Bobbs-Merrill, 1944-53-61.
Childhood of Famous Americans Series. The
childhood and youth of the girl who became the
fourth President's wife, with a few pages about
her rescue of the painting and state papers from

the White House when the British burned it in
1814. (E)

1237 Nolan, Jeannette Covert. Dolley Madison. Julian
Messner, 1958. An engrossing biographical novel
of Dolley Payne Todd Madison who often acted as
hostess for Thomas Jefferson and was the friend of
eight other Presidents (1768-1849). She was
honored toward the end of her life by a seat in the
House of Representatives. Her saving of Madison's
papers (with records of the Constitutional Conven-
tion) was of supreme importance. (YA)

1238 Wilkie, Katherine E. and Moseley, Elizabeth R.
Father of the Constitution: James Madison. Jacket
by Jules Gotlieb. Julian Messner, 1963. A biography of the staid, serious fourth President who,
more than any other man, was responsible for the
U.S. Constitution and the Bill of Rights. (YA)

JOHN QUINCY ADAMS

1239 Hoehling, Mary. Yankee in the White House: John
Quincy Adams. Julian Messner, 1962. Biography
of a great statesman (1767-1848), son of President
John Adams and his wife Abigail, Secretary of
State under James Monroe, and sixth President of
the United States--afterwards a congressman from
Massachusetts. (YA)

1240 Hoyt, Edwin P. John Quincy Adams. Ill. with photographs of paintings. Reilly and Lee, 1963. A
biography of the sixth President of the U.S. who,
though not popular, was an expert on foreign affairs and an able diplomat. (YA)

1241 Kerr, Laura. Louisa: The Life of Mrs. John Quincy
Adams. Funk and Wagnalls, 1964. A biographical
novel about this First Lady (1776-1853) during the
years 1825-29, when her husband was 6th President
of the U.S. His public life contained many other
important assignments in all of which she was a
very great asset. (YA)

1242 Lomask, Milton. Son of the American Revolution:
John Quincy Adams. Jacket by Frank Aloise.
Farrar, Straus and Giroux, 1965. Any biography
of any member of the Adams family is inevitably
also a history of that particular Adams' period.
As sixth President of the U.S. he was (and still
is) the only President's son to attain that office.
Two matters of especial interest in this book

concern 1) John Quincy's opposition to the War of
1812 and 2) his important role in the Amistad
Case, in which African slaves, who had been stolen
by the Spanish, mutinied and landed in Long Island
in 1841 and finally obtained freedom through Adams'
plea to the Supreme Court. (YA)

1243 Weil, Ann. John Quincy Adams, Boy Patriot. Ill. by
William Moyers. Bobbs-Merrill, 1945-63. Childhood of Famous Americans Series. The unusual
childhood of the sixth President who, when he was
only 11 (in 1778) went to Europe with his father
John Adams, Minister to France. At 14, John
Quincy was secretary to the American Minister to
the Netherlands. Chronology, glossary, questions
on the book, and things to look up and to do included. (E)

ANDREW JACKSON

1244 Myers, Elisabeth P. Andrew Jackson. Ill. with
photographs. Reilly and Lee, 1970. A carefully
researched political biography of the seventh
President (1767-1845), who has had an "Age"
named after him. (YA and Up)

1245 Parlin, John. Andrew Jackson, Pioneer and President. Ill. by William Hutchinson. Garrard Press,
1962. A Discovery Book. The story of the General called "Old Hickory" who became the seventh
President of the United States. (E)

1246 Stone, Irving. The President's Lady: A Novel about
Rachel and Andrew Jackson. Doubleday, 1951.
This dual biographical novel covers the late 18th
and early 19th centuries, the turbulent years of
early American politics, the Battle of New Orleans,
Indian affairs, and the final incorporation of Louisiana and Florida. It treats both Rachel and Andrew
with sympathy and compassion. (A)

1247 Vance, Marguerite. The Jacksons of Tennessee. Ill.
by Nedda Walker. E. P. Dutton, 1953. A dual
biography in fictional form of Andrew Jackson,
1767-1845, and his greatly maligned wife, Rachel.
(YA)

MARTIN VAN BUREN

1248 Hoyt, Edwin P. Martin Van Buren. Reilly and Lee,
1964. A biography of the 8th President (1782-

1862) who was largely responsible for the emergence
of the political system of compromise which brings
order out of widely divergent interests. Especially recommended to readers with an interest in
practical politics. (YA)

JAMES K. POLK

1249 Severn, Bill. Frontier President: The Life of
James K. Polk. Ives Washburn, 1965. A biography of one of our "apt to be forgotten Presidents," the 11th, whose administration (1845-49)
expanded America's frontiers by the annexation of
Texas and the addition of far western states to the
Union, adding more than 500,000 square miles to
the area of the nation. (YA)

ZACHARY TAYLOR

1250 Hoyt, Edwin. Zachary Taylor. Reilly and Lee,
1966. A biography of the 12th President, primarily a military man with few qualifications for
the presidency. More interesting than his brief
16 months in office is his military career in the
Black Hawk, Seneca and Mexican Wars. (YA)

FRANKLIN PIERCE

1251 Hoyt, Edwin P. Franklin Pierce: the Fourteenth
President. Ill. with photographs. Abelard-
Schuman, 1972. As a compromise candidate,
Pierce could satisfy no one, but it is a question
whether any President at that time could have
coped successfully with rising tensions caused by
the problems of slavery and states' rights. (YA
and Up)

JAMES BUCHANAN

1252 Hoyt, Edwin P. James Buchanan. Ill. with portraits
and engravings. Reilly and Lee, 1966. This
scholarly biography of the bachelor President
(1791-1878) merits careful reading by students of
American government and politics and the slavery
problem. The 15th President was a strict Constitutional Constructionist with faith in legal
processes. (YA and Up)

ABRAHAM LINCOLN

1253 Andrews, Mary Raymond Shipman. The Perfect Trib-
      ute. Ill. by Rudolph Ruzicka. Charles Scribner's
      Sons, 1905-56. This little book is itself a tribute
      to Abraham Lincoln and the beauty and strength of
      his Gettysburg Address. (All Ages)
1254 Baker, Nina Brown. The Story of Abraham Lincoln.
      Ill. by Warren Baumgartner. Grosset and Dunlap,
      1952. One of many good biographies (1809-65).
      (I)
1255 Bragdon, Lillian J. Abraham Lincoln, Courageous
      Leader. Ill. by Edward Shenton. Abingdon, 1960.
      A Portrait. (I)
1256 Bulla, Clyde Robert. Lincoln's Birthday. Ill. by
      Ernest Crichlaw. Crowell, 1965. A brief bi-
      ography with especially interesting illustrations.
      (E)
1257 Cary, Barbara. Meet Abraham Lincoln. Ill. by Jack
      Davis. Random, n.d. Step-Up Books. Short
      Biography. (E)
1258 Cavanah, Frances. Abe Lincoln Gets His Chance. Ill.
      by Paula Hutchison. Rand-McNally, 1959. Fic-
      tion, with plenty of Lincoln humor, about the man,
      from his birth (in 1809) to his election in 1860.
      (I)
1259 Colver, Anne. Abraham Lincoln for the People. Ill.
      by William Moyers. Garrard, 1960, A Discovery
      Book. A short and intimate portrait of the 16th
      President. (E)
1260 Daugherty, James. A. Lincoln. Ill. with lithographs
      in two colors by the author. Viking, 1943. A
      big book about a big man, in which Lincoln is the
      American dream personified. (YA and Up)
1261 D'Aulaire, Ingri and Edgar. Abraham Lincoln. Ill.
      by the authors. Doubleday, 1939 and 1957. A
      picture book biography. (E)
1262 Eifert, Virginia S. The Buffalo Trace: Lincoln's
      Ancestors. Ill. by Manning de V. Lee. Dodd
      Mead, 1955. The first of four biographical novels
      about Lincoln, this one covering the years 1780 to
      1810 and the pioneering lives of his grandfather
      Abraham and his grandmother, Bathsheba on the
      Kentucky frontier. (YA)
1263 _____. Out of the Wilderness: Young Abe Lincoln
      Grows Up. Ill. by Manning De V. Lee. Dodd
      Mead, 1956. The second book of the Lincoln

series, 1811-31. (YA)

1264   . Three Rivers South: A Story of Young Abe Lincoln. Ill. by Thomas Hart Benton. Dodd Mead, 1953. The third book of the Lincoln series, about Abraham's flatboat trip along the Sangamon, Illinois and Mississippi Rivers, 1831. (YA)

1265   . With a Task Before Me: Abraham Lincoln Leaves Springfield. Ill. by Manning De V. Lee. Dodd Mead, 1957-66. The fourth book, 1832-61. (YA)

1266 Ervin, Janet Halliday. More than Halfway There. Ill. by Ted Lewin. Follett, 1970. A new kind of Lincoln story about a boy who meets up with lanky, strong young Abe and learns from him the importance of education and of Abe's determination to "become somebody" in spite of his father Thomas' reluctance to let him go his own way. (I)

1267 Fisher, Aileen. My Cousin Abe. Ill. by Leonard Vosburgh. With a foreword by Paul M. Angle. Thomas Nelson, 1962. A novel based on (among other sources) interviews given by Dennis Hanks to Lincoln's law partner, Herndon, who incorporated them into his biography of Lincoln. This novel gives the reader a sense of familiarity with all the Lincoln kin, and is written with the flavor of the period in speech and manner. (YA and Up)

1268 Foster, Genevieve. Abraham Lincoln: An Initial Biography. Ill. by the author. Charles Scribner's Sons, 1950. (I)

1269   . 1861: Year of Lincoln. Ill. by the author. Charles Scribner's Sons, 1970. The first year of Lincoln's administration is presented in its world-wide context, clearly written and vividly illustrated. (I)

1270 Frisby, Margaret. Tad Lincoln and the Green Umbrella. Ill. by Darrell Wiskur. Children's Press, revised edition, 1969. First published in 1944. A thoroughly delightful story of mischievous Tad and his loving father, full of humor and containing an unusual plot. (I)

1271 Gorham, Michael. The Real Book about Abraham Lincoln. Ill. by Elinore Blaisdell. Doubleday, 1951. Familiar stories, with the addition of a chronology--"Real Dates in the Life of Abraham Lincoln"--and a postscript, "Things Lincoln Really Said." (I)

1272 Gutman, Adele. When Lincoln Went to Gettysburg.

Ill. by Emil Weiss. Aladdin Books, 1955. The
story line follows the activities of Captain Eckert,
the conductor on the local train bringing Lincoln
from Hanover Junction to Gettysburg on November
18, 1863. The book as a whole sets the stage for
the immortal address--all the local color, the
music, the activities of the Marines guarding the
President, the telegrapher who learned of his coming, and, on Lincoln's part, his concern for his
sick little Tad back in Washington. (I and YA)

1273 Horgan, Paul. Citizen of New Salem. Ill. by
Douglas Gorsline. Farrar, Straus and Cudahy,
1961. The story of Lincoln's young manhood in
New Salem, Illinois, from the age of 21 to 28
(1830-1837). (YA)

1274 Houser, Richard and Donald B. Hyatt. Meet Mr.
Lincoln. Project Twenty, National Broadcasting
Co., 1960. Golden Press, N.Y. A television
program in hard covers--a visual story of Lincoln
and his times. (I and Up)

1275 Judson, Clara Ingram. Abraham Lincoln, Friend of
the People. Ill. by Robert Frankenberg, with
photographs from the Chicago Historical Society
Lincoln Dioramas. Follett, 1950. (I and YA)

1276 Kelly, Regina Z. Lincoln and Douglas Debates: The
Years of Decision. Ill. by Clifford Gear. Landmark, Random, 1954. Largely a political
biography of Lincoln from the time he entered
politics until he was elected President. Also a
biography of Douglas and the story of the beginning of the Republican Party. (I and YA)

1277 Latham, Frank B. Abraham Lincoln. Ill. with
photographs. Franklin Watts, 1968. A serious
biography of Lincoln's years in politics and his
difficult problems during the Civil War. An excellent map of the boundaries of the Northern,
Southern and Border states. (YA and Up)

1278 McNeer, May. America's Abraham Lincoln. Ill. by
Lynd Ward. Houghton Mifflin, 1957. A biography
of Lincoln's whole life, 1809-65. (I and YA)

1279 Miers, Earl Schenck. That Lincoln Boy. Ill. by
Kurt Werth. World, 1968. A fresh narration of
Lincoln's years from birth (1809) to young man-
hood when he first entered politics, by an eminent
Lincoln scholar. Enjoyable reading for all ages.
(I)

1280 Neyhart, Louise A. Henry's Lincoln. Ill. by Charles

Banks Wilson. Holiday House, 1945. A story
about a famous Lincoln-Douglas debate in Freeport,
Ill. in 1858 and a young boy who started out as a
Douglas supporter but changed his mind after hearing the debate and "went for Lincoln." (E and I)

1281 Nolan, Jeannette Covert. Abraham Lincoln. Ill. by
Lee Ames. Julian Messner, 1953. An absorbing
biography in lively narrative form. (YA)

1282 Norman, Gertrude. A Man Named Lincoln. Ill. by
Joseph Cellini. G. P. Putnam's Sons, 1960.
A See and Read Book. (E)

1283 North, Sterling. Abe Lincoln: Log Cabin to White
House. Ill. by Lee Ames. Random House, 1956.
A fine, sensitive narration of Abe's boyhood and
young manhood. (I and YA)

1284 Ostendorf, Lloyd. A Picture Story of Abraham
Lincoln. Ill. with 160 drawings and photographs
by the author. Lothrop, Lee and Shepard, 1962.
(I)

1285 Pauli, Hertha. Lincoln's Little Correspondent. Ill.
by Fritz Kredel. Doubleday, 1951. The true
story of 11-year-old Grace Bedell and the letter
she wrote to Lincoln, suggesting that he raise
whiskers. The letter still hangs on the wall of
Lincoln's house at the corner of 8th and Jackson
Streets in Springfield, Ill. (I)

1286 Randall, Ruth Painter. I, Mary. Ill. with photographs and portraits. Little Brown, 1959. A
sympathetic biographical novel of Kentucky-bred
Mary Todd Lincoln, the President's wife. (YA)

1287 Sandburg, Carl. Abe Lincoln Grows Up. Ill. by
James Daugherty. Harcourt, Brace and World,
1926. Reprinted from "Abraham Lincoln, the
Prairie Years," being the first 27 chapters of
Sandburg's original two-volume biography. A
classic, not to be missed. (YA and Up)

1288 Stevenson, Augusta. Abe Lincoln, Frontier Boy. Ill.
by Clotilde Embree. Bobbs-Merrill, 1932.
Stories Children Can Read. (E)

1289 _____. Nancy Hanks, Kentucky Girl. Ill. by Paul
Laune. Bobbs-Merrill, 1954. Childhood of
Famous Americans Series. A fictional recreation
of the childhood of Abraham Lincoln's mother.
(E and I)

1290 Stone, Irving. Love is Eternal. Doubleday, 1954,
Pocket Books, 1956. A biographical novel of
Lincoln's marriage mainly from his wife's view-

point. Poor Mary Todd Lincoln has always been the
subject of much cruel criticism, not all of which is
justified. (A)

1291 Wahl, Jan. Abe Lincoln's Beard. Ill. by Fernando
Krahn. Delacorte, 1971. A picture book apparent-
ly intended for very young children, but its style,
that of an old album of daguerrotypes, may please
older readers more. (All Ages)

1292 Weaver, John D. Tad Lincoln, Mischief Maker in the
White House. Ill. by Robert Handville. Dodd
Mead, 1963. A dual biography of father and son,
Abraham and Tad, completely faithful to fact and
recorded sayings, many taken from the childhood
memories of Julia Taft Bayne's book, "Tad Lincoln's
Father" (Little Brown, 1931). (I and YA)

1293 Wilkie, Katherine E. Mary Todd Lincoln, Girl of the
Bluegrass. Ill. by Leslie Goldstein. Bobbs-Merrill, 1954-60. Childhood of Famous Americans
Series. A highly imaginative story of the young
girl who became Mrs. Abraham Lincoln, with
questions, vocabulary etc. (E and I)

ANDREW JOHNSON

1294 Foster, G. Allen. Impeached! The President Who
Almost Lost His Job. Ill. with photographs and
prints. Criterion Books, 1964. The story, written
in lively mid-20th-century manner, of the impeachment of the 17th President of the U.S., Andrew
Johnson, by the House of Representatives, and
his trial by the Senate. In the author's opinion,
Johnson's real "crime" lay in trying to follow the
advice of Abraham Lincoln, "with malice toward
none," and the final chapter draws the analogy
between two President Johnsons who followed assassinated Presidents into office--Andrew and
Lyndon. (YA)

1295 Lomask, Milton. Andy Johnson: The Tailor Who Became President. Jacket by Douglas Gorsline.
Farrar, Straus and Cudahy, 1962. A sympathetic
biography of the man (1809-75) who became President (the 17th) after Abraham Lincoln's death, was
impeached by the House of Representatives, and
barely saved from complete dishonor by the Senate
trial. (YA)

ULYSSES S. GRANT

1296 Meyer, Howard N. Let Us Have Peace: The Life of
      Ulysses S. Grant. Ill. from Bettmann Archives.
      Macmillan, 1966. This author has nothing good to
      say of Grant's predecessor, Andrew Johnson, and
      places the blame for the evils of the reconstruction
      years almost entirely upon his shoulders, but he
      also claims that General Grant did not make a great
      President. The portion of the biography dealing
      with his presidency and reconstruction problems is
      particularly interesting now, almost a century later.
      (YA and Up)

1297 Reeder, Colonel Red. Ulysses S. Grant, Horseman
      and Fighter. Ill. by Ken Wagner. Garrard, 1964.
      A Discovery Book. President Grant was born in
      Ohio in 1822 (he died in 1885) but his name is
      closely associated with Galena, Illinois, where he
      worked in a hardware store after taking part in the
      Mexican War and where, in later years, the people
      gave him a house which is now open to the public.
      (E)

1298 Renick, Marion. Steve Marches With the General. Ill.
      by Pru Herric. Charles Scribner's Sons, 1962.
      An amusing story in which a boy of today learns
      how to do research on a Civil War hero (Ulysses
      S. Grant), how to write a script for a pageant (the
      complete script as performed by Steve's class is
      included) and how to put on a play. From all this
      emerges a biography of Grant (1822-85). (I)

1299 Thomas, Henry. Ulysses S. Grant. G. P. Putnam's
      Sons, 1961. A well arranged and fair story of
      the life of the Civil War general and two-term
      President. (YA)

RUTHERFORD B. HAYES

1300 Myers, Elizabeth P. Rutherford B. Hayes. Ill. with
      photographs. Reilly and Lee, 1969. A biography
      of the 19th President (1822-1893) who was neither
      colorful nor exciting but who was conscientious and
      believed that "He serves his party best who serves
      his country best." (YA and Up)

JAMES A. GARFIELD

1301 Feis, Ruth S. B. Mollie Garfield in the White House.
      Ill. with family pictures and memorabilia. Rand
      McNally, 1963. A very specialized kind of family
      portrait by the granddaughter of President James
      A. Garfield (20th President and second to be as-
      sassinated), mainly about 14-year-old Mollie's
      short year in the White House, but also largely
      about the President himself as a husband and
      father. (YA and Up)

1302 Severn, Bill. Teacher, Soldier, President: The Life
      of J. A. Garfield. Ives Washburn, 1964. This
      biography of the 20th President who served for less
      than 11 months before being assassinated by a dis-
      appointed office seeker, forcibly presents the evils
      of the spoils system which prevailed at that time,
      and portrays Garfield as an honest and courageous
      public servant. (YA and Up)

GROVER CLEVELAND

1303 Hoyt, Edwin P. Grover Cleveland. Ill. with photo-
      graphs. Reilly and Lee, 1962. A biography of
      the President who served two terms but not con-
      secutively, terms during which the great Silver Bat-
      tle was in full force, the Pullman strike occurred,
      and American imperialism which he opposed was
      rearing its head. Corruption in government was
      rampant when he first took office and he dealt with
      it firmly and courageously. (YA)

THEODORE ROOSEVELT

1304 Cavanah, Frances. Adventure in Courage: The Story
      of Theodore Roosevelt. Ill. by Grace Paull. Rand
      McNally, 1961. This biography takes Teddy (1858-
      1919) from his sickly, asthmatic childhood to his
      arrival at the White House. (I)

1305 Garraty, John. Theodore Roosevelt: The Strenuous
      Life. Ill. with 140 illustrations, cartoons, paint-
      ings, photographs, etc.--American Heritage, 1967.
      A pictorial biography of the 26th President, suc-
      ceeding McKinley who was the third victim of as-
      sassination. (YA)

1306 Judson, Clara Ingram. Theodore Roosevelt, Fighting
      Patriot. Ill. by Lorence F. Bjorklund. Follett,

1953. A fine, comprehensive biography of this
remarkably colorful and active man (1858-1919),
the 26th President, with particular attention to his
interest in conservation, his encouragement of civil
service reform, and his insistence on military pre-
paredness: "Speak softly and carry a big stick."
(YA)

1307 Looker, Earle. The White House Gang. Ill. by James
Montgomery Flagg. Fleming H. Revell, 1929.
Told by one of the gang of which young Quentin
Roosevelt was the leader during his father's term
in the White House, this book will have especial
appeal to grandparents who grew up in the golden
years of the gang. A book for the whole family.
(I and Up)

1308 Monjo, R. F. N. The One Bad Thing about Father.
Ill. by Rocco Negri. Harper and Row, 1970. An I
Can Read History Book. The "one bad thing" was
that Father, Theodore Roosevelt, happened to be
President of the United States, so that his family
of rambunctious children had to be somewhat restrained in their activities. A very funny book
indeed. (E)

WILLIAM HOWARD TAFT

1309 Myers, Elisabeth P. William Howard Taft. Ill. with
photographs and cartoons. Reilly and Lee, 1970.
Between the flamboyant Teddy Roosevelt and the
scholarly Wilson, Taft (1857-1930) has not, perhaps,
received enough attention or credit for his integrity,
diplomacy and sound hard work. At least so it
seems from this carefully researched biography.
(YA and Up)

WOODROW WILSON

1310 Peare, Catherine Owens. The Woodrow Wilson Story,
An Idealist in Politics. Thomas Y. Crowell, 1963.
Biography of the intellectual 28th President (1856-
1924) which includes a clear account of America's
entry into World War I and ends sadly with Wilson's illness and inability to persuade America to
join the League of Nations. (YA)

HERBERT HOOVER

1311   Pryor, Helen B. <u>Lou Henry Hoover, Gallant First
        Lady</u>. Ill. with photographs. Dodd Mead, 1969.
        Mrs. Hoover was an inspiring example of many
        other First Ladies who combined home and civic
        responsibilities. Highly educated, and active in
        many organizations and relief causes, Lou Henry
        Hoover (1874-1944) is best remembered for her
        leadership in the Girl Scouts movement. (YA)

1312   Steinberg, Alfred. <u>Herbert Hoover</u>. Jacket by
        Charles Waterhouse. G. P. Putnam's Sons, 1967.
        A biography of the great humanitarian (1874-1964)
        and 31st President, which includes much important
        history of his times such as the Boxer Rebellion in
        China, two World Wars and the great Depression.
        He never dramatized his own achievements nor
        defended himself against unjust criticism and was
        fortunate in living long enough to be recognized for
        his greatness. (YA)

FRANKLIN D. ROOSEVELT

1312a   Blassingame, Wyatt. <u>Eleanor Roosevelt</u>. Ill. by
        Paul Frame. G. P. Putnam's Sons, 1967. It is
        interesting to note that here, as in the cases of
        Abigail Adams and Dolley Madison, there are more
        books for young readers on the White House Lady
        than on her husband. A very simple See and Read
        Book. (E)

1313   Davidson, Margaret. <u>The Story of Eleanor Roosevelt</u>.
        Ill. with photographs. Four Winds, 1968. The
        story of a truly remarkable woman defined in The
        Random House Dictionary as "U.S. diplomat, au-
        thor and lecturer" and, in parentheses, "Wife of
        Franklin Delano Roosevelt." (1884-1962). In this
        book we see her first as a painfully shy, unloved
        little girl; later, as a woman with a dominating
        mother-in-law and a husband stricken by polio who
        needed constant encouragement; and finally, as a
        woman of diverse and important activities after her
        husband's death. (I and YA)

1313a   Eaton, Jeanette. <u>The Story of Eleanor Roosevelt</u>.
        Ill. with 42 photographs. William Morrow, 1956.
        This biography was written during Mrs. Roosevelt's
        lifetime, when she was 72, which gives it some
        advantages and some disadvantages over the

biography written by Margaret Davidson, after her
death. They both tell the same story of the development of a shy, homely little girl into one of
the great Americans. (YA)

1314 Goodsell, Jane. Eleanor Roosevelt. Ill. by Wendell
Minor. A Crowell Biography, 1970. A short,
easy-to-read book. (E)

1315 Hickok, Lorena. The Road to the White House:
F.D.R.--The Pre-Presidential Years, with a
foreword by Eleanor Roosevelt. Ill. with photographs. Jacket by Leon Leiderman. Chilton,
1962. The story of Roosevelt's childhood and
youth, his early political interest, marriage and
children, his service as Assistant Secretary of
the Navy during World War I, his struggle to re-
cover from polio, and his years as governor of
New York. (YA)

1316 Johnson, Gerald W. Franklin D. Roosevelt: Portrait
of a Great Man. Ill. with 30 photographs and
decorations by Leonard Everett Fisher. Morrow,
1967. A fine biography (1882-1945) including a
brief political history of the first 45 years of the
20th century. (I and YA)

1317 Peare, Catherine Owens. The F.D.R. Story. Ill.
with photographs. Jacket by Robert Hallock.
Crowell, 1962. A biography of special interest
for its delineation of the development of Roosevelt's dynamic personality, showing childhood in-
fluences, the effect of his illness and physical
handicap, and the crucial years of his political
career. (YA)

1318 Steinberg, Alfred. Eleanor Roosevelt. Ill. by Andre
Le Blanc. G. P. Putnam's Sons, 1959. The
word "inspiring" must seem overused in these
notes on biographies, but most of them are just
that--especially in the case of this ugly duckling
who grew into not a swan but a very great woman.
(I and YA)

1319 Sullivan, Wilson. Franklin Delano Roosevelt. Ill.
with photographs and cartoons. American Heritage,
1970. A pictorial biography (1882-1945) of the
32nd President of the United States. (I and YA)

1320 Wise, William. Franklin Delano Roosevelt. Ill. by
Paul Frame. G. P. Putnam's Sons, 1967. A
See and Read Beginning to Read Biography, with
a list of "key words." (E)

SAILING SHIPS AND SEAMEN

PIRATES--The 17th Century

1321 Lawson, Robert. Capt. Kidd's Cat. Ill. by the author. Little Brown, 1956. "Being the True and Dolorous Chronicle of Wm. Kidd, Gent., and Merchant of New York, Late Captain, the Adventure Galley ... [and] of the Vicissitudes attending his Unfortunate Cruise in Eastern Waters, of his incarceration in Newgate Prison, of his Unjust Trial and Execution. As Narrated by His Faithful Cat McDermot Who Ought to Know." Obviously a highly humorous story of the famous privateersman, hanged for a pirate, and an explosion of the myth of his hidden treasure. (I and YA)

1322 Monjo, F. M. Pirates in Panama. Ill. by Wallace Tripp. Simon and Schuster, 1970. A legend about the pirate Henry Morgan, and of how small Benito and Brother John saved the Altar of Gold from the hands of pirates. (E)

1323 Syme, Ronald. Sir Henry Morgan, Buccaneer. Ill. by William Stobbs. Morrow Junior Books, 1965. This reckless and highly successful Welshman carried out his piratical deeds against Spain in the waters around the West Indies and ended his turbulent life as lieutenant governor of Jamaica, dying there of over-indulgence in food and drink. (I)

PIRATES--The 18th Century

1324 Beatty, John and Patricia. Pirate Royal. Macmillan, 1969. A novel in which the principal character is Sir Henry Morgan's accountant and scrivener who, after having been falsely accused of theft, is sent to America as an indentured servant but is abducted by a captain of Morgan's fleet. (YA)

1325   Best, Herbert.   Not Without Danger.   Ill. by Erick
         Berry.   Viking Press, 1951.   A grand adventure
         story set in the Colony of Jamaica in the period of
         the American Revolution.   A Connecticut boy,
         running away from the law (on account of having
         put hornets inside the proclamation scroll of the
         sheriff) becomes involved with pirates, smugglers
         and the crooked manager of a big sugar plantation.
         (I and YA)
1326   Hyde, Lawrence.   Under the Pirate Flag.   Ill. by
         Victor Mays.   Houghton Mifflin, 1965.   A thrilling
         adventure story in which a Nova Scotian lad stows
         away on a pirate ship which has a brutal captain,
         and with a few exceptions, a savage crew.   (I and
         YA)
1327   Meader, Stephen W.   The Black Buccaneer.   Ill. by
         Edward Shenton and the author.   Harcourt, Brace
         and World, 1920-48.   A rousing good story of pirates,
         kidnapping, sea battles and hidden treasure.   (I
         and YA)
1328   Miers, Earl Schenck.   Pirate Chase.   Ill. by Peter
         Burchard.   Colonial Williamsburg Inc., 1965.   An
         exciting story (what pirate story isn't) about the
         infamous Blackbeard who captures the fictional
         hero who, in turn, is later in on the capture of
         the pirate.   A legend with a factual basis of es-
         pecial interest for its depiction of the relationship
         between "respectable merchants" and pirates, and
         the heroic defense against piracy by Governor
         Spotswood of Virginia.   (I and YA)
1329   Norton, Andre (Alice Mary).   Scarface.   Ill. by
         Lorence Bjorklund.   Harcourt, Brace and World,
         1948.   "Being the Story of One Justin Blade,
         later of the Pirate Isle of Tortuga, and how Fate
         did justly deal with him to his great Profit."   A
         humdinger of a pirate story with suspense and
         mystery to the very end.   (YA)
1330   Wellman, Manley Wade.   Carolina Pirate.   Ives Wash-
         burn, 1968.   This story is set in the time of the
         "War of Jenkins' Ear" (1739-41) and is based on
         the commercial rivalry between England and
         Spain.   It is purely fictional but true to the spirit
         of the times, a good sea yarn in which a 19-year-
         old, skipping a ship of his father's business part-
         ner, is captured by pirates who take over the ship
         and force him to be the navigator.   (YA)
1331   Wibberley, Leonard.   Flint's Island.   Ill. with a

map. Farrar, Straus and Giroux, 1972. A sort
of sequel to Stevenson's "Treasure Island" which
Wibberley "felt compelled to write," turning it,
however, into an American story in which the
leading character comes from Salem, Mass. The
story includes a few of Stevenson's pirates, particularly Long John Silver. (I and YA)

PIRATES--The 19th Century

1332   Sperry, Armstrong. Black Falcon. Ill. by the author.
       John C. Winston, 1949. A splendid historical
       novel about Jean Lafitte, the protagonist a 16-
       year-old boy, son of the captain of a ship sunk by
       the British. The father is killed and the boy taken
       prisoner, but he escapes and joins LaFitte's band
       on the island of Grand Terre. The novel is cli-
       maxed by the Battle of New Orleans. (I and YA)
1333   Tallant, Robert. The Pirate Lafitte and the Battle
       of New Orleans. Ill. by John Chase. Random
       House Landmark, 1951. There are many myster-
       ies about Jean Lafitte (and his brother Pierre),
       but there seems to be no question about his patri-
       otism and support of Andrew Jackson in the fighting
       in December of 1814 and January of 1815. (I and
       YA)
1334   Turkle, Brinton. Obadiah the Bold. Viking Seafarer
       Edition, 1965. The story of a small Quaker boy
       in Nantucket in the mid-19th century who thought
       he would like to be a pirate. (E)
1335   Watson, Sally. Jade. Jacket by Michael Lowenbein.
       Holt, Rinehart and Winston, 1969. A Virginia
       girl aged 17 is so obstreperous that she is sent
       off to Jamaica to the control of an aunt and uncle.
       However when yellow fever strikes there she is
       sent home in what turns out to be a slave ship.
       And from there the plot certainly thickens. Suffice
       it to say that after being captured by a band of
       pirates led by a "lady pirate" (Anne Burney, an
       actual character) she becomes a half pirate herself.
       What a story! It beats all, but the author gives
       factual basis in an epilogue. (YA)
1336   Wellman, Manley Wade. Flag on the Levee. Ill. by
       William Ferguson. Ives Washburn, 1955. A novel
       of New Orleans just preceding the War of 1812--
       of duelling and conflict between Creoles and

Americans, of Jean Lafitte, and of plots of Aaron
Burr, of the Mardi Gras, and the foreign flavor
of New Orleans as it impresses a young man from
Carolina who comes there to learn his uncle's
business. (YA)

1337 _____. The River Pirates. Ives Washburn, 1963.
A rip-roaring story of piracy on the Mississippi
River, Aaron Burr's conspiracy, and a clever boy
who outwits the pirates in the end. A lot about
guns and fisticuffs. (I and YA)

PIRATES--The 20th Century

1338 Stahl, Ben. Blackbeard's Ghost. Ill. by the author.
Houghton Mifflin, 1965. A thoroughly spooky and
entertaining story of the infamous pirate, Teach,
and how he returns to a Carolina town in the
1960s to save his old castle from being torn down
to be replaced by a gas station. (I and YA)

THE REVOLUTIONARY ERA

1339 Bailey, Ralph Edgar. Fighting Sailor: The Story of
Nathaniel Fanning. Jacket and frontispiece by
Franz Altschuler, maps by James MacDonald.
Morrow Junior Books, 1966. A biography of a
young American who, after serving with John Paul
Jones in the Bonhomme Richard in its encounter
with the Serapis, was in command of French
privateers, and was twice captured by the British
but escaped to engage in diplomatic adventures,
encouraged by Ben Franklin. Glossary of sea
terms, bibliography and index. (I and YA)
1340 Cluff, Tom. Minutemen of the Sea. Ill. by Tom
O'Sullivan. Follett, 1955. The story, too long
untold, of the heroism of the farmers, fishermen
and woodsmen of Machias, Maine, who, five days
before the Battle of Bunker Hill, captured the
British ship, Margaretta, striking the first blow on
sea for American liberty. (I and YA)
1341 Haislip, Harvey. Sea Road to Yorktown. Doubleday,
1960. The third novel of a series ("Sailor Named
Jones" and "The Prize Master") whose hero, Midshipman Tommy Potter, rejects Ben Franklin's
orders to return home from France and instead

signs on the Princess, a privateer, finally effective
in the American victory at Yorktown. (YA and Up)

1342 Johnston, Johanna. Paul Cuffee, America's First Black
      Captain. Ill. by Elton C. Fax. Dodd Mead, 1970.
      A biography of a dauntless man (1759-1817). (E
      and I)

1343 Meader, Stephen W. A Blow for Liberty. Ill. by
      Victor Mays. Harcourt, Brace and World, 1965.
      An orphaned, indentured boy of Cape May County,
      New Jersey, joins the crew of a privateer schoon-
      er, and, after some narrow escapes in sea battles,
      is able to pay off his indenture with his share of
      prize money. (YA)

1344 _____. Guns for the Saratoga. Ill. by John O'Hara
      Cosgrove II. Harcourt, Brace and World, 1955.
      A story of the early American navy, in which a
      15-year-old boy, son of an ironmaster, delivers
      nine-pounders for the navy's new sloop-of-war, the
      Saratoga and signs on as a midshipman. The
      names of the Saratoga's crew were all taken from
      her actual muster. (YA)

1345 O'Connor, Patrick (Wibberley). Gunpowder for Wash-
      ington. Ives Washburn, 1956. A young lieutenant
      is sent to the West Indies to bring back 80 tons of
      gunpowder and runs into all sorts of surprises.
      (YA)

1346 Rink, Paul. John Paul Jones: Conquer or Die. Ill.
      by Tran Mawicke. G. P. Putnam's Sons, 1968.
      An American Pioneer Biography (1747-92). (I)

1347 Sperry, Armstrong. River of the West. Ill. by
      Henry C. Pitz. John C. Winston, 1952. Although
      not truly of the Revolution, this is a fine historical
      novel of the sea and the Boston men who sailed
      around the Horn to establish trade for furs on the
      north Pacific coast, and then traded with China.
      The story is of a young man who with Robert Gray
      in 1792 discovered the river of the West which he
      named "Columbia" after the vessel from which he
      discovered it, and thereby laid the claim to Ore-
      gon. Dangers from storm, scurvy, and hostile
      Indians make the novel one of constant action and
      tension. (I and YA)

1348 Syme, Ronald. Captain John Paul Jones, American
      Fighting Seaman. Ill. by William Stobbs. William
      Morrow, 1968. A short biography of the young
      Scot (1747-92) who became an American naval cap-
      tain. Special attention is given to the battle

between the Bonhomme Richard and the British
Serapis. (I)

1349 Wibberley, Leonard. Sea Captain from Salem.
Farrar, Straus and Cudahy, Ariel Book, 1961.
The third in the Treegate series on the American
Revolution ("John Treegate's Musket" [243] and
"Peter Treegate's War [244] were the first and
second), a story whose leading character is
"Peace of God Manley," first met in "Peter Tree-
gate's War." Franklin, in Paris, asks Captain
Manley to harry British shipping in the English
Channel. Humor, good nautical detail, and many
narrow escapes [see also 272 and 1362].

THE EARLY 19th CENTURY (War of 1812)

1350 Andrews, Mary Evans. Lanterns Aloft. Ill. by
Arthur Harper. Longmans Green, 1955. A side-
light on the War of 1812 as it affected Maryland's
eastern shore, with a well-developed plot and an
historical note and "Ship Talk" at the end. (I)

1351 Beyer, Audrey White. Capture at Sea. Ill. by H.
Tom Hall. Alfred A. Knopf, 1959. An 11-year-
old lad and his older cousin are taken by the
British from an American ship and put to work on
an English man-of-war, fighting against the French.
Their only chance to escape comes after the beginning of the War of 1812. (I)

1352 DuSoe, Robert C. The Boatswain's Boy. Ill. by
Arthur Harper. Longmans Green, 1950. A first-
rate sea story about a boy kidnapped on his way
to report as a midshipman on the U.S.S. Constitution, about his fearsome experiences aboard a
British Navy ship, and the violent battles en-
countered before he finally reports to Stephen
Decatur on the U.S.S. United States. (YA)

1353 Forester, C. S. The Captain from Connecticut. Little, Brown, 1941. A rattling good novel of the
sea in which the American captain and a British
one are interned together, by the French, on the
island of Martinique. (A)

1354 Hanson, Harry. Old Ironsides. Ill. by Alter Buehr.
Random House, Landmark, 1955. The adventures
of a famous ship, beginning with a race with a
British ship in which Old Ironsides showed her
speed--then the victory over the Barbary Pirates,

and, most excitingly, the victory over the British
ship Guerrierre in the War of 1812. (I and YA)

1355 Haywood, Charles F. No Ship May Sail. Nichols-
Ellis Press, 1942. A novel of seafaring during
the Jeffersonian Embargo in which a young Salem
captain outwits, outfights and outsails French privateers, Barbary pirates and the naval might of
England. (A)

1356 Mays, Victor. Action Starboard. Ill. by the author.
Houghton Mifflin, 1956. An exciting War of 1812
story in which an American brig breaks through
the British blockade, outruns a British privateer,
and turns privateer herself, and in which young
Toby Ives learns a great deal about seamanship
and the ways of seamen. Informative illustrations
of celestial navigation, the plans of the brig
Cormorant, and the equipment of a six-pound can-
non. A glossary of sea terms at the end should
really be studied at the beginning. (I and YA)

1357 Meader, Stephen. Clear for Action. Ill. by Frank
Beaudouin. Harcourt, Brace and World, 1940.
A story of two young American sailors impressed
into the British navy and their adventures before
and after their escape to an uninhabited island in
the Caribbean. (I and YA)

1358 Prudden, T. M. The Frigate Philadelphia. Ill. by
John C. Wonsetler. D. Van Nostrand, 1966.
Though the principal character is fictional, the
war against the Barbary pirates, Stephen Decatur's
daring action, and many of the other characters
are historical. (YA)

1359 Roberts, Kenneth. The Lively Lady. Doubleday,
Doran, 1941. "A Chronicle of Arundel, of Pri-
vateering, and of the Circular Prison on Dart-
moor." A novel about privateersmen in the War
of 1812. (A)

1360 Smith, Bradford. Stephen Decatur, Gallant Boy.
Ill. by Raymond Burns. Bobbs-Merrill, 1955.
Childhood of Famous Americans Series. Poor health
in childhood resulted in Stephen's being taken to
sea at an early age by his sea captain father, and
from then on nothing could deter him from a naval
career. (E and I)

1361 Werstein, Irving. The Cruise of the Essex; An Incident from the War of 1812. Macrae Smith, 1969.
The "incident" is actually only one of many daring
exploits of Captain David Porter (1780-1843), but

possibly the most "outlandish" one, for his was
the first American warship to round the Horn into
the Pacific and visit the Cannibal Isles (the Mar-
quesas and other south sea islands).   The book is
a biography of Captain Porter (1780-1843), with
the Pacific adventures as the focal point, and as
entertainingly written as fiction.   (YA)

1362   Wibberley, Leonard.   Leopard's Prey.   Jacket by
Enrico Arno.   Farrar, Straus and Giroux, 1971.
The fifth of the Treegate series, following "Tree-
gate's Raiders" [272] in which the grandson of
John Treegate and God's Peace Manley is acci-
dentally impressed on the British ship Leopard as
a powder boy during the period leading up to the
War of 1812.   (YA)

1363   Wilson, Hazel.   Tall Ships.   Ill. by John O'Hara
Cosgrove II.   Little, Brown, 1958.   The town of
Portland, Maine, was suffering badly because of
what was called "Jefferson's Embargo," and 16-
year-old Ben Wingate set out for Washington with
an older companion to try to persuade Jefferson
to lift it.   Almost there (in his father's longboat)
he was impressed by some British officers and
spent the next four years on a British ship until
it tangled with Stephen Decatur's ship, the United
States.   (I)

WHALING STORIES

1364   Alter, Robert Edmond.   Red Water.   Ill. by Steele
Savage.   G. P. Putnam's Sons, 1968.   A whale
of a story about a 17-year-old shanghied in the
1820s by some vicious seamen onto a whaler
which they scheme to "lose" for insurance.   With
a glossary of pidgin English and an author's note
concerning the basis of what seems like an im-
plausible plot.   (YA)

1365   Gould, Jean.   Young Mariner Melville.   Ill. by Donald McKay.   Dodd Mead, 1956.   The adventurous
youth of the author of "Moby Dick" which provided
much of the material for his writings.   (YA)

1366   Meader, Stephen.   Whaler 'Round the Horn.   Ill. by
Edward Shenton.   Harcourt, Brace and World,
1950.   A 16-year-old boy survives the wreck of
his whaling boat and is marooned on a Hawaiian
Island.   Good material on Hawaii as well as on

the dangers of whaling. (I and YA)
1367 Melville, Herman. Moby Dick; or, The White Whale
      (1851). Ill. by Robert Shore. Macmillan, 1962.
      With an afterword by Clifton Fadiman. The Amer-
      ican classic of whaling with its symbolism of good
      and evil, in a beautiful edition with powerful il-
      lustrations. (There are many editions.) (A)
1368 Ritchie, Rita. Rogue Whaler. Jacket by Frank Aloise.
      W. W. Norton, 1966. This combination of a mys-
      tery story with a story of whaling in the 1830s
      results in suspense plus a good deal of informa-
      tion about whales and their capture. (I and YA)
1369 Sperry, Armstrong. Danger to Windward. Ill. by
      the author. Holt, Rinehart and Winston, 1947.
      Danger indeed from a crooked step-uncle; from a
      cousin who is the vicious captain of The Good In-
      tent, rightfully belonging to the 15-year-old hero;
      and from whales, gales and cannibals. (YA)
1370 Webb, Christopher. Quest of the Otter. Jacket by
      Ernest Kurt Barth. Funk and Wagnalls, 1963.
      What one seeks is not always found but the search
      sometimes reveals something quite different, yet
      of equal or greater value. Paul Joplin sets off
      on the whaler Otter in 1842 or thereabouts, hoping
      to find his father, reported to have been lost in
      the south seas. (I and YA)

THE CIVIL WAR AT SEA

1371 Beatty, Jerome. Blockade. Ill. by Suzanne Verrier.
      Doubleday, 1971. A true story, based on the
      diary of young Steve Blanding of Providence,
      Rhode Island, who, after enlisting in the Union
      Navy in 1862, was assigned to the gunboat Louisi-
      ana, which was sent to blockade the North Carolina
      port of Little Washington. (I)
1372 Meader, Stephen. Phantom of the Blockade. Ill. by
      Victor Mays. Harcourt, Brace and World, 1962.
      A 17-year-old sailor aboard a Confederate block-
      ade runner escapes capture by the skin of his
      teeth, as the Gray Witch makes its many voyages
      to bring back from Bermuda rifles, powder and
      medicine for Lee's army in exchange for southern
      cotton. (YA)
1373 Merriwether, Louise. The Freedom Ship of Robert
      Smalls. Ill. by Jack Morton. Prentice-Hall,

1971.   The story of Robert Smalls' journey to
freedom, with 15 other runaway slaves, on a captured gunboat.   (YA)

1374   Sterling, Dorothy.   Captain of the Planter: The Story
of Robert Smalls.   Ill. by Ernest Crichlow.
Doubleday, 1958.   The story of how "that boy,"
Robert Smalls (1839-1915), a young slave, delivered
the Planter into Union hands and how he later held
a seat in Congress and became a landholder.   (YA)

THE 19th CENTURY--GENERAL

1375   Arntson, Herbert.   Adam Gray, Stowaway: A Story
of the China Trade.   Ill. by Henry S. Gillette.
Franklin Watts, 1961.   An adventure story,
based on actual history of two ships, the Tonquin
and the New Hazard, which begins and ends in
New York.   With a glossary of sailing ship terms.
(I and YA)

1376   Capron, Louis.   The Blue Witch.   Jacket and Ill. by
Douglas Gorsline.   Henry Holt, 1957.   A suspenseful story of ships in the China trade in the
1830s; of "wreckers" off Key West, Florida; of
hurricanes, and Indian massacres.   A young
Vermonter is enticed by a step-uncle of dubious
repute into investing his father's money in the
China trade and becoming involved in some very
shady deals.   (I and YA)

1377   Coatsworth, Elizabeth.   The Captain's Daughter.
Macmillan, 1950 and 1963.   A victorian love story
about a young lady sent on a long sea voyage to
the Orient by her father who objects to the young
man Janet wants to marry.   The charm of the
book lies in the details of sea travel in the days
of clipper ships.   (YA)

1378   Corbett, Scott.   One By Sea.   Ill. by Victor Mays.
Little Brown, 1965.   A boy whose widowed father
is at sea, falls into the hands of conspirators
against his father's life and runs terrifying risks
to reach and warn his father.   (I and YA)

1379   Duncan, Fred B.   Deepwater Family.   Ill. with contemporary photographs.   Pantheon, 1969.   With
an afterword by Karl Kortum.   In this unusual
story of family life on one of the last three-
masted deepwater sailing ships, the reader may
experience the thrills and dangers of voyages

around the horn and to many exotic ports as re-
called by the author who spent the first 11 years
of his life at sea, with his captain father, his
mother and brothers and sisters, toward the end
of the nineteenth century. (YA and Up)

1380 Fritz, Jean. I, Adam. Ill. by Peter Burchard.
Coward McCann, 1963. A novel about a 16-year-
old in 1850 who has to make a difficult choice of
direction in his life. Should it be on land or sea?
The choice is complicated by a sense of duty to
his parents, by economic circumstances and by a
serious accident. In the end, a problem of self-
understanding. (I and YA)

1381 Gendron, Val. Outlaw Voyage. Ill. by Leonard
Vosburgh. World, 1955. "The exciting adventures
of young Joshua Small in the days of the mighty
Clipper Ships" pretty well sums up this skillfully
plotted tale of a Cape Cod lad who signs up as
first mate on a "slaver." (YA)

1382 Latham, Jean Lee. Authors Aweigh: The Story of
David Glasgow Farragut. Ill. by Eros Kieth.
Harper and Row, 1968. "Damn the torpedos, full
steam ahead." An exciting biography of the great
admiral (1801-1870) who first went to sea as a
midshipman, under Captain David Porter, when he
was ten years old. Good naval detail. (I)

1383 _____. Carry On, Mr. Bowditch. Ill. by John
O'Hara Cosgrove II. Houghton Mifflin, 1955. A
biographical novel of Nathaniel Bowditch (1773-
1838), whose book "The American Practical Navigator" is still the sailor's Bible and standard
text in the U.S. Naval Academy, though Bowditch
himself had very little formal schooling. (I and
YA)

1384 _____. David Glasgow Farragut. Ill. by Paul
Frame. Garrard, 1967. A Discovery Book. A
midshipman at age ten, and appointed prize master
of a captured British ship at age 18. (E)

1385 _____. Trail Blazer of the Seas. Ill. by Victor
Mays. Houghton-Mifflin, 1956. The exciting and
inspiring life story of Matthew Maury (1806-73),
whose name is little remembered but who fought
all his life, against bitter opposition, for his
ideas which, according to Baron Von Humboldt,
were the foundation of a new science--the physical
geography of the sea. Though recognized by
eminent scientists and rulers of many European

countries, he was "retired" from the U.S. Navy
at the age of 47, under "the Act to promote the ef-
ficiency of the Navy" but with instructions to carry
on his duties with one third of his former pay.
Nevertheless he continued to blaze the trail for the
laying of the Atlantic cable.   (I and YA)

1386   McCague, James.   When Clipper Ships Ruled the Seas.
Ill. by Victor Mays.   Garrard, 1968.   A story of
the building of clipper ships and of some famous
ones (particularly the Flying Cloud and its voyage
around the Horn), with illustrations that make all
sea stories about that period vivid.   (I)

1387   Meader, Stephen W.   The Voyage of the Javelin.   Ill.
by John O'Hara Cosgrove II.   Harcourt, Brace,
1959.   A story of high adventure for a young man
under 18 in the great age of clipper ships (the
1850s), when they raced each other around the
Horn, traded for furs with hostile Indians on the
Northwest coast, picked up tea cargo in China, and
fought pirates.   (I and YA)

1388   O'Dell, Scott.   The Dark Canoe.   Ill. by Milton Johnson.   Houghton Mifflin, 1968.   A novel about the
search for a sunken ship, the Amy Foster, led by
a mad captain who identifies himself with Ahab of
"Moby Dick."   (YA)

1389   Orrmont, Arthur.   The Indestructable Commodore
Matthew Perry.   Jacket by Stephen Voorhies.
Julian Messner, 1962.   A biography of a naval of-
ficer and diplomat (1794-1859), notable for his
opening of Japan to the western world in 1853, his
part in the founding of Liberia, his pioneering of
naval sanitation, his promotion of the steam navy,
and his victory with Winfield Scott at Santa Cruz.
(YA)

1390   Rink, Paul.   To Steer by the Stars: The Story of
Nathaniel Bowditch.   Jacket by Tim Lewis, endpapers and frontispiece courtesy of Peabody Museum
of Salem.   Doubleday, 1969.   The story of Bowditch's development of the science of celestial navigation and his faith in its truth.   (YA)

1391   Robertson, Keith.   The Wreck of the Saginaw.   Ill. by
Jack Weaver.   Viking, 1954.   Enlivened by imagined
dialogues, this is a true story of a wreck on Mid-
way Island in 1870 and the superhuman effort of five
crew members who sailed a small gig 1500 miles to
Hawaii to get help for the 88 men marooned on the
desert island.   (I and YA)

1392 Walton, Elizabeth Cheatham. Voices in the Fog.   Ill.
       by Shirley Hughes. Abelard Schuman, 1968.
       Twelve-year-old twin girls run into dangerous ad-
       ventures in trying to solve the mystery of their
       father's and uncle's business of ship stores on
       Cape Cod, at Falmouth, in the 1840s.   (I)
1393 Webb, Christopher. The Ann and Hope Mutiny.   Funk
       and Wagnalls, 1966.   A boy from New Bedford
       becomes embroiled in a mystery surrounding the
       appearance of a ship in the south seas with all
       sails set, yet nary a soul aboard.   Based on the
       story of the Mary Celeste.   (I and YA)

TURN OF THE CENTURY/20th CENTURY

1394 Kipling, Rudyard. "Captains Courageous" (1897).   A
       Magnum Easy Eye Book, 1967, Lancer Books.
       The spoiled son of a railroad and shipping tycoon
       falls overboard from a luxury liner near the Grande
       Banks of Nova Scotia.   Rescued by a fisherman
       from the fleets off the Banks, he has three months'
       rugged experience at sea before he can get home,
       an experience which changes his outlook and per-
       sonality greatly for the better, and provides good
       entertainment for the reader.   (The title, by the
       way, is intentionally placed in quotation marks as
       Kipling took the phrase from an Elizabethan bal-
       lad.)   (I and YA)
1395 Mowat, Farley. The Black Joke.   Ill. by Victor
       Mays.   Little Brown, 1962.   An action-packed
       story of whiskey smuggling in the 1930s, in which
       a group of boys have some wild adventures on the
       ship Black Joke, off the coast of Newfoundland.
       (YA)
1396 Vance, Marguerite. Courage at Sea.   Ill. by Lorence
       F. Bjorklund.   E. P. Dutton, 1963.   A fictional
       story of the sinking of the Titanic on April 10,
       1912.   An unathletic and timid boy suddenly dis-
       plays his real mettle in the crisis.   (I)

SCIENCE

1397   Aliki (Brandenberg). A Weed Is a Flower: The Life
       of George Washington Carver. Ill. by the author.
       Prentice-Hall, 1965. A picture story of the great
       botanist and chemist, who came near to being
       abandoned as a baby (1860?-1943). (E)
1398   Baker, Rachel and Joanna Baker Merlin. America's
       First Woman Astronomer, Maria Mitchell. Ill.
       with photographs. Julian Messner, 1960. Bio-
       graphy (1818-89) of a woman who, at the age of
       ten, in her father's absence, rated a chronometer
       for a ship captain, sighted an undiscovered comet
       at the age of 29, and in 1922 was elected to the
       Hall of Fame. (YA)
1399   Berry, Erick (Best). Stars in My Pocket: A Novel
       Based on Events in the Life of Maria Mitchell,
       America's First Woman Astronomer. John Day, 1960.
       Daughters of Valor Series. A story of Maria
       Mitchell's girlhood with just a bit about her suc-
       cess and fame in later years. (I)
1400   Bontemps, Arna. The Story of George Washington
       Carver. Ill. by Harper Johnson. Grosset and
       Dunlap, 1954. Biography, mainly about Carver's
       childhood and young manhood and the education for
       which he worked so hard. (I)
1401   Bragdon, Lillian. Luther Burbank, Nature's Helper.
       Ill. by Frederick T. Chapman. Abingdon, 1959.
       Biography of the great horticulturalist and plant
       breeder (1849-1926) and the story of his seeming
       miracles in grafting, cross pollenization and the
       actual creation of new plants. (I)
1402   Douglas, William O. Muir of the Mountains. Ill.
       by Harve Stein. Houghton Mifflin, 1961. Bi-
       ography of the great naturalist, explorer and
       writer (1838-1914), intrepid mountain climber,
       discoverer of glaciers, and early conservationist,
       written by a Supreme Court Justice who is also
       a mountain climber and conservationist. Born in
       Scotland, his youth spent in Wisconsin, Muir be-

came a world citizen. For dog lovers there is an
especially interesting chapter in this book about
Muir's dog, Stickeen and an ice bridge. (I)

1403 Douty, Esther. America's First Woman Chemist,
Ellen Richards. Jacket by Jules Gotlieb. Julian
Messner, 1961. Biography (1842-1911) of one of
the first women to combine homemaking with a
career, and the first to study at the Massachusetts
Institute of Technology. (YA)

1404 Epstein, Sam and Beryl. George Washington Carver.
Ill. by William Mayers. Garrard, 1960. A Discovery Book. The story of a sickly little slave
baby who might easily have been abandoned but
was fortunately saved to become a great botanist
and chemist, recognized by Presidents and others.
(E)

1405 Forsee, Aylesa. Louis Agassiz, Pied Piper of Science. Ill. by Winifred Lubell. Viking, 1958. See
entry 1416. (YA)

1406 Frisbee, Lucy Post. John Burroughs, Boy of Field
and Stream. Ill. by Gray Morrow. Bobbs-Merrill,
1964. Childhood of Famous Americans Series.
The story of the boyhood of a great naturalist and
writer about nature, who once said, "The most
precious things in life are near at hand, without
money and without price." (E and I)

1407 Garst, Shannon and Warren. Ernest Thompson Seton,
Naturalist. Jacket by Gerald McCann. Julian
Messner, 1959. Biography of a man (1860-1946)
who always believed in turning defeats into victories,
and who did that time and time again. His father's
floggings sent him into the woods for solace; poor
health prevented him from going to college but led
him to study art; and boy vandals who defaced the
fences of his beautiful estate gave him the idea
which resulted in his forming the Boy Scouts. (YA)

1408 Graham, Shirley. Dr. George Washington Carver,
Scientist. Ill. by Elton C. Fox. Julian Messner,
1944. A biographical novel about the great man
who was saved, half dead, from slave-snatchers as
a baby, and who, by his own efforts achieved fame
for his contributions to U.S. agriculture and the
science of nutrition. Like Booker T. Washington,
who called him to serve at Tuskegee Institute, he
believed in the dignity of labor and the Biblical
words, "The earth is the Lord's and the fullness
thereof." (I and YA)

1409 Hayden, Robert C. Seven Black American Scientists.
      Addison-Wesley, 1970. Included in this book are
      biographies of Benjamin Banneker, George Wash-
      ington Carver, Ernest E. Just, Daniel Hale Wil-
      liams, Matthew A. Henson, Charles R. Drew, and
      Charles H. Turner. (YA and Up)
1410 Lewis, Claude. Benjamin Banneker: The Man Who
      Saved Washington. Ill. by Ernest Crichlow.
      McGraw-Hill, 1970. A self-educated free Negro
      (1731-1806) Banneker was a mathematician,
      astronomer, calculator of several almanacs, and,
      in 1791, through his remarkable memory, was able
      to draw plans that had been laid down by L'Enfant
      (whose services had been terminated and who had
      carried all his plans and papers away with him) for
      the building of the city of Washington, D.C. (I and
      YA)
1411 Manber, David. Wizard of Tuskegee: The Life of George
      Washington Carver. Ill. with photographs. Mac-
      millan, 1967. An inspiring biography (1864-1943)
      of the great Negro chemist and botanist, whose
      discoveries have led to hundreds of useful products
      from the soil, particularly from the peanut and the
      sweet potato. (I and YA)
1412 Means, Florence Crannell. Carver's George. Ill. by
      Harve Stein. Houghton Mifflin, 1952. A biography
      of the great Negro botanist and chemist, 1864-
      1943. (I)
1413 Peare, Catherine. Albert Einstein: A Biography for
      Young People. Ill. with photographs. Henry Holt,
      1949. Biography (1879-1955) of the German-born
      physicist who lived there until forced out by the
      Nazis in 1933, when he came to the United States
      where he took out citizenship in 1936. He became
      a life member of the Institute for Advanced Studies
      in Princeton, New Jersey. The genius who de-
      veloped the theory of relativity, he was also a
      staunch pacifist. (YA)
1414 Swift, Hildegarde Hoyt. The Edge of April: A Bi-
      ography of John Burroughs. Ill. by Lynd Ward.
      William Morrow, 1957. A "dramatized" rather
      than fictional biography according to its author,
      this brings the subject (1837-1921) to a kind of
      living reality. (YA and Up)
1415 _____. From the Eagle's Wing: A Biography of
      John Muir. Ill. by Lynd Ward. William Morrow,
      1962. A dramatized biography (1838-1914) of the

mountain climber, carpenter, naturalist, conservationist and writer, with an introduction by Eleanor
Roosevelt. (YA and Up)

1416 Tharp, Louise. Louis Agassiz, Adventurous Scientist
Ill. by Rafaello Busoni. Little Brown, 1961.
Imagine letting yourself be lowered 120 feet inside
of a glacier, or jumping over crevasses in the
Jungfrau or studying sea life in the Magellan
Strait. Such were only a few of the daring adventures of Louis Agassiz, born in Switzerland in
1807, but an American from 1846 until his death
in 1873. Trained in medicine, he became famous
as an ichthyologist, zoologist, geologist, and, above
all, a teacher. (YA)

1417 Wilkie, Katharine E. Maria Mitchell. Ill. by Paul
Kennedy. Garrard, 1966. A Discovery Book.
The story of a little girl who learned astronomy in
her own attic, under her father's guidance. When
she was 29, she discovered a comet and received
a medal from the King of Denmark in 1848. (E)

SLAVERY, CIVIL RIGHTS, BLACK HISTORY

COLLECTIVE BIOGRAPHIES

1418 Hughes, Langston. <u>Famous American Negroes.</u> Ill.
with photographs. Dodd Mead, 1954. Phillis
Wheatley, poet; Richard Allen, founder of the African Methodist Episcopal Church; Ira Aldridge,
actor; Frederick Douglass, fighter for freedom;
Harriet Tubman, underground railroad conductor;
Booker T. Washington, founder of Tuskegee; Daniel
Hale Williams, physician; George Washington Carver, agricultural chemist; Robert S. Abbott, cru-
sading journalist; Paul Lawrence Dunbar, poet;
W. C. Handy, father of the blues; Charles C.
Spaulding, business executive; A. Philip Randolph,
labor leader; Ralph Bunche, statesman and political
scientist; Marian Anderson, concert singer; Jackie
Robinson, first Negro in Big League baseball.   (YA)

1419 Johnston, Johanna. <u>A Special Bravery.</u> Ill. by Ann
Grifalconi. Dodd Mead, 1967. Minibiographies of
Crispus Attucks, James Forten, Benjamin Ban-
neker, Henry Brown, Harriet Tubman, Frederick
Douglass, Robert Smalls, Booker T. Washington,
George Washington Carver, Matthew Henson, Mary
McLeod Bethune, Jackie Robinson, Marian Ander-
son, Ralphe Bunche, and Martin Luther King.
(E and I)

1420 Rollins, Charlemae. <u>They Showed the Way: Forty</u>
<u>American Negro Leaders.</u> Thomas Y. Crowell,
1964. Robert S. Abbott, Ira Frederick Aldridge,
Richard Allen, Crispus Attucks, Benjamin Ban-
neker, James Beckwourth, Mary McLeod Bethune,
George Washington Carver, Joseph Cinque,
Frederick Douglass, Charles Richard Drew,
William Edward Burchardt DuBois, Paul Lawrence
Dunbar, Jean Baptiste Pointe DeSable, Deborah
Garnet, Henry Highland Garnet, Archibald Henry
Grimke, William C. Handy, Matthew A. Henson,
James Weldon Johnson, Edmonia Lewis, Jan Ernest
Matzeliger, Hugh Nathanial Mulzac, Skipper

Pompey, Gabriel Prosser, Norbert Rillieux,
Peter Salem, Robert Smalls, Henry Ossawa Tan-
ner, Harriet Tubman, Nat Turner, Maggie Lena
Walker, Booker T. Washington, Phillis Wheatley,
Burt Williams, Daniel Hale Williams, Carter
Goodwin Woodson, Charles Young. (I and YA)

1421 Sterling, Philip and Rayford Logan. Four Took
Freedom. Ill. with drawings by an unnamed
artist; Jacket by Charles White. Doubleday, 1967.
Biographies of: Harriet Tubman, Frederick
Douglass, Robert Smalls, and Blanche K. Bruce.
(I and YA)

1422 Sterne, Emma Gelders. They Took Their Stand.
Ill. with photographs. Crowell-Collier Press,
1968. Profiles of 12 courageous white southerners
who devoted their lives to the struggle for equal
rights: John Laurens, Sophia Auld, Angelina
Grimke, John Fairfield, George Henry Thomas,
James Hunnicutt, Claude Williams, Myles Horton,
Anne Braden, The Rev. Dunbar Ogden, Robert
Zellner. And there were many others. There
were also Levi Coffin, the underground railroad
Quaker, and Joseph Gelders, Myles Horton, Anne
and Carl Braden who tried to bring Negroes into
the white community. These people endured
prison--sometimes even death--and always ostra-
cism from white supremacists and even some
moderate southerners. (YA)

INDIVIDUAL BIBLIOGRAPHIES

1423 Ansley, Delight. The Sword and the Spirit: A Life
of John Brown. Ill. by Robert Hallock. Thomas
Y. Crowell, 1955. A sympathetic biography of
the fanatical Brown (1800-59) showing also his
serious mistakes and lack of practical planning.
His meetings with other abolitionists, especially
Frederick Douglass, are significant in showing the
violent against the non-violent approaches. (YA
and Up)

1424 Bernard, Jacqueline. Journey Toward Freedom:
The Story of Sojourner Truth. Ill. with photo-
graphs and engravings. W. W. Norton, 1967.
A biographical novel about "a giant of a woman"
(1797-1883), born in slavery in the Hudson River
Dutch country, who, when free, became a great

abolitionist and also champion of womens' rights,
prison reform, and better conditions for working
people. (YA)

1425 Bontemps, Arna. Frederick Douglass: Slave--Fighter
--Freeman. Ill. by Harper Johnson. Alfred A.
Knopf, 1959. A fictionalized account of the life
(1817-95) of the famous Negro, based on his
autobiography. (I)

1426 Booker, Simeon. Susie King Taylor, Civil War Nurse.
Ill. by Harold James. McGraw-Hill, 1969. A
biography (1847-1912) of one who, starting as a
little slave girl, worked as a nurse for the famous
slave regiment in the Civil War (under Thomas
Wentworth Higginson) and also the story of the
overcoming of illiteracy by Blacks who had been
denied educational opportunity. (I)

1427 Clayton, Ed. Martin Luther King, the Peaceful Warrior. Ill. by David Hodges. Prentice-Hall, 1964.
A brief biography (1929-64) of the preacher of non-
violence, who constantly faced not only imprisonment but threats on his life, enduring all but the
last. (I)

1428 Davidson, Margaret. Frederick Douglass Fights for
Freedom. Ill. by Ann Grifalconi. Four Winds,
1968. A well-written and beautifully illustrated
biography (1817-95). (I)

1429 deKay, James. Meet Martin Luther King, Jr. Ill.
with photographs and drawings by Ted Burwell.
Random, 1969. Step-Up Books. A moving story
of the life of the Negro leader (1929-68) who won
a Nobel prize for his peaceful rebellion against
Jim Crow laws and who was assassinated and
deeply mourned by all. (E)

1430 Douglas, Frederick. Life and Times of Frederick
Douglass. Adapted by Barbara Ritchie. Thomas
Y. Crowell, 1966. The autobiography (1817-95)
of the great man who rose from slavery to become
a highly respected American lecturer and statesman
and who was able to greatly help his own people.
(I and YA)

1431 Douty, Esther M. Forten the Sailmaker: Pioneer
Champion of Civil Rights. Ill. with photographs.
Rand McNally, 1968. This Civil Rights pioneer
was indeed pioneering (1765-1842). Though free,
rich and successful himself (he lived in Pennsylvania), he fought against the lot of his enslaved
people and also against the ideal of colonizing

Blacks in Africa. (YA)
1432 Felton, Harold W. Mumbet: The Story of Elizabeth
      Freeman. Ill. by Donn Albright. Dodd Mead,
      1970. Briefly told, this is the story of a woman
      (1744?-1829), a dauntless slave for 30 years, who
      was the first Negro to win her freedom through the
      courts of Massachusetts. (I)
1433 Felton, Harold W. James Weldon Johnson. Ill. by
      Charles Shaw. Dodd Mead, 1971. The story of a
      black boy, raised in poverty, but with plenty of
      love, in Jacksonville, Florida, who grew up to be
      a distinguished poet and author, teacher, editor,
      lecturer, diplomat, and successful writer of popular
      songs, and one of the founders of the N.A.A.C.P.
      Included are the words and simplified guitar arrange-
      ment of his "Lift Ev'ry Voice and Sing." (I)
1434 Griffin, Judith Berry. Nat Turner. Ill. by Leo Carty.
      Coward McCann, 1970. The tragic story of the
      young Negro (1800-31) who led a slave rebellion in
      1831, an unsuccessful one resulting not only in his
      capture and execution, but also in harder lots than
      ever for many slaves. (I)
1435 Hennessy, Maurice and Edwin Sauter Jr. A Crown
      for Thomas Peters. Ives Washburn, 1964. A bio-
      graphical novel of a young Negro, captured by the
      British in the early 18th century and sold into
      slavery in Charleston, S.C., whence he finally
      escaped by the underground railroad. He eventual-
      ly returned to Sierra Leone as a leader of fugitive
      slaves. (YA)
1436 Iger, Eve Marie. John Brown: His Soul Goes March-
      ing On. Ill. with photographs. Young Scott, 1969.
      A well narrated and illustrated biography (1800-59),
      leaving it up to the reader to judge Brown's actions.
      Was he the man so greatly admired by such aboli-
      tionists as Emerson and Thoreau, or were his
      violent methods wrong, as some other abolitionists
      felt? (I and YA)
1437 Killens, Oliver. Great Gittin' Up Morning: A Bi-
      ography of Denmark Vesey. Doubleday, 1972. The
      life story (1767-1822) of the free Black man in the
      Charleston of the early 1800s who was determined
      that slavery should be done away with and believed
      that this could only happen through killing every
      white man, woman and child in Charleston, first,
      after which he hoped the movement would spread
      farther. Except for the first chapter which is

largely fictional, the book is based on "The
Trial of Denmark Vesey" and other sources.   (YA)

1438   Lacy, Leslie Alexander.   Cheer the Lonesome
Traveller: The Life of W.E.B. DuBois.   Ill. by
James Barkley and Photographs.   Dial, 1970.   A
fair, factual biography of the founder, in 1909, of
the N.A.A.C.P., who was born in Great Barring-
ton, Mass., in 1868, and who died in Ghana in
1963, having joined the Communist Party.   (YA
and Up)

1439   McConnell, Jane T.   Cornelia: The Story of a Civil
War Nurse.   Ill. by Dorothy Bayley Morse.
Crowell, 1959.   A biography of Cornelia Hancock
(1840-1926), a Quaker and early civil rights
worker in Washington where she helped and nursed
the freed slaves.   She was also a teacher and
founder of the Laing School in Mt. Pleasant, S.C.,
a social worker in Philadelphia, and a pioneer in
urban housing problems.   (YA)

1440   Meltzer, Milton.   Thaddeus Stevens and the Fight for
Negro Rights.   Thomas Y. Crowell, 1967.   A
biography (1792-1868) and history that needs and
deserves careful reading, and provides an excellent background for an understanding of the current
problems of race relations.   (YA and Up)

1441   Millender, Dharathula H.   Martin Luther King, Boy
With a Dream.   Ill. by Al Fiorentino.   Bobbs-
Merrill, 1969.   Childhood of Famous Americans
Series.   The story of King's childhood and youth
and his courage in leading the non-violent move-
ment for civil rights (1929-1968).   (I)

1442   Nolan, Jeannette Covert.   John Brown.   Ill. by
Robert Burns.   Julian Messner, 1950.   The
story of his life and mission from the time he
was 12 in 1812 until he was hanged for the insur-
rection at Harper's Ferry.   (YA)

1443   Petry, Ann.   Harriet Tubman, Conductor on the Underground Railroad.   Jacket by Ernest Crichlow.
Thomas Y. Crowell, 1955.   A biography of Harriet and a short history of slavery in the United
States.   (YA)

1444   Pitrone, Jean Maddern.   Trailblazer: Negro Nurse
in the American Red Cross--The Life of Frances
Reed Elliott.   Jacket by Karolina Harris.   Harcourt, Brace and World, 1969.   Biography of a
Negro nurse (1882-1965) and a story of dedication
to the nursing profession and the overcoming of

the obstacle of racial prejudice to obtain a place
in the Red Cross; a story too of the prejudice of
some Negros against the lighter skinned members
of their race, and of the support of white friends.
(YA)

1445 Sterling, Dorothy. The Making of an Afro-American:
Martin Robeson Delany, 1812-85; The Story of the
Father of Black Nationalism. Doubleday, 1971.
An extremely important book for its content, which
is presented in exciting narrative form. (YA and
Up)

1446 Swift, Hildegarde Hoyt. The Railroad to Freedom.
Ill. by James Daugherty. Harcourt, Brace and
World, 1932-60. A biographical novel of Harriet
Tubman (1821-1913), conductor on the underground
railroad, Civil War nurse, and spy. (YA)

1447 Underwood, Betty. The Tamarack Tree. Ill. by Bea
Holmes. Houghton Mifflin, 1971. A novel based
on the trials which beset Miss Prudence Crandall
when she established a school "for young ladies
of color" in Canterbury, Conn., in 1833. (YA)

1448 Winders, Gertrude Hecker. Harriet Tubman, Freedom Girl. Ill. by William T. Plummer. Bobbs-
Merrill, 1969. Childhood of Famous Americans
Series. Mainly the story of Harriet's life as a
slave girl, with only a short section about her
later life. (I)

1449 Wise, Winifred. Fanny Kemble: Actress, Author,
Abolitionist. Ill. with a portrait by Thomas
Sully. G. P. Putnam's Sons, 1966. The biography
of an English actress (1809-1893) who married an
American, Pierce Butler, and lived with him for
some time on his Georgia plantation where she
saw slavery at its near-worst if not its absolute
worst. Her account of it, published in England
during the Civil War was a strong influence
against England's aiding the Confederacy. (YA)

1450 Yates, Elizabeth. Prudence Crandall, Woman of Courage. Ill. by Nora S. Unwin. E. P. Dutton, 1955.
A biographical novel about a most courageous young
Connecticut woman (1803-1890) who in 1833, against
threats of violence (often carried out) against her
house, and long dreary trials and even imprisonment, opened a school for "young ladies and little
misses of color" in Canterbury, Connecticut.
Florence's married name was "Philleo" and you
may find her thus listed in libraries. (YA)

1451 _____. Amos Fortune, Free Man. Ill. by Nora
      S. Unwin. E. P. Dutton, 1950. A biography of
      a Negro (1710-1801), born free in Africa, enslaved
      in America, freed at the age of 59, and a success-
      ful tanner through his later years. His loving
      spirit and care for others, his buying freedom for
      some, and his skill in the tanning business secured
      for him a fine reputation, recorded on his tomb-
      stone in Jaffrey, New Hampshire. (YA)

SLAVERY; THE UNDERGROUND RAILROAD

1452 Allee, Marjorie. Susanna and Tristram. Ill. by
      Hattie Longstreet Price. Houghton Mifflin, 1957.
      A novel about a young Quaker lady and her younger
      brother who become dangerously involved in the
      underground movement to transport slaves to
      Canada after the Fugitive Slave Law made it pos-
      sible for owners to recapture them in free states.
      (YA)

1453 Bacmeister, Rhoda. Voices in the Night. Ill. by
      Ann Grifalconi. Bobbs-Merrill, 1965. A good
      underground railroad story in which a little New
      England girl of 11 plays an important part in
      eluding the slave catchers. (I)

1454 Bacon, Martha. Sophia Scrooby Preserved. Ill. by
      David Omar White. Atlantic Monthly Press, 1968.
      A highly imaginative story of a little African girl
      and her incredible adventures and accomplishments:
      from her childhood among Africa's wild beasts,
      through enslavement in New Haven, Conn., capture
      by pirates and still more adventures. (I and YA)

1455 Beyer, Audrey. Dark Venture. Jacket by Leo and
      Diane Dillox. Alfred A. Knopf, 1968. A story
      of a 12-year-old African boy captured by alien
      tribesmen of Africa (who sell him into slavery)
      which ends with him in New England, still a slave
      but to a kindly young doctor. (YA)

1456 Bradbury, Bianca. The Undergrounders. Ill. by Jon
      Nielsen. Ives Washburn, 1966. Story of a school-
      boy's part in the rescue of runaway slaves, after
      the passage of the Fugitive Slave Law. (YA)

1457 Brown, Frances Williams. Looking for Orlando.
      Jacket by H. Lawrence Hoffman. Criterion, 1961.
      A tightly plotted novel about the underground rail-
      road and two "ex-southern" young men who become

involved in its purpose. (YA)

1458   Buckmaster, Henrietta (Henkle). Flight to Freedom:
       The Story of the Underground Railroad. Thomas Y.
       Crowell, 1958. A tense account of the Negro
       struggle for equality, showing the dissension in the
       matter of civil rights in the north as well as the
       south. (YA and Up)

1459   Burchard, Peter. Bimby. Ill. by the author. Cow-
       ard McCann, 1968. A short tense novel about a
       boy facing the reality of slavery and about his
       dream of freedom.

1460   Butler, Beverly. The Silver Key. Dodd Mead, 1961.
       A well plotted historical romance set in the Welsh
       settlements near Ripon, Wisconsin, when the un-
       derground railroad had stations in that state. (YA)

1461   DeAngeli, Marguerite. Thee, Hannah. Ill. by the
       author. Doubleday, 1940. The story of a little
       Quaker girl who resents having to wear a plain
       "scoop" bonnet instead of a flowered one, until
       she learns that her bonnet symbolizes something
       important for escaping slaves. (E and I)

1462   Douglas, Marjory Stoneman. Freedom River. Ill. by
       Edward Shenton. Charles Scribner's Sons, 1953.
       A book, full of details of the Florida country, about
       a Negro living there at the time Florida became a
       slave state, and a white boy who saves him from a
       slave dealer. (YA)

1463   Fisher, Aileen. A Lantern in the Window. Ill. by
       Harper Johnson. Thomas Nelson, 1957. A top-
       notch underground railroad story in which a 12-year-
       old boy outguesses the slave catchers. (I)

1464   Forman, James. Song of Jubilee. Jacket by David
       Hodges. Farrar, Straus and Giroux, 1971. A novel
       of a Negro growing up as a rather favored slave
       but suffering insults and degradation more than
       physical brutality, and of his hopeless love of a
       white girl. (YA)

1465   Freedman, Florence. Two Tickets to Freedom: The
       True Story of Ellen and William Craft, Fugitive
       Slaves. Ill. by Ezra Jack Keats. Simon and
       Schuster, 1971. The miraculous escapes of hus-
       band and wife, first from their southern master,
       and then because of the Fugitive Slave Law, from
       slave catchers in the north. (YA)

1466   Fritz, Jean. Brady. Ill. by Lynd Ward. Coward
       McCann, 1960. A sensitive and suspenseful story
       about the underground railroad and a boy's growing
       understanding of the importance of keeping a
       secret. (I and YA)

1467 Goodman, Walter. Black Bondage: The Life of Slaves
     in the South. Ill. with photographs. Farrar,
     Straus and Giroux, 1969. Clearly, unemotionally,
     but dramatically, this book sums up the many evils
     of slavery as an institution and makes for under-
     standing of current racial tensions. (YA)
1468 Hamilton, Virginia. The House of Dies Drear. Ill.
     by Eros Keith. Macmillan, 1968. A mystery of
     "now and then," almost a ghost story, about a
     family moving into a house once occupied by an
     eccentric abolitionist who built into it secret tun-
     nels, doors and hiding places for escaping slaves
     traveling the underground railroad. (YA)
1469 Hildreth, Richard. Memoirs of a Fugitive. Ameri-
     ca's first antislavery novel adapted by Barbara
     Ritchie. Jacket by James Barclay. Thomas Y.
     Crowell, 1971. This adaptation of a much longer
     novel, published in 1836, includes a note about its
     adaptation. It is possible that "Uncle Tom's
     Cabin" may have owed much of its background to
     Hildreth's book which, however, is a much strong-
     er indictment of the institution of slavery than
     Mrs. Stowe's. (YA and Up)
1470 Knight, Michael (adaptor). In Chains to Louisiana:
     Solomon Northup's Story. E. P. Dutton, 1971.
     This painful to read, courageous book was first
     published in 1853 as "Twelve Years a Slave:
     Narrative of Solomon Northup, a Citizen of New
     York, Kidnapped in Washington City in 1841 and
     Rescued in 1853 from a Cotton Plantation near
     the Red River in Louisiana." (YA)
1471 Kristof, Jane. Steal Away Home. Ill. by W. T.
     Mars. Bobbs-Merrill, 1969. A terribly exciting
     story about two Negro boys, aged 12 and 9, who
     take the underground railroad all the way from
     South Carolina to near Philadelphia to join their
     father, a freed Negro. (I)
1472 Lawrence, Jacob. Harriet and the Promised Land.
     Ill. by the author. Simon and Schuster, 1968.
     A ballad and picture book about Harriet Tubman,
     the conductor on the underground railroad. (E and
     I)
1473 Lester, Julius. Long Journey Home: Stories from
     Black History. Dial, 1972. Six well-constructed
     short stories, dramatic and poignant, about the
     condition of slavery. (YA and Up)
1474 _____. To Be a Slave. Ill. by Tom Feelings.

Dial, 1968. Stories mainly told by ex-slaves in
the 1930s for the Federal Writers' Project, but
some written up by abolitionists before the Civil
War--all true tales of what it was like to be a
slave, from the time of the settlement of Jamestown to the Emancipation. (YA)

1475 Meadowcroft, Enid La Monte. By Secret Railroad.
Ill. by Henry C. Pitz. Thomas Y. Crowell, 1948.
A suspenseful story of a white boy's part in res-
cuing his Negro friend from slavers who captured
him even though he had been freed, and of the courage of the railroad conductors and the dangers they
ran even in Chicago in the year of Lincoln's election. (I)

1476 Meltzer, Milton (editor). In Their Own Words.
Thomas Y. Crowell, 1964. A history of the American Negro, 1619-1865. A collection of stories,
told by the slaves themselves, beginning with the
true story of life (or living death) in a slave ship
in 1619. An invaluable "Calendar of Negro History,
1619-1865" concludes the book. (YA and Up)

1477 Monjo, F. N. The Drinking Gourd. Ill. by Fred
Brenner. Harper and Row, 1970. An I Can Read
History Book. A story of the underground railroad and how a mischievous little boy foiled the
slave catchers. (E)

1478 Steinman, Beatrice. This Railroad Disappears. Ill.
by Douglas Gorsline. Franklin Watts, 1958. A
story of suspense, as all underground railroad
stories are, about a 13-year-old boy who wanted
to be a conductor on the disappearing railroad
that sent so many slaves on their way to Canada.
(I)

1479 Sterne, Emma Gelders. The Long Black Schooner.
Ill. by Paul Giovanopoulos. Follett, 1953-68. A
remarkable story, based on newspaper accounts
and court testimonies, about a "shipment" of African Negroes who managed to reach Connecticut
and finally, through the efforts of John Quincy
Adams, to gain their freedom to stay there or go
home to Africa. (YA)

1480 Stowe, Harriet Beecher. Uncle Tom's Cabin. Adapted
by Anne Terry White. Original illustrations.
George Braziller. A Venture Book, 1966. The
adaptation simply removes some of the long flowery
descriptive or moralizing passages of the original,
but the melodrama and sentimentality are still

there, and in spite of them, it remains a very
important book. (YA)

1481 Twain, Mark. Pudd'nhead Wilson. A Bantam paperbound edition of the novel originally published in
1893, with an introduction by Langston Hughes. A
detective novel, mainly concerned with the evil effect of the institution of slavery on the master as
well as the slave. (A)

1482 Vining, Elizabeth Gray. The Taken Girl. Cover by
Donald A. Mackay. Viking, 1972. The principal
character is a 14 to 16-year-old girl, "taken" from
an orphanage to "help out," first in an unhappy
household, and then in a very happy Quaker one in
which John Greenleaf Whittier, 30 years old, and
an ardent abolitionist, ia a boarder. (YA)

1483 Wells, Helen. Escape by Night: A Story of the Underground Railroad. Ill. by George L. Connelly.
John C. Winston, 1953. Two children work as
conductors on the railroad, with their Marietta,
Ohio, home as a station. In a preface, the author
confirms the authenticity of the story's events and--
with the changing of a few names--that of the people in the story, including Salmon Chase, Abraham
Lincoln and others. (I and YA)

1484 Witheridge, Elizabeth. And What of You, Josephine
Charlotte? Ill. by Barbara McGee. Atheneum,
1969. A novel about a sensitive, educated 17-
year-old slave, treated by her mistress almost as
a sister, but always in dreadful fear of being married off to a slave she detests and sold with him.
In her attempt to escape by underground railroad,
she encounters white slave kidnappers. Good
suspense and insight into various southern attitudes
toward slavery in the early 1800s. (I and YA)

1485 Wriston, Hildreth. Susan's Secret. Ill. by W. T.
Mars. Farrar, Straus and Cudahy, 1957. About
the underground railroad and an 11-year-old girl in
Vermont. (I)

RECONSTRUCTION AND AFTERMATH

1486 Bontemps, Arna. Chariot in the Sky: A Story of the
Jubilee Singers. Jacket by Ken Jordan. Holt,
Rinehart and Winston, 1951-71. A book about 11
singers, all born in slavery, who, to save their
college (Fisk) from having to close for lack of

funds, went on concert tour soon after the Civil
War, and in 1871 singing songs of slavery in world
capitols and even having their picture painted by
Queen Victoria's court painter. (YA)

1487 Meltzer, Milton. Freedom Comes to Mississippi:
The Story of Reconstruction. Ill. with contemporary prints and photographs. Follett, 1970. Taking
this one deep southern state as an example, the
author shows how, for a time, freedom did come
to Mississippi and why it failed to thrive. (YA)

1488 Place, Marian T. Rifles and War Bonnets: Negro
Cavalry in the West. Jacket by Victoria Dudley.
Ives Washburn, 1968. The story, told as a story,
of the Ninth and Tenth Cavalry of the U.S. Army,
made up of Negro soldiers with white officers;
how Colonel Benjamin Guerson tried his utmost to
obtain proper equipment and food for them and
recognition of their accomplishments in the Indian
warfare of the '78s and '80s. These so-called
"buffalo soldiers," after a difficult beginning,
proved to be excellent fighters. (YA)

1489 Sayre, Anne. Never Call Retreat. Thomas Y.
Crowell, 1957. A novel of Reconstruction days in
which a Quaker family moves south to Alabama to
try to help both Whites and Blacks to restore their
devastated lands and learn to live together in peace;
their encounter with hatred and bigotry and their
lesson in how to treat the wounds of the Civil War.
(YA)

1490 Werstein, Irving. This Wounded Land: The Era of
Reconstruction 1865-77. Delacorte, 1968. Dell
paperbound, 1970. Neither fiction nor biography,
this book seems to fit in because of its important
subject and highly readable style. (YA)

1491 Wibberley, Leonard. The Wound of Peter Wayne. Ill.
by Douglas Gorsline. Farrar, Straus and Cudahy,
1955. A novel about how the bitterness of a young
southern veteran of the Civil War is strangely
healed by his experiences in the gold fields of
Colorado. Also about Reconstruction in Georgia
and the beginnings of the Ku Klux Klan. (YA)

SPIES AND SECRET SERVICE

THE 18th CENTURY

1492 Bakeless, Katherine and John. Spies of the Revolu-
       tion. Jacket by Peter Burchard. J. B. Lippin-
       cott, 1962. A glossary of "spy words" begins this
       book about Washington's espionage system. Ex-
       cept for poor Nathan Hale and, possibly, Lydia
       Darragh, most of the spies told about here have
       never been well known nor will be, for a spy is of
       necessity an unsung hero but all too often not
       unhung. Though it cannot be proven, the author
       of this book suggests that the final American vic-
       tory was made possible by couragious spies in the
       service of a clever commander, General George
       Washington. (YA)
1493 Bothwell, Jean. The Mystery Candlestick. Ill. by
       Fermin Rocker. Dial, 1970. An 11-year-old
       boy finds himself involved in a spying operation
       against the Redcoats while two British officers
       quarter their horses in his barn. (I)
1494 Cooper, James Fenimore. The Spy (1821). With il-
       lustrations of contemporary scenes and a fore-
       word by Curtis Dahl. Dodd Mead Great Illustrated
       Classics, 1946. A novel of espionage and love,
       about a Yankee peddler performing as a double
       spy. (A)
1495 Emery, Anne. A Spy in Old Detroit. Ill. by H. P.
       Vestal. Rand McNally, 1963. A good diagram
       of the fort and map of the area make it easy to
       follow the action of this English-French-Indian con-
       flict and the siege of Fort Detroit by Chief Ponti-
       ac, the great Indian strategist. A foreword tells
       of Pontiac's victories and an author's note gives
       the factual basis of the story. (I and YA)
1496 _____. A Spy in Old Philadelphia. Ill. by H. B.
       Vestal. Rand McNally, 1958. A skillfully plot-
       ted story about rebels pretending to be Tories
       and about a 16-year-old boy who helps to trap a

traitor. A map of the Philadelphia area clarifies
the action. A fictional hero but factual basis. (I
and YA)

1497 _____. A Spy in Old West Point. Ill. by Lorence
P. Bjorklund. Rand McNally, 1965. The story of
Major Andre and the treachery of Benedict Arnold,
involving a fictional Patriot. A good map and au-
thor's note add to the realism and authenticity.
(I and YA)

1498 Epstein, Samuel and Beryl. Jackknife for a Penny.
Ill. by Coward McCann, 1958. A young Colonial,
pretending to be a Tory, runs into all kinds of
danger while getting secret messages and warnings
to the Patriots. Set in Long Island. (I)

1499 Faulkner, Nancy. Journey into Danger. Ill. by Jon
Nielsen. Doubleday, 1966. An exciting novel with
a factual basis about spy activities while General
Howe was in Philadelphia, in particular the participation of a young girl patriot. (YA)

1500 Lancaster, Bruce. The Secret Road. Jacket by
Charles W. Andres. Little Brown, 1952. An
adult novel about the actual secret service system
set up by General Washington in 1778. Some of
the story of the capture of Major Andre is based
on fact and some on legend. (A)

1501 Lawrence, Isabelle. A Spy in Williamsburg. Ill. by
Manning de V. Lee. Rand McNally, 1955. Published with the approval and collaboration of
Colonial Williamsburg. A suspenseful story of
pre-Revolutionary days in Williamsburg in which a
12-year-old blacksmith's son plays the leading role.
Excellent and authentic details of the blacksmith's
craft and Colonial Williamsburg. (I)

1502 Main, Mildred Miles. Hail, Nathan Hale. Jacket and
ill. by Stephen J. Voorhis. Abingdon, 1965. A
fictional biography of the young American spy. The
author's statement explains that it is not known who
betrayed him, so she has invented the betrayer.
(I)

1503 Mann, Martha. Nathan Hale, Patriot. Ill. by Victor
J. Dowling. Dodd Mead, 1944. A biographical
novel about young Hale (1755-76) based on the few
known facts concerning him. (YA)

1504 Stevenson, Augusta. Nathan Hale, Puritan Boy. Ill.
by Leslie Goldstein. Bobbs-Merrill, 1959. Childhood of Famous Americans Series. A story mainly about Hale's Puritan boyhood. The ruckus over

his haircut seems amazingly similar to the matter
of hairstyles in the 1960s. The story of his ill-
fated spying activity is included near the end, and
his last words, "I regret that I have but one life
to lose for my country," have survived for almost
200 years. (E)

1504a Voight, Virginia Frances. Nathan Hale. Ill. by
Frank Alois. G. P. Putnam's Sons, 1965. Poor
young Hale (1755-1776) volunteered to be a spy at
a time when spies had no preparation or defenses
such as secret writing or contacts with other patriots behind the British lines. (E)

1505 Wise, William. The Spy and General Washington.
Ill. by Peter Burchard. E. P. Dutton, 1965. A
little known story about a spy named John Honey-
man who may have been responsible for the success of Washington's crossing of the Delaware on
Christmas of 1776. (I)

THE 19th CENTURY

1506 Beatty, Patricia. Blue Stars Watching. Jacket and
endpapers by Franz Altschuler. William Morrow,
1969. An unusual Civil War spy story about a
Confederate conspiracy in California and the beginning of the Union Secret Service. A brother
and sister are sent to their aunt in San Francisco
to escape the dangers of the war in Delaware and
there become involved in even greater peril in the
seemingly harmless setting of their aunt's toyshop.
Almost all of the characters are fictional, but the
events are based on extensive research. (I and
YA)

1507 Emery, Anne. A Spy in Old New Orleans. Ill. by
Emil Weiss. Rand McNally, 1960. A story of a
boy who spies for Jean Lafitte while searching for
his uncle in the Bayou country of Louisiana. The
Battle of New Orleans is the climax of the story.
(I)

1508 Grant, Dorothy Fremont. Rose Greenhow, Confederate Secret Agent. Ill. by Douglas Grant. P. J.
Kenedy, 1961. A sympathetic biography of this
Civil War Confederate spy (1814-64), depicting
her more as a staunch states-righter than a supporter of slavery. (YA)

1509 Hoehling, Mary. Girl Soldier and Spy: Sarah

Edmunson. Julian Messner, 1959. A biography as exciting and absorbing as any fiction, of a girl member of the Michigan infantry who worked as an army nurse, at the same time repeatedly defying capture as she spied on Confederate movements and plans. A vivid portrayal of the horror of the Civil War, based on her published diary. (YA)

1510 Neal, Harry Edward. The Story of the Secret Service. Ill. with photographs. Grosset and Dunlap, 1971. This book telling in lively narrative style of "How its agents protect Presidents, outwit counterfeiters and forgers, guard securities and combat crime" begins its stories in 1864 and carries it up to the present. (I and YA)

1511 Nolan, Jeannette Covert. Belle Boyd, Secret Agent. Julian Messner, 1967. A novel about the young confederate spy. (YA)

1512 _____. Spy for the Confederacy: Rose O'Neal Greenhow. Julian Messner, 1960. A biographical novel about the ardent secessionist woman (1814-64). (YA)

1513 Orrmont, Arthur. Mr. Lincoln's Master Spy: Lafayette Baker. Jacket by Al Orbaan. Julian Messner, 1966. A biography of an unsung hero of the Civil War whose most famous achievement was in finding the man who shot Lincoln, and who died, unfairly judged, at the age of 42. An excellent Civil War spy story. (YA and Up)

1514 Sobol, Donald J. The Lost Dispatch. Ill. by Anthony Palumbo. Franklin Watts, 1958. A story of military strategy and espionage about a dispatch (concerning General Lee's plans) found by a Union soldier, which turned the tide at the bloody battle of Antietam. How the dispatch was lost in the first place provides the basis for a highly imaginative plot. (YA)

1515 Wise, William. Detective Pinkerton and Mr. Lincoln. Ill. by Hoot von Zitzewitz. E. P. Dutton, 1964. How the Pinkerton detective agency foiled the plots to sabotage the Philadelphia, Wilmington and Baltimore Railroad and assassinate Lincoln on the way to his inauguration. (I)

1516 Young, Rosamund McPherson. The Spy with Two Hats. David McKay, 1966. A fine Civil War story, based on the actual experiences of a Timothy Webster, who went into the south as a supposed friend of the Confederacy but actually as a secret agent for the Union, under Pinkerton. (YA and Up)

SPORTS

1517 de Grummond, Lena Young, and Lynn de Grummond
Delaune. Babe Didrikson, Girl Athlete. Ill. by
James Ponter. Bobbs-Merrill, 1963. Childhood
of Famous Americans Series. The childhood of the
little tomboy who grew up to make records in
several sports, some never as yet equaled (1913-
1956). (I)

1518 Durant, John with Les Etter. Highlights of College
Football. Ill. with prints and photographs.
Hastings House, 1970. The book begins with the
ancient history of the game in Greece, and carries
through the season of 1969, with the interesting
statistics at the end. It would be unwieldy to list
all the names of the football heroes, but the name
of Walter Camp must be specially noted as the
Father of American Football (1859-1925). (YA
and Up)

1519 _____. Highlights of the Olympics. Third Edition,
revised and enlarged, Hastings House, 1969. The
first 75 pages are truly historical (beginning with
the Greeks); continues up through 1950. (YA)

1520 _____. The Sports of Our Presidents. Ill. with
photographs and original drawings by Joshua Tal-
ford. Hastings House, 1964. The appendix gives
a list of sports with the names of the Presidents
who participated or showed interest in them; also
physical descriptions, terms of office, religious
affiliations and college graduating classes. (I and
YA)

1521 Fall, Thomas (Snow). Jim Thorpe. Ill. by John
Gretzer. Thomas Y. Crowell, 1970. The story
of an Oklahoma Indian (Sac and Fox family,
1888-1953) who won the decathlon gold medal in
the 1912 Olympic Games. (E)

1522 Hubler, Richard. Lou Gehrig, the Iron Horse of
Baseball. With an introduction by Grantland Rice.
Houghton Mifflin, 1941. The story of a shy,
modest boy of German parentage who grew up to
be the Yankees' great first baseman and the idol

of all American boys. A list of baseball records
(as of 1941) and the "Complete Baseball Record of
Lou Gehrig" are appended. (YA)

1523 Lovelace, Delos W. Rockne of Notre Dame. Ill.
with photographs. G. P. Putnam's Sons, 1931.
A thorough and authoritative biography (1888-1931)
of the great coach, including accounts of his Norwegian forebears and background; the three main
"breaks" that secured his fame, his religious
conversion, and his strong influence on the game
of football. Appendix One: "Rockne's Complete
Record of Games as Head Coach"; Appendix Two:
Football Lettermen at Notre Dame Under Rockne."
(YA and Up)

1524 Luce, Willard and Celia. Lou Gehrig, Iron Man of
Baseball. Ill. by Dom Lupo. Garrard, 1970.
The short but highly successful life of the Yankees'
great first baseman (1903-41) who, at the time
when he benched himself because of illness, had
appeared in more consecutive games than any other
player in the history of baseball. (I)

1525 Mann, Arthur. The Jackie Robinson Story. Ill. with
photographs. Grosset and Dunlap, 1956. A combination sports and civil rights story as Robinson
(1919-1972) was the first Negro to play in the
major leagues. It might also be called the "Branch
Rickey Story," for it was Rickey's determination,
courage, strategy, and just plain common sense
that helped to bring about this breakthrough in race
relations in the 1940s. Includes a "Lifetime Bat-
ting List" at the end. (YA and Up)

1526 Owens, Jesse, with Paul Neimark. The Jesse Owens
Story. G. P. Putnam's Sons, 1970. A truly thrilling autobiography of a man (1913-) who started
out as a sickly, spindly, poverty-stricken son of
a Negro sharecropper, became an Olympic champion
in track events, and is now a successful business-
man, devoting much of his time to worthy causes.
(I and YA)

1527 Rosenburg, John. The Story of Baseball. Ill. with
photographs. Random, 1962-4-6. A history of
the game from the beginning in the 19th century to
the recent past, with its highlights and leading
players; a list of those in the Hall of Fame at the
end. A big book, well arranged and generously
illustrated. (I and YA)

1528 Stoutenburg, Adrien and Laura Nelson Baker. Snow-

shoe Thompson.   Ill. by Victor DePauw.   Charles
Scribner's Sons, 1957.   A biographical novel of
Norwegian-born John Thompson (1828-76), the
"mailman of the Sierras" before the coming of the
transcontinental railroad, who was also known as
the "father of American skiing."   (YA)

1529   Sullivan, George.   Knute Rockne, Notre Dame's Football Great.   Ill. by Dom Lupo.   Garrard, 1970.
An inspiring biography of the Norwegian-born coach
(1888-1931) who, in the words of Damon Runyan,
"with his marvelous Notre Dame teams, and through
his powerful personality made football the national
institution it is today."   (I)

1530   Van Riper, Guernsey.   Babe Ruth, Baseball Boy.   Ill.
by Seymour Fleishman.   Bobbs-Merrill, 1954 and
1959.   Childhood of Famous Americans Series.
The boyhood of this historic sports figure was spent
in St. Mary's Industrial School because his parents
simply couldn't handle him, and the moral and
emotional handicaps he had to overcome, particularly his quick temper, made him even more heroic
than the story of his 60 home-runs.   (E and I)

1531   _____.   Knute Rockne, Young Athlete.   Ill. by Paul
Laune.   Bobbs-Merrill, 1952.   Childhood of Famous
Americans Series.   A story of his boyhood determination to play football in spite of his parents' concern about it being too rough a sport and how hard
he worked to buy his first football pants.   (E and I)

COLLECTIVE BIOGRAPHIES

1532 Buckmaster, Henrietta (Henkle). Women Who Shaped
History. Ill. with photographs. Macmillan, 1966.
Biographies of: Dorothy Dix, Prudence Crandell,
Elizabeth Cady Stanton, Elizabeth Blackwell,
Harriet Tubman, Mary Baker Eddy. (YA)

1533 Crawford, Deborah. Four Women in a Violent Time.
Crown, 1970. Jacket by W. T. Mars. The exciting stories of women who were far ahead of
their times in their pursuit of freedom of belief
and equality with men: Anne Hutchinson (1591-
1643), Mary Dyer (1591?-1660), Lady Deborah
Moody (1600-59), and Penelope Stout (1622-1732).
(Two unfortunate errors in the first chapter should
be noted: Elizabeth I of England is mistakenly
called the direct successor of Henry VIII, and
James I as Elizabeth's nephew.) (YA)

1534 Gersh, Harry. Women Who Made America Great.
Ill. by Mel Silverman. J. B. Lippincott. Foreword by Esther Peterson. Stories of Maria
Mitchell, astronomer; Mary Bethune, educator;
Lillian Wald, social worker; Abigail Scott Dunning,
champion of women's rights; Mary Jones, labor-
leader; Anna Zenger, journalist; Mildred Didrick-
son Zaharias, athlete; Dr. Elizabeth Blackwell,
medicine; Margaret Bourke-White, photographer;
and Harriet Tubman, rescuer of slaves. (YA)

1535 Johnson, Dorothy. Some Went West. Jacket by
Lorence F. Bjorklund. Ill. with photographs.
Dodd Mead, 1965. This book of stories about
lesser known pioneer women contains so many
names that only the most prominent can be listed
here: Cynthia Ann Parker, Fanny Keely, the
German Sisters (all captured by Indians), Mary
Richardson Walker, the sisters of Providence,
"Mercer's Belles" (who went west to work and to
marry), Harriet Sanders, Electa Plummer and
Maria Virginia Slade (who married badmen), Dr.

262

Bethenia Owens-Adair (a real rebel), Isabella Bird
and Elizabeth Custer (adventurers), Catherine Weldon, Nannie Anderson, Grace Snyder. A "Postscript" tells of how truly "harried" the housewives
of the 19th century were. (YA)

1536 Ross, Nancy Wilson. Heroines of the Early West.
Ill. by Paul Caldone. Random Landmark, 1944-60.
The first chapter of this unusually well-done book
is in the form of a tribute to the courage and endurance of these pioneer women. Some of the
names are familiar--Sacajawea and Narcissa Whitman, for instance, have had many books written
about them, but others have been included only in
anthologies, if even there. Almost all, however,
in spite of danger, and fatigue managed to write
letters or keep diaries and thus their stories have
come down to us. Among these writers there are
biographical sketches of Mary Richardson Walker,
missionary; Sister Loyola and the five nuns who
accompanied her all the way from Belgium, and
that earliest of Suffragists, Abigail Scott Dunniway,
through whose efforts Oregon gave the vote to
women in 1912.

1537 Stoddard, Hope. Famous American Women. Ill.
with photographs and prints. Thomas Y. Crowell,
1970. Biographical sketches of 42 women of the
19th and 20th centuries: Jane Addams, Louisa May
Alcott, Marian Anderson, Susan B. Anthony, Ethel
Barrymore, Clara Barton, Mary McLeod Bethune,
St. Francis Xavier Cabrini, Willa Cather, Mary
Cassatt, Agnes de Mille, Emily Dickinson,
Dorothea Dix, Isadora Duncan, Amelia Earhart,
Mary Baker Eddy, Margaret Fuller, Lillian Gil-
breth, Martha Graham, Edith Hamilton, Oveta
Culp Hobby, Malvina Hoffman, Helen Keller,
Dorothea Lange, Susanne Langer, Mary Lyon,
Margaret Mead, Edna St. Vincent Millay, Maria
Mitchell, Constance Baker Motley, Lucretia Mott,
Rosa Ponselle, Eleanor Roosevelt, Florence
Sabin, and Margaret Sanger. (YA)

1538 Vance, Marguerite. The Lamplighters, Women in
the Hall of Fame. Ill. by Luis Pellicer. E. P.
Dutton, 1960. Foreword by Sarah Gibson. Short
biographies of the following eight women in the
Hall of Fame: Emma Willard (1787-1870), pioneer in education for women, Mary Lyon (1797-1849),
founder of Mt. Holyoke College; Harriet Beecher

Stowe, author of "Uncle Tom's Cabin," Charlotte
Saunders Cushman (1816-76), actress; Maria
Mitchell (1818-89), America's first woman astronomer; Susan B. Anthony (1820-1906), leader in many
causes: temperance, abolitionism, and particularly woman's suffrage; Frances Elizabeth Willard
(1839-1902), suffrage and temperance leader; and
Alice Freeman Palmer (1855-1902), educator,
president of Wellesley College. (YA)

FEMINISM AND FEMINISTS

1539   Beatty, Patricia.   Hail Columbia.   Ill. by Liz Dauber.
       Morrow Junior Books, 1970. An extremely enter-
       taining story of a high-flying Aunt in 1893 Oregon
       who is a suffragist, a Lucy Stoner (keeping her
       maiden name after marriage), a Unitarian, and, in
       general, a reformer and fighter for women's rights.
       How she attacks some of the evils of the city, and
       even enlists her own brother in her fearless ac-
       tivities makes a hilarious tale, completely fictional,
       but not impossible as the "Author's Note" indicates.
       (I)
1540   _____. Me, California Perkins.   Ill. by Liz
       Dauber.   Morrow Junior Books, 1968.   The story
       of a 12-year-old girl in 1882, living in a house
       made of bottles in the Mojave Desert, near San
       Bernardino, California, and her problems in se-
       curing an education.   Humorous and authentic. (I)
1541   Bolton, Carole.   Never Jam Today.   Atheneum, 1971.
       A period piece in which Maddy Franklin--aged 17
       in 1916, a high school graduate (aged 20 at the
       end)--joins the militant branch of the suffrage move-
       ment, suffering jailing and forced feeding as a con-
       sequence.   World War I, the 1919 flu epidemic and
       three proposals of marriage make her life a tem-
       pestuous one.   (YA)
1542   Burt, Olive.   First Woman Editor: Sarah J. Hale.
       Jacket by Jon Nielsen.   Julian Messner, 1960.
       Biography of an amazing woman (1788-1879), the edi-
       tor of Godey's Ladies' Book, and promoter of all
       kinds of good causes, who tried to erase the word
       "female" from the American vocabulary. (YA)
1543   _____. Petticoats West.   Julian Messner, 1963.
       A love story based on the historical importation of
       females from the East to the Washington territory,

to bring some of the amenities of life to the almost
exclusively male frontier--the "Mercer Belles." (YA)

1544 Caudill, Rebecca. Barrie and Daughter. Ill. by
Berkeley Williams Jr. Viking, 1951. A novel of a
young mountain woman in southeastern Kentucky, in
the early years of the 20th century, and her rebellion against the only two futures open to her: housekeeping and teaching. (YA)

1545 Clarke, Mary Stetson. Petticoat Rebel. Ill. by Robert
MacLean. Viking, 1964. A revolutionary period
novel about the beginning of education for girls, in
which a young woman of Gloucester, Mass. finds
a part to play in the fight for liberty. (YA)

1546 Coigny, Virginia. Margaret Sanger: Rebel with a
Cause. Doubleday, 1969. A biography (1883-1966)
of a slight, attractive, very feminine woman who
was forced to undergo arrest and imprisonment for
trying to give out birth control information. A
story of complete dedication to a cause, and the
reward of finally seeing that cause accepted and
promoted by prominent people of almost all countries and races. (YA)

1547 Faber, Doris. Oh Lizzie! The Life of Elizabeth Cady
Stanton. Lothrop Lee and Shepard, 1972. Biography (1815-1902) of a woman who combined a busy
life in the home and care for her children with public speeches and other work in the cause of women's
rights, along with Lucretia Mott who was older,
and Susan B. Anthony who was younger, and other
suffragists of the 19th century. (YA)

1548 Hall, Elizabeth. Stand Up, Lucy. Ill. by Beth and
Joe Krush. Houghton Mifflin, 1971. A candidate
for secretary of the ninth grade becomes imbued
with suffragist fervor (never say "suffragette") and
suddenly finds herself in the paddy wagon as a
result of her part in demonstrations.

1549 Holberg, Ruth Langland. At the Sign of the Golden
Anchor. Ill. by Jane Castle. Doubleday, 1947.
The story of a brave, adventursome little girl,
near the end of the War of 1812, who resents being
a girl until she learns that girls have their uses
too. (I)

1550 Meltzer, Milton. Tongue of Flame: The Life of Lydia
Maria Child. Thomas Y. Crowell, 1965. A biography (1802-1880) based chiefly on Mrs. Child's
own writings, of an abolitionist and crusader in many
movements. (YA)

1551   Monsell, Helen Albee.   Susan Anthony: Girl Who
       Dared.   Ill. by Al Fiorentino.   Bobbs-Merrill,
       1954.   Childhood of Famous American Series.
       Biography (1820-1906).   When the 19th amendment
       was passed in 1919, giving women the right to
       vote, many people said that it should have been
       named the Susan B. Anthony Amendment, as Mrs.
       Anthony had worked toward that end for 50 years,
       and in 1892, became the president of the National
       Woman's Suffrage Association.   (E and I)
1552   Sterling, Dorothy.   Lucretia Mott, Gentle Warrior.
       Jacket and endpapers by Ernest Crichlow.   Double-
       day, 1964.   This little Quaker mother of six
       (1793-1880) and grandmother of 19 was an inde-
       fatigable and indomitable fighter for the cause of
       human rights--the abolition of slavery and votes
       for women.   (YA and UP)
1553   Wise, Winifred.   Rebel in Petticoats.   Chilton, 1960.
       A dramatically narrated biography of Elizabeth
       Cady Stanton (1815-1902), that early advocate of
       women's rights, and the story of the obstacles she
       overcame in her pursuit of that cause.   Mother of
       seven, she nevertheless managed to make her mark
       in the vanguard of the female rebellion.   (YA)

AUTHOR INDEX

Adams, Samuel Hopkins 340, 459, 460
Agle, Nan Hayden 982
Agle, Nan Hayden (with Bacon Frances Atchison) 779
Albrecht, Lillie V. 88, 121, 196
Alderman, Clifford Lindsey 89, 157, 888, 983
Aldis, Dorothy 90, 391
Aldrich, Bess Streeter 643
Alexander, Lloyd 158
Aliki (Aliki Brandenberg) 941, 1397
Allee, Marjorie Hill 1452
Allen, Edward 868
Allen, Henry see Henry, Will
Allen, Leroy 1001
Allen, Merritt Parmalee 61, 139, 248, 273, 341- 345, 476-478, 1002
Allen, T. D. 346, 1160
Alter, Robert Edmond 140, 438, 1003, 1364
Altschuler, Joseph A. 1064
Alvarez, Joseph 1203
Anderson, A. M. 984
Anderson, Bertha 91
Anderson, Betty Baxter 479
Anderson, Levere 1065
Anderson, Lonzo 92
Andrews, Mary Evans 1350
Andrews, Mary Raymond Shipman 1253
Andrist, Ralph K. 274
Andrus, Vera 644
Angell, Pauline K. 761
Angell, Polly 461

Ansley, Delight 1423
Appel, Benjamin 715, 735
Apsler, Alfred 541
Archer, Jules 869, 716
Archer, Marian Fuller 577
Armstrong, William H. 578, 780
Arnold, Elliott 1004, 1024
Arntson, Herbert E. 1375
Ashabramer, Brent K. (with Russell G. Davis) 1069, 1070
Asimov, Isaac 1107
Averill, Esther 275, 985
Avery, Lynn 276
Ayers, James Sterling 781; and 942 with Rebecca Caudill

Bachman, Evelyn Trent 645
Bacmeister, Rhoda W. 1453
Bacon, Frances Atchison (with Nan Hayden Agle) 779
Bacon, Martha 1454
Bailey, Bernardine 15
Bailey, Jean 579
Bailey, Ralph Edgar 159, 462, 542, 1339
Bakeless, John 277
Bakeless, Katherine and John 1492
Baker, Betty 26-28, 439, 463, 1025, 1026
Baker, Elizabeth 580
Baker, Laura Nelson 880; and 859, 860, 1528 with Stoutenberg
Baker, Nina Brown 16, 29,

TITLE INDEX

281

BIOGRAPHICAL INDEX

Billy the Kid   553
Bird, Isabella   1535
Birdseye, Clarence   1119
Black Hawk   1023, 1027,
   1048
Blackwell, Elizabeth   1164,
   1532, 1534
Blue Jacket   1035
Bly, Nellie   871
Bolivar, Simon   1143, 1146
Bonaparte, Elizabeth Pat-
   terson   309
Boone, Daniel   275, 278,
   282, 291, 297, 300
Booth, Edwin   806
Booth, Evangeline   932
Booth, John Wilkes   806
Bourke-White, Margaret
   1534
Bowditch, Nathaniel   1384,
   1390
Boyd, Belle   1511
Braden, Anne and Carl
   1422
Bradford, William   104,
   117
Bradstreet, Anne   822
Brant, Joseph   1012,
   1014
Brewster, William   114
Bridger, Jim   341, 345, 374
Bridgman, Laura   1169
Brown, Henry   1419
Brown, John   1423, 1436,
   1442
Brown, Tabitha   371
Bruce, Blanche K.   1421
Buchanan, James   1205, 1252
Buffalo Bill (see Cody), Wil-
   liam
Bunche, Ralph   1418, 1419
Bunyan, Paul   946, 950, 951,
   953, 966, 968, 971
Burbank, Luther   1401
Burnette, Frances Hodgson
   817
Burr, Aaron   306, 319, 305

Burr, Theodosia   305
Burroughs, John   1406, 1414
Byrd, Richard E.   770, 773

Cabeza de Vaca, Alvar
   Nuñez   28, 31, 50a, 57
Cabot, John   17
Cabrillo, Juan Rodriguez
   35
Cabrini, St. Frances Xavier
   1537
Camp, Walter Chauncey   1518
Carlota, Empress   1193,
   1196
Carnegie, Andrew   1139,
   1141, 1142
Carson, Kit   342, 362, 387
Carson, Rachel   857
Cartier, Jacques   62, 68
Carver, George Washington
   1397, 1400, 1404, 1408,
   1409, 1411, 1412, 1418,
   1420
Cassatt, Mary   797, 1537
Castenadas, Pedro de   42
Castillo, Bernal Diaz del
   38, 50a
Cather, Willa   828, 1537
Catlin, George   795
Champlain, Samuel de   57,
   69
Chapman, John   see Apple-
   seed, Johnny
Child, Lydia Maria   1550
Christophe, Jean Henri
   1151, 1153
Cinque, Joseph   1420
Clark, George Rogers   168
Clark, William   274, 277,
   284
Clay, Henry   422, 426
Clemens, Olivia Langdon
   859
Clemens, Samuel   see
   Twain, Mark
Cleveland, Frances

SPECIAL INDEX FOR HORSE LOVERS